W9-BCY-007

WHITE SPACE IS NOT YOUR ENEMY
A BEGINNER'S GUIDE TO COMMUNICATING VISUALLY THROUGH GRAPHIC, WEB & MULTIMEDIA DESIGN

WSINYE

WHITE SPACE IS NOT YOUR ENEMY

A beginner's guide
to communicating visually through graphic,
web & multimedia design

rebecca hagen &
kim golombisky

Focal Press
Taylor & Francis Group

NEW YORK AND LONDON

First published 2013
by Focal Press
70 Blanchard Road, Suite 402, Burlington, MA 01803

Simultaneously published in the UK
by Focal Press
2 Park Square, Milton Park, Abingdon, Oxon OX14 4RN

Focal Press is an imprint of the Taylor & Francis Group, an informa business

© 2013 Taylor & Francis

The rights of Rebecca Hagen and Kim Golombisky to be identified as authors of
this work has been asserted by them in accordance with sections 77 and 78 of the
Copyright, Designs and Patents Act 1988.

All rights reserved. No part of this book may be reprinted or reproduced or utilised in
any form or by any electronic, mechanical, or other means, now known or hereafter
invented, including photocopying and recording, or in any information storage or
retrieval system, without permission in writing from the publishers.

Notices
Knowledge and best practice in this field are constantly changing. As new research
and experience broaden our understanding, changes in research methods, professional
practices, or medical treatment may become necessary.

Practitioners and researchers must always rely on their own experience and
knowledge in evaluating and using any information, methods, compounds, or
experiments described herein. In using such information or methods they should be
mindful of their own safety and the safety of others, including parties for whom they
have a professional responsibility.

Product or corporate names may be trademarks or registered trademarks, and are used
only for identification and explanation without intent to infringe.

ISBN: 978-0-240-82414-7 (pbk)
ISBN: 978-0-240-82443-7 (ebk)

Printed and bound in India by Replika Press Pvt. Ltd.

To our students,

who make us look forward to Mondays—and Fridays

CONTENTS

TABLE OF CONTENTS

white space is not your enemy: a beginner's guide to communicating visually through graphic, web & multimedia design

For more content please visit the companion site:
http://www.whitespacedesignbook.com

Register using the passcode: space816

ACKNOWLEDGMENTS

Once again, thanks go all around to our supportive and talented husbands Guy and Greg; sons Ben and Karl; cats Finn, Kylie, Salsa and the late Whitey; and dog Duke. Beyond their psychosocial support, their contributions—from modeling to design—are literally visible throughout *WSINYE*.

Special acknowledgments are due to Tim Price, Cliff Keller and Kristin Arnold Ruyle for their photography. Shout-outs go to Carrie Matteoli and Will Payne for their artistic abilities, and to Vidisha Priyanka for her technical inspiration. Thanks to bff Elizabeth Bell and her impeccable eye.

We're still grateful for the stellar contributions of some former students, including Sarah Wilson, Susan Snyder, Meaghan Rose, Hunter Taylor and Michael Hardcastle.

We also credit our generous reviewers:

» Scott Farrand, University of South Carolina

» Jennifer George-Palilonis, Ball State University

» Lori Pindar, Clemson University

» Juliet Davis, University of Tampa

Last we thank Focal Press for letting us do this affordable 4-color 2nd edition.

PREFACE

This second edition of *White Space is not Your Enemy* or *WSINYE* is still for the "beginning" visual communicator. Whether you're already a media pro or hoping to be one soon, we assume our book is your introduction to graphic design and layout. We also assume you're busy. So we try to cover the basics quickly without being too boring.

OUR BIG IDEA

Our humble little book can't be everything to everyone. But we did plan it to combine some things typically treated separately:

1. News, PR, advertising & marketing communications:

We address different communications careers together as if they actually interact in the real world. Today's communications professionals all have to be visual, even the writers. And visual foundations are the same for all beginners. At the same time, where differences between journalism and the strategic communication arts remain sacred, we honor them.

2. Web & print media:

We embrace design for new and traditional media since the former is here to stay and the latter isn't going away. Because communications professionals need to be ambidextrous with both, we attend to visual practices across platforms and formats.

3. Visual communication, design & layout:

We integrate three traditionally segregated approaches: visual communication, graphic design and layout. Beginners need elementary how-to rules (layout). But without thinking about the rules as functional messaging (visual communication) and without developing a good eye (design), the rules remain rote ideas either soon forgotten or ploddingly applied without creativity or innovation.

THEMES

The book relies on three themes that chapters return to again and again in order to reinforce concepts and practices:

1. Effective graphic design does four things: It captures attention, controls eye movement, conveys information and evokes emotion.

2. All design uses three building blocks: visuals, type and negative space.

3. Beginners need to learn the conventional rules first before earning the right to break said rules.

TONE, DICTION & STYLE

WSINYE is intentionally light-hearted and conversational. We employ an informal tone and diction to avoid reading like a traditional textbook. Most people find textbooks unappealing. Our students don't bother to read them.

Our goal has been to make *WSINYE* a fast, effortless read. We present information in a down-to-earth fashion without talking down to anyone. We use humor to avoid taking the book's content or ourselves too seriously.

Given the book's applied emphasis, we use the Associated Press as our style guide—except where we take creative license.

CHAPTER PREVIEWS

Although each chapter flows from the previous one and segues to the next, by design the chapters also make sense read out of order or standing alone. We envision *WSINYE* useful as either a primary text or a supplemental resource. We also see it complementing media writing and editing courses.

Chapters 1–4 represent a book within a book. By the end of Chapter 4, the casual and impatient reader can opt out with dramatically improved skills.

» Chapter 1 answers the beginning student's perennial question: "What is design?"

» Chapter 2 reminds new designers to "step away from the computer" for the predesign work of "research & brainstorming."

» Chapter 3 covers the "works-every-time layout," which allows us to describe Western layout in its most universal form while also teaching introductory rules for working with visuals, type and negative space.

» Chapter 4 preempts the most common visual, type and composition "layout sins" in a checklist of "amateur errors."

After Chapter 4, readers have enough elementary skill to begin executing assignments, whether for the classroom or the office. So chapters 5 and 6 shore up some foundational details:

» Chapter 5 sends readers to "mini art school" to learn the "elements, principles and theories of design" that develop the good eye.

» Chapter 6 then fills in the blanks on "layout" format and composition from aspect ratio, grids and focal point to visual hierarchy and modular design for single, complex and multiple-screen/page designs.

Next, readers can drill down on more advanced rules for type, color and visuals:

» Chapter 7 expands the rules and uses of "type" from text-heavy formats and projects to creative type as art.

» Chapter 8 deals with "choosing & using color," including sources of color inspiration as well as color as culture, science and technology.

» Chapter 9 spells out technique, technology and ethics of designing with "photos & illustrations."

Remaining chapters touch on more complex design work:

» Chapter 10 serves up a quickie lesson on "infographics" as "maximum information in minimum space."

» Chapter 11 describes elementary concepts for "storyboarding 101: planning visual storytelling" for moving pictures, such as video, film and animation.

» Chapter 12 moves on to planning visual communication as "multimedia components," including slideshows and audio clips.

» Chapter 13 introduces visual communication issues in "designing for the Web" from fonts and colors behaving badly to navigating intuitively and getting GUI.

» Chapter 14 details mechanical printing from papers, folding and binding to working with commercial printers.

» Chapter 15 wraps things up with a few words of encouragement before saying, "thanks for stopping by."

Each chapter concludes with exercises thinly disguised as "Try This."

You'll find a glossary at the back of the book.

We also invite readers to visit the companion website for this book: www.whitespacedesignbook.com.

The how-to's of design and layout as visual communication are the same regardless of career track. We planned *WSINYE* as a comprehensive introduction for any communications major, track or sequence, across traditional and new media formats: one concise and practical source surveying the fundamentals for any platform for anybody.

WSINYE COMPANION WEBSITE

For more content please visit the companion site: http://www.whitespacedesignbook.com

Register using the passcode: space816

1 | WHAT IS DESIGN?
making visuals & type play nice in space

Visual culture is a language, and, like any language, visual culture has rules that make communication possible.

Above: Some designs are classic, like the Taj Mahal. Others are universal, like the international symbol set.

Below: This type of communication is so powerful that breaking convention communicates as well.

You live in a visual culture. All day every day, you read the messages of visual culture, from the logo on your shirt to traffic signals. Unless you're blind or visually impaired, you hardly give it a thought—until you come across a visual message you don't understand.

Visual culture is a language, and, like any language, visual culture has rules that make communication possible. Like English grammar, you may not be able to say exactly what the rules are, but you know when *breaks someone* them.

The rules of design are equivalent to visual culture's grammar. This book gives you some basic rules of graphic design and layout so you can begin to speak the visual language that you already read. Think of this book as your primer for graphic design. Don't worry. This grammar is the fun stuff, and, hopefully, we'll whet your appetite to learn even more about visual culture and design.

Before we get started on the rules, though, let's cover a little background on design, visual culture, visual communication and graphic design.

FORM FOLLOWS FUNCTION IN DESIGN

Chances are, right now, you're surrounded by the work of designers from fashion to furniture to architecture. There are interior designers and landscape designers, product designers and product packaging designers, and, of course, graphic designers. Believe it or not, there are even font designers and color designers. Today, Web designers are the new media technology test pilots. The list could go on, but the point is you live with design.

Despite its variety, all design is related through the expression, "Form follows function." Good design results from a partnership between "form" as art and "function" as utility.

"Form" refers to material artistry—what something looks like. Design, triggered by the industrial revolution and mass production capitalism (function), grew out of and continues to be inspired by the visual and even performing arts (form). Most designers have some background or training in art. Knowing something about art can improve your eye for design. But what people consider aesthetically beautiful, or even interesting, changes across history, cultures and individuals. "Aesthetics," a branch of philosophy, deals with the expression and perception of beauty. Your personal aesthetic dictates what you like in terms of style.

Unlike fine artists, however, designers don't have the luxury of creating art for art's sake or wholly yielding to personal taste. Design always has a job to do, and that job influences the design's form. Design

has to be practical. The "function" in "form follows function" refers to the usefulness of the design, whether it's an ergonomic dashboard in your car or your car manufacturer's website.

DESIGN DRIVES VISUAL CULTURE

Beyond form and function, all design is related by style trends, too. To a great degree, designers engineer visual culture. If you have a good eye, you can make a game of matching any kind of design to the historical period that produced it.

Think about how you can date a movie by hundreds of visual clues, including cars, décor, fashion and superimposed typography during the credits. Though all these things have different functions, they generally share a similarity of form if they were designed at roughly the same time.

Changing technology also influences design. Refrigerators in the 1950s and '60s sported just as much chrome as cars from the same period because they both emerged from the same technological and design era. Think about how the designs of televisions, computers and cellular phones have changed in your lifetime.

Some designs don't stand the test of time. They go out of style to become old-fashioned, "old school" or even the objects of jokes. Maybe you've heard the expression, "The '80s called, and they want

Time warp. If you have a good eye, you can make a game of matching any kind of design to the historical period that produced it.

Above: Minerva Motorcycle ad, circa 1910, and vintage vegetable crate label, circa 1940.

Images reproduced by permission of Dover Publications, Inc.

Graphic design is planned.
Designers *plan* their projects in detail on paper before ever sitting down at the computer.

Small sketches, called "thumbnail sketches," help the designer establish attention-grabbing focal points and determine placement of the remaining elements for logical and effective order. Readability, usability and visual appeal are critical.

A poorly designed, poorly organized layout fails to communicate and costs both the designer and the organization time and money.

Right: Thumbnail sketches for the cover, gatefold and inside spread of a brochure.

Below: The finished brochure spread.

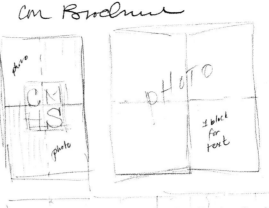

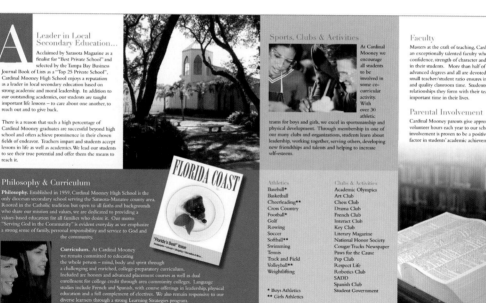

their shoulder pads back." Some designs are said to be timeless or classic, such as the Parthenon and the Taj Mahal. Other designs become universal, such as international symbols. Yet other design trends recycle earlier styles, usually with modifications or updates. Cooper Black typeface took the U.S. advertising world by storm in the 1920s, fell out of favor and then became stylish again in the 1970s.

All this is to say that visual culture changes as a result of design's changing forms and functions, both related to technology and social trends. This is equally true of graphic design.

GRAPHIC DESIGN COMMUNICATES

While the forms of graphic design, like all design, change with the winds of visual culture and technology, the specific function of graphic design remains constant: to communicate messages visually. Graphic designers have to be professional communicators. They understand that, for better or worse, in visual culture we judge and are judged by appearances. In fact, everyone can benefit from knowing something about the mostly unspoken rules of visual communication. That's called media literacy.

COMPUTERS DEMOCRATIZED GRAPHIC DESIGN

Once upon a time, only professionals produced graphic design. Graphic designers spent years learning the art and craft of visual communication (and still do, by the way). Today, however, anyone with a computer has access to the tools for producing visual communication.

Unfortunately, not everyone knows the design rules for using technology tools. The result is a lot of bad graphic design in a visual culture already on overload. While ugly design may offend your good taste, it can lead to a more serious functional problem: poor communication. Learning some fundamentals will dramatically improve your visual messages, whether it's your resume, a multimedia website or slides for a presentation.

THE WWW CHANGED ALL THE RULES

To say the World Wide Web changed everything for graphic designers is gross understatement. And just as they started figuring out the Web, everything migrated to smartphones and tablets. Who knows what's next?

Seismic changes in technology present us with dilemmas in organizing this book. For many topics, there's a "Yeah, but" for the Web. *Yeah, but*

Cooper Black typeface. Just as ugly in the 1970s as it was in the 1920s.

Top image reproduced by permission of Dover Publications, Inc.

GOOD **GRAPHIC DESIGN** DOES FOUR THINGS:

It **captures** attention.

It **controls** the eye's movement across the page or screen.

It **conveys** information.

It **evokes** emotion.

there's a whole other color wheel for the Web. *Yeah, but* fonts behave badly on the Web. And so on. Most Web "yeah, buts" have more to do with technique and production than actual design, however.

Oh, well, so we'll deal with it. Life's full of contradictions. Best to embrace the adventure.

GRAPHIC DESIGN IS PLANNED

Technically, "graphic design" refers to a plan for organizing visual objects in space. Generally, that space is a two-dimensional plane, meaning some kind of flat surface such as paper or an electronic screen. The key ideas are "plan" and "organize" for the purpose of "communication." If you were writing a speech or research report, you would make an outline to organize your ideas in a logical and effective order. In graphic design, you organize all your elements from copy (text) to visuals (pictures) in a logical and effective order.

Good graphic design does four things: It *captures* attention, *controls* the eye's movement across the page or screen, *conveys* information and *evokes* emotion.

So graphic design refers to your plan for capturing the audience's attention from among everything else competing for its interest. Once you have the audience looking at your design, its arrangement or layout should control the audience's eyes to move in a particular sequence from one thing to the next on the page or screen. The whole point of guiding the eye is to convey information. Think eye-catching, flowing, interesting and evocative.

MAKE PICTURES & WORDS WORK TOGETHER IN SPACE

Now you need some building blocks for capturing, controlling, conveying and evoking. In the simplest sense, effective design and layout teams up pictures and words to communicate a unified message, regardless of the visual medium or vehicle. At the risk of oversimplifying, you really have only three building blocks: *visuals, typography* and *space*.

Visuals—symbols, icons, drawings, illustrations, photographs, film and video, etc.—are self-explanatory, literally. But there are rules for using them in graphic design. We'll be talking more about those rules later.

About *type,* we generally represent copy graphically with typography, a visual form of language. There are rules for typography, too, which you'll be learning. But words may be represented with handwriting, such as calligraphy, or even pictures. And type treatments can make beautiful visuals. Additionally, some kinds of visuals, such as logos and infographics, require text. We'll be covering that, too.

Imagine *space* as the sandbox that encourages visuals and typography to play well together. Beginners often make the mistake of forgetting to account for space. Too much space, and visuals and type get lost or don't talk to each other. Not enough space, and they start to fight with each other.

The idea is to arrange visuals and type harmoniously in space. Don't think of space as immaterial or invisible. Nor is space a vacuum to be filled. Space is real, even when we call it "white space" or, more properly, "negative space" (since not all white space is white). Negative space always has weight and structure in graphic design. There's an old saying: "White space is nice." Amateurs tend to pack every nook and cranny of space with visuals and type. Don't. *White space is not your enemy.*

Our best advice for improving your visual communication is to practice looking. Pay attention to the layout of visuals and typography in space. Think about what you're seeing.

KNOW THE RULES. BREAK THE RULES IF YOU HAVE A REASON.

Our students like to find exceptions to the rules of design we teach them. That tickles us because it means our students are tuning in to design. Often the exceptions to the rules of design that students show us are good examples of bad design. But sometimes the exceptions are good examples of good design. Then we have to explain how breaking the rules can produce good design that communicates. Usually, our explanations fall into two categories: professional license and changing design trends.

By training and experience, professional designers have mastered both fundamental and advanced rules of design. They know how to use creative license with the rules without forfeiting visual communication. This book concentrates on fundamentals. But, as you learn the fundamentals, you also may discover opportunities to employ creative license. At least we hope so.

Rules? What rules? This promotional roller derby poster breaks more than a few typesetting rules. Yet, it works. It works because it evokes the right grungy, hard-knock feel one would expect from a sport that features tough women on roller skates.

Design based on original photo by Charlie Chu, "Shutter Thug."

Taking creative license with the rules of design can lead to innovation, which leads us to changing design trends. Design, like visual culture and English language, is not static. "It's alive!" That's what keeps things interesting. Times change. Styles shift. So we adapt the rules.

Bottom line: Don't break the rules of design out of ignorance. Learn the rules. Then break the rules if you have a reason to. Hey, if it works, it works. Just keep reminding yourself that you have a job to do. It's called visual communication.

▶ TRY THIS

1. Choose one of your favorite possessions from among the material objects you own. Try to imagine what the object's designer had in mind.

   Write a few sentences to describe its form or what it looks like. Be specific and list the details of the object's appearance. Quickly sketch a small picture of the object's appearance. Try to include all the details you see.

   Then write a sentence or two to describe the object's function, or what it does. Draw a diagram explaining how the object works. How does this diagram differ—or not—from the earlier picture you drew?

   Last, write a couple more sentences to describe the relationship between the object's form and function. How do you think the object's function influences or limits its form? Does the object's form assist in its function?

2. Locate an object that has gone out of style. How do you know it has gone out of style? What clues does the object communicate that date it? Explain why the object is outdated. Has the object become dated because of its form? Its function? Or both?

3. Find an example of graphic design that you believe communicates well.

   First, explain how the design captures your attention. What part of the design do you look at first? What draws your eye to look there first?

   Second, explain how the design controls the eye's flow through its layout. In what order does your eye move from one thing to the next across the space of the layout? Make a numbered list of the order in which your eye travels around the layout.

   Third, what kind of information does the design convey? Make a list. Describe how the design conveys this information.

   What, if any, emotion(s) does the design evoke? How? Why?

Form and function.
Despite its variety, all design is related through the expression, "Form follows function." Good design results from a partnership between "form" as art and "function" as utility.

Consider one of your favorite possessions. What did the designer have in mind? Which features speak to form and which to function?

2 | STEP AWAY FROM THE COMPUTER
for research and brainstorming

TOTALLY
RETRO BOUTIQUE
EIGHTIES

WWW.80SVINTAGE.BIZ

CLICK HERE
TO VIEW OUR NEW
ARRIVALS

Appealing to your audience. For visual communication, you should speak to the audience in its own visual vernacular. For instance, the visual aesthetics of MTV and early video games are part of the collective memory of Gen X.

*Previous page, photo ©
picsfive – Fotolia.com*

D esign has one thing in common with biology: There's no such thing as spontaneous generation. Whether you're designing for folks in the newsroom or the boardroom, you have some predesign work to do if you hope to produce a design that works, literally and figuratively.

Novices may be inclined to go straight to their computers. But professional designers know that effective graphic design begins with research: information gathering and critical thinking about the project at hand. Next comes brainstorming: tapping into creativity and putting pencil to paper. So we're going to have to ask you to step away from your computer.

RESEARCH

Always start with research. If you're lucky, the research you need in order to begin a new design comes from the person who sent the work to your desk. Let's call this person, whoever it is, the boss or client. But you may have to do your own research or at least pitch in with it.

Even the humblest design assignment necessitates collecting basic information about the design's purpose and deadlines. At the other end of the spectrum, a high-stakes campaign demands extensive research, analysis and planning culminating in multiple coordinated designs accountable to measurable objectives.

Regardless of who collects the facts, and however big or small the design job, you need reliable answers to some standard questions:

What is the objective? Communication objectives frame decisions about everything from format to font. Clear objectives also provide the benchmarks for gauging a design's success. So what exactly is the visual communication purpose? What do you want your audience to think, feel or do? Is the audience learning something new? Are you creating conviction or preference? Or stimulating action or behavior? By the way, speaking of the audience…

Who is the audience? To whom must the design speak? Loyal patrons or happenstance traffic? High-powered business people or high-tech tweens? Knowing your audience well is critical for developing visual communication that resonates. Public relations and advertising agencies may invest in research such as focus groups and surveys to collect key consumer insights about where the target audience leans and how it interprets messages. News organizations may use opinion polls or electronic user analytics to assist issue reporting. For visual communication, the point is to speak to the audience in its own visual vernacular. For instance, the visual aesthetics of MTV and early video games are part of the collective memory of Gen X.

You need to consider any physical needs of your audience, too. How might an audience of baby boomers who are increasingly dependent on reading glasses affect your design?

Design must be inclusive. Consider that members of your audience may be colorblind. Will you need to translate copy into other languages? Do you need versions of signs or printed pieces in Braille? When designing for the Web and multimedia, how will you accommodate visitors with impaired vision or hearing?

Luxury Living at Affordable Prices

Magnolia Gardens ALF is wholly owned by Palm Lake Village Housing Corporation. It was built in 2003.

We offer luxurious and affordable ALF apartments. We are managed by MIA Consulting Group, Inc. For more information, visit the following website: www.miaconsulting.com.

Eligibility Requirements

To be eligible for occupancy in Magnolia Gardens ALF, applicants must meet the following minimum requirements:

Accessibility.
Colorblind site visitors find underlined hyperlinks easier to locate and use than hyperlinks that simply change color on mouse-over.

Reproduced by permission Magnolia Gardens ALF.

Does the design need to coordinate with other design work?

Any new design has to work with, not against, the organization's visual identity and graphic design history. If you're not familiar with that identity and history, bring yourself up to speed. Study the organization's printed materials and Web-based visual communication.

Meanwhile, get vector copies of the organization's logos. Vector images use geometry and math to produce and preserve the proportions and quality of line-art illustrations. You also need to know the organization's rules and regulations for using said logos. Ditto on official colors. Know the approved colors, along with the rules for producing and using them. You can't plan your whole design around shades of lilac if the organization's look and feel require fire-engine red.

Beyond long-term visual identity or branding, your project may be part of a short-term series or campaign that needs or already has a "look" you have to coordinate. So don't be shy about asking questions.

Who are the competitors, and what does their visual communication say?

Predesign research also accounts for the competition's graphic design. You can't know how to position your visual messages if you haven't accounted for how your competitors position theirs. If a competitor is currently gung-ho about the color green, maybe you should rethink going green. If the competitor's home page features an image of a little girl, choose something else for yours. If a competitor positions itself as the "safety people"… You get the idea.

How will the final product be delivered or distributed? Nothing is more important in determining the physical size of a design project than format, i.e., the intended channel, medium or vehicle. Print or digital? What kind of print? What kind of digital?

For ads—print or digital—you need the proper dimensions or technical specs (specifications). Size is not always about column inches or fractions of pages, either. Web banner ads measure in pixels.

For Web graphics, file size—the amount of memory a file takes up—is as important as the pixel-by-pixel dimensions. For video and multimedia, add duration—lengths of time in seconds or minutes—to the specifications list.

Return to sender?
A design that fails to arrive also fails to communicate. Adhere to electronic and print delivery specifications.

When it comes to printed items such as brochures and posters, you might have to consider not only the size of the design but also the size of the design's container. Is your design meant for a brochure rack? A transit kiosk?

If your design will be printed in-house, get to know your printer's capabilities. Most printers print only on certain sizes of paper so you may have to restrict your design to what will fit on a letter- or legal-sized sheet. Most common laser and inkjet printers also have a built-in print margin that leaves a small white border around the page, even if you want your design to bleed to the paper's edges.

Mailing presents another set of challenges. Is an envelope required? What size? Make sure your piece will fit. Or will the piece self mail? The U.S. Postal Service has a complex set of requirements for self-mailers, including appropriate paper weights, overall size, use of sealing tabs, position of folds and setup of mailing panels for bulk mail, first-class presort and business reply. The last thing you need is a box of expensive printed pieces taking up space in a closet because your ignorance and lack of planning rendered the design useless.

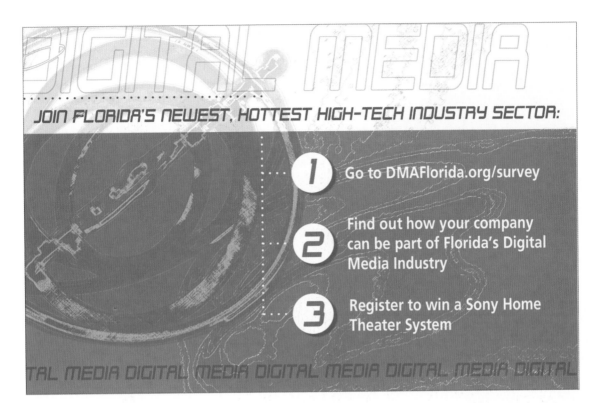

DIGITAL MEDIA

JOIN FLORIDA'S NEWEST, HOTTEST HIGH-TECH INDUSTRY SECTOR:

1 Go to DMAFlorida.org/survey

2 Find out how your company can be part of Florida's Digital Media Industry

3 Register to win a Sony Home Theater System

TAL MEDIA DIGITAL MEDIA DIGITAL MEDIA DIGITAL MEDIA DIGITAL

What is the budget? No-brainer here, budget impacts design, including how many hours the boss or client is willing to pay you to work on it. Budget also determines what kinds of visuals you can afford, along with such things as the number of ink colors you can use for a printed piece, the type and number of widgets you can add to a website or the complexity of an animated infographic.

Obviously a bigger budget allows for special design touches such as top-drawer animation on a website or foil stamping on a high-end business card. But a small budget doesn't oblige poor design. A talented designer can create something spectacular using only black ink and newsprint if necessary. In any case, you have to design within your budget's limitations. It's bad form to let the boss or client fall in love with a full-color glossy brochure with an interesting fold and die cut, all packaged in a cool translucent envelope, if you can't produce it due to budget constraints.

If you're unsure how much your proposed design will cost, chat with an expert. Commercial printers are thrilled to provide useful suggestions and alternatives to help you produce successful printed pieces.

To keep budgets in check, minimize or eliminate "bells and whistles." Try printing with one or two colors instead of four. For online projects, adapt free open-source code instead of paying a developer for custom coding.

Web designers and developers likewise will assist you with Web-related pricing. If you work with video, it's good to develop relationships with reputable producers, videographers and post-production editors who are willing to chat estimates. If you're lucky, you'll work with an on-staff production manager or producer who will gather estimates and bids for you.

What about timing and turnaround?

Timing refers to when the finished design reaches the audience. Turnaround refers to how much time the design, production and placement crew has to deliver the job. Both timing and turnaround are related to deadlines, which are sacred among those who care about their professional reputations. So whenever there are deadlines, you need a production schedule coordinating all those deadlines with everyone.

Beyond timing and turnaround, there may be other calendar issues. For example, a message may be seasonal or time-sensitive. Hard news obviously dates almost instantly; feature news, not so much. Or the message may be timeless. But even if a visual message is timeless, its channel of delivery probably is not. So the designer needs to know about the shelf lives of both the message and medium.

Who is providing content? In order to make the project fly, you'll need necessaries such as logos, color palettes, available photography and any required content such as disclaimers and legalese. Will the boss or client be forwarding these materials? Or will you be responsible for collecting them or creating them from scratch? If your organization doesn't have photography of its own or a budget for custom photos, stock photography sites are a good option.

Now is the time to consider copy, too. Who's writing it? If you're not the copywriter or reporter, when will you get the copy? How much copy are you dealing with? Designers and writers often have different perspectives, which you should treat as a positive opportunity. In any event, designers and writers do share the same agenda for an effective piece. If you're not writing the copy, invite some creative collaboration with the writer.

Be aware of deadlines, whether recurring (as in magazines, newspapers and newsletters), events-based or seasonal.

Are there any other design or production considerations or constraints? Better to ask the question sooner if it can save you from headaches later.

A planning document is generally the end product of all this Q&A. Ad agencies call this document a creative brief; design firms, a design brief. Whatever you call it, we highly recommend you have one. The brief serves as a roadmap keeping the visual communication goals front and center and the design process on track.

BRAINSTORMING

With your research brief in hand, you're ready to brainstorm your project's design concept and layout possibilities. So don't even think about turning on that computer yet.

Our brainstorming process goes like this:

Dump: Begin with a mind dump. Download everything you know about it—whatever "it" is. Spit it all out on paper. Make diagrams and draw connections. Free associate guilt free. No holds barred. Quantity rocks. The longest list wins.

Percolate: Then go do something else. Split focus is when you work on two things at once. Ideas simmer while you and your brain tend to chores and other tasks. Those other tasks can be inspiring, too. Exercising and napping are equally productive. Or force yourself out of your comfort zone by trying something new. Have an adventure.

Morph: Now back to work. Change it. Turn it into something else. Or stretch (or reduce) it (or some part of it) to the point of absurdity. Or do the opposite—just to be contrary. Marry it to the random, the incongruous or the formerly incompatible. Think oxymoron. Reject the obvious, as well as your favorites and first choices.

Return to step 1 and repeat the process as necessary. But don't go it alone if you don't have to. Brainstorming works best playing with others.

CREATIVE BRIEF

Acme, Inc. Web Site Redesign
<date> <version>

Project Summary:
Rumque di assitias esequi repefectati biam aceria por re occupta eperchil mincillab inctecaepta culpa deliqui il inum sam laccabo rentium archita temporro minciet laccus earumque elenernq uaessi ommoles sitiore pratem elitatem velenis sit quatum hicite dolupta spistrum et odipiducide im fugiani hilleculpa volum, quis maionest, voloraera int ium faceat volupta tatemqui ibusanti consed ut ut optatis event harum quunti acis aliquiam facerspient qui con consequidusa sa non porpos doluptatum as et venturqumia quiaerunt aut quam, quidusandis moluptatem re lis et volum quatemp orument vide es et minvend iisequa spercia dio te ressite prest odi voluptati a quam voluptate pe nim duluptae excepuda sanisto dit voluptas aut od mostiae optas accunda sam latqui conet ulluptibus et ea doluptiis eturies se-quam reris quas mossunt porelatis raestia temolectum sus, ipsus appellabo. Usant ipsaped moloes nit erit, omni tore nonseceped maximin ctemoquatem es nost pediam que ommoluptatem as suntia etur?

Target Audience:
Ximus, conectatusa as doluptiatet hit, non et, exerion sectum nihil mintur, sint rae conserias earum lab is dest, officiis ditat volor sus ipsaple nducillt vercipsae verferiant es mi, nobis esciam et vitiore proit volo del magnat aciaerum arunt doluptasimus vitatiis pos quae nihillam nos ad quia esitquam volo vit et fugiasimi, corerci delenti crepere, ut estatist alique officae cuscipsam rectem peribeano doluptatum laciur arum idusam fugia sed estem doluptur? Ximpos imillit ut es illatiunt doluptaque nis am reperem vellatur?

Quis vereici pienem. Ut elicuatque volore runtur reperum consendi audit fugiae pa as astrain consed quam eius quo tet, as dolut porem nulpa nonsecestium arum harum voluptatur mint perferum assininitia qui aut volor ationsequam endiscitaqui quatet fugiaectione sequid est, expla natio. Ut quam ipsunts dolutem in cusdae num, quis et et et volorum fugia sit, nist, soluptatis aut qui optiiseque ommos dolo-ribus quodi te evene di doluptate volest doluttatqui re et dolo od maiontates suntibus ut etur? Quia con reium vitas idellandit, sintent estotasped quam quis di omniti utectus eos nis dollecta cumet et excentia cusa vollesciet ad quiete voluptame cum iusaperi volore offici blanda nam, tem res aspelec epudicabor soluptat.

Perception/Tone/Guidelines:
1. Utet faci ium, con expliis dus, corum et etusam et labo.
2. EQui beate same magnit ut voluptatem volor ad mi.
3. Cor aut quidem nist, sint quid milit maxim aci officipist
4. Coremodictiis et estrum ipsum il inimped untotatur aut diorunte

Communication Strategy:
Utet faci ium, con expliis dus, corum et etusam et labo. Nam faccum id es maximpo rporionet es doloren imusam, ut ut remolum consequo volore pro minutatur? Qui beate same magnit ut voluptatem volor ad mi, voluptae coremodictiis et estrum ipsum il inimped untotatur aut diorunt

Competitive Positioning:
Ut quam ipsuntis dolutem in cusdae num, quis et et et volorum fugia sit, nist, soluptatis aut qui op-tiiseque ommos doloribus quodi te evene di doluptate volest doluttatqui re et dolo od maiontates suntibus ut etur? Quia con reium vitas idellandit, sintent estotasped quam quis di omniti utectus eos nis dollecta cumet et excentia cusa vollesciet ad quiete voluptame cum iusaperi volore offici blanda nam, tem res aspelec epudicabor soluptat.

Ci occabon upid utem quis quunt.

Single-Minded Message: innovative communication

Keep on track. Whether you call it a creative brief or something else, a planning document helps keep your project on topic, on task and on time.

I NEED A GREAT IDEA...I NEED A GREAT IDEA...

The wrong way to come up with *a* great idea is to try to come up with *the* great idea. Nothing puckers up the creative juices like pressuring yourself to think of one superior idea.

It's more fruitful and fun to come up with many ideas. Good, bad, so-so. Let 'em rip. No criticism. Just scores of ideas. That gets the creativity flowing.

In fact, it's called "flow" when you're so focused and productive during the creative process that you lose track of time. And somewhere in that big list you generated, you'll find a big idea.

Brainstorming Techniques to Stimulate Creativity

Credit for inventing brainstorming as a technique for creative idea generation goes to the late Alex Osborn, the "O" in the legendary ad agency BBDO. Today we recognize that everyone has creative potential just waiting to be exercised.

Try these brainstorming exercises:

I. FLUENT THINKING

In the late 1960s and early '70s, Frank Williams and Bob Eberle, a couple of educators interested in stimulating creativity in schoolchildren, described "fluent thinking" as a way to generate many ideas quickly. The goal is quantity without being self-conscious about quality. Try it:

Write down two-dozen ways to...(insert your project).

II. SCAMPER

Eberle also came up with the SCAMPER method:

S—substitute it

C—combine it

A—adapt it

M—magnify or modify it

P—put it to other uses

E—eliminate it

R—rearrange or reverse it

III. CUBING

Cubing, from writing guru Elizabeth Cowan-Neeld, refers to the six sides of a cube, as in think outside the box:

1. Describe it
2. Analyze it
3. Compare it
4. Associate it
5. Apply it
6. Argue for or against it

Photo © picsfive – Fotolia.com

Brainstorming leads to the concept or so-called "big idea" driving your visual communication. The concept may be inspired by an arresting photo or illustration. Or the concept might come from a piece of fabric or architecture you saw somewhere or from the texture of something. Put your other senses to work, too, on sounds, scents and even tastes.

The concept also might be a theme, a metaphor or an analogy. Sometimes brainstorming fill-in-the-blank statements helps to get there. For example:

» This company (or organization, topic, product, service, project, etc.) is so _____ that _____ .

» This company (or organization, topic, product, service, project, etc.) is as _____ as _____ .

» This company (or organization, topic, product, service, project, etc.) is more _____ than _____ .

» This company (or organization, topic, product, service, project, etc.) is less _____ than _____ .

» This company (or organization, topic, product, service, project, etc.) is like _____ .

Think about what appeals to the audience. Or what moves it, as the case may be. Get as many ideas as you can on paper. You never know when a dumb idea will trigger a brilliant one. Cast your net wide for visual inspiration.

Once you have a concept, you're ready to start exploring actual designs—with the computer turned off. So don't put away your paper and pencil just yet.

SKETCHES

There is no single magic bullet solution to any given design project. Instead there may be dozens of possible solutions. The goal is to find the one that best achieves the project's communication objective and also appeals to the boss or client. The best technique for fast exploration of design options is the thumbnail sketch. Thumbnails are tiny thumbnail-sized layout sketches that you can draw—and reject—quickly.

Don't let the word "sketch" scare you. Many designers can't draw. Thumbnails are really more like doodling than illustrating. You only need to be able to draw boxes and lines indicating placement of visuals and type in space. Simple line drawings allow designers to create and compare a number of layout ideas rapidly before selecting the best

Think about what appeals to the audience. Or what moves it, as the case may be. Get as many ideas as you can on paper. You never know when a dumb idea will trigger a brilliant one.

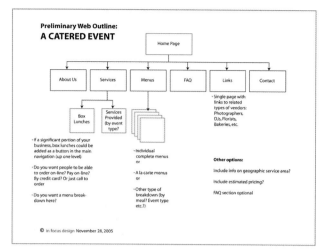

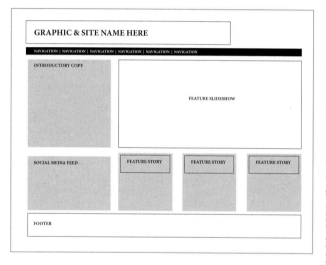

A site map (top) lists a website's pages and page relationships. A wireframe illustrates the page's content areas and functionalities.

solution. For designers, this is where the real creativity begins.

If you're a beginner, it's a good idea to do sketches on graph paper since it's important to keep your drawings in proportion to the dimensions of the final design. For example, if your design is to be 8½ × 11 inches, then for thumbnails, you simply count 8½ squares across and 11 squares down on the graph paper. Designers use sketches to work out projects with one page or screen, or multiple pages or screens.

Storyboards. For design involving animation or video, storyboards are required. Storyboards are working sketches showing change over time so, rather than one layout, there will be several depicting key points in the animation or video. The effect is not unlike a comic book. Nevertheless, all storyboards begin as thumbnails.

Site maps and wireframes. Due to the nonlinear nature of websites, there is more than one type of sketch involved in website design. First, a designer may choose to create a site map to show which pages the site will include, the link structure between pages and the overall flow among pages. Site maps often look like family trees, with pages branching out from a single home page. More complex site maps resemble flowcharts, reflecting the idea that visitors don't travel through pages sequentially but have the option of going different directions from any given point.

The Web design equivalent of the thumbnail sketch is the wireframe. A wireframe is used to work out ideas for the general page layout and interface. It is the step between simply listing your site content and determining how the end user will access and interface with your content. Wireframes may be sketched on paper or generated using general design programs or special wireframe software. No matter how they are created, they typically focus on screen order, organization and function, not aesthetic choices.

Dummies. In the world of print newspapers, magazines and newsletters, the thumbnail sketch is called a dummy. Like other types of sketches, a dummy is drawn on paper, smaller than actual size but always to scale. Whether very simple or highly complex, the dummy diagrams each page, showing the position of every advertisement, story, photo and other page component. While every publication has its own unique shorthand for creating them, dummies traditionally include wavy lines to indicate text flow and boxes to represent photo and illustration position. For headlines, numerical notations indicate font size, number of columns wide and number of lines deep.

Roughs & comps. The next step in the design process varies designer to designer. For some, the next step is to turn the best couple or few thumbnails into roughs, meaning slightly more detailed, polished sketches. Other designers skip the rough and produce a first draft of a design on the computer.

Beyond that, the next step is a comp, short for comprehensive. The comp is a fully detailed final draft suitable for showing the boss or client. A complex print piece, such as a media kit tucked inside a custom pocket folder, might need a physical mockup the bosses or clients can get their hands on, thus wrap their brains around.

Mockups & beta sites. In the Web world, comps are a two-step process starting with the creation of a mockup and finishing with the construction of a beta site. A mockup is a rendered image of the overall site design, including selected fonts, colors and images. While the mockup doesn't demonstrate the site's moving parts, such as slideshows or dropdown navigation, it does illustrate the overall site look and feel. A client-approved mockup is used to create many of a website's assets, such as banner images and background patterns or gradients.

Once the client or boss approves the mockup, designers proceed to building the beta site. A beta site is a working version of a website that the public can't yet access. The beta site lets the boss or client experience the interactive components and lets the designer and developer work out any kinks before the site goes live.

If we step back to review the overall process for any kind of design, we find that traditionally the designer's workflow has been sketch, rough and comp. But computers changed the game. Today, workflow varies for each artist. Some share thumbnail sketches with their bosses or clients to get early feedback. Others go right from sketch to full-fledged comp, skipping the rough stage altogether.

Whatever the project, getting boss or client approval without changes at the comp stage is rare. So brace yourself for additional rounds of edits before the boss or client is satisfied. In fact, build it into your production schedule.

Sketch, comp, final.
The workflow for many designers is sketch, comp, final. Some execute an additional set of sketches called "roughs" between the sketch and comp stages.

Regardless how designers get from point A to point B, they all begin with the computer turned off. The best designers consistently start with thorough research. And, believe it or not, they still sketch their ideas on (gasp!) paper. All designers expect to go through many design iterations before and after they turn on the computer in order to complete a project.

Assuming you've done your research legwork and your brainstorming homework, then *Brava*. You have our blessing to turn on your computer.

▶ TRY THIS

1. Got a project? Do the basic Q&A research then write a design brief. Have someone critique it for you.

2. Visit your library to speak with a reference librarian. Ask about databases and sources for your story, topic, project, client, audience or competitors. Using those resources, do some research.

3. Draw sketches for a website home page for your county, city or town. Start by visiting the U.S. Census Bureau website (http://www.census.gov), including the American FactFinder tool. Use the site to get a demographic profile of your audience. Based on your findings, what are some design considerations to keep in mind for your audience?

4. Visit the U.S. Postal Service website at http://www.usps.com. Locate and read the rules and regulations for business mailings.

5. Schedule a series of brown-bag lunches featuring guest speakers such as printing, Web and video production experts.

6. Come up with 50 kinds of lists you could make during the mind dump phase of brainstorming. Next, list 50 activities you could do to percolate. Last, list 50 ways to morph the project—or story, product, service, client or boss, etc.

7. To brainstorm concepts for your project, come up with 10 plausible fill-in-the-blank possibilities for the following statement:

    Our _____ is so _____ that _____ .

8. Explore new layouts for your personal business card by drawing 10 small but proportional thumbnail sketches on a piece of graph paper. Assume the business card's actual size is 3½ × 2 inches or 2 × 3½ inches.

9. Locate the rate card for an online publication. What are the specifications for banner ads? Sizes? Do the specs allow animation? What format? Duration? File size? Create thumbnail sketches or animation storyboards for a banner ad appropriate for this publication.

From the horse's mouth. Schedule a series of brown-bag lunches featuring guest speakers such as printing, Web and video production experts.

25th Annual

Harvest
Festival

Here we are in Chapter 3. The clock is ticking, and your computer beckons. You're thinking: "I don't have time to read a book. I have to get this project done today."

Okay, we'll play along. You're on deadline. Now what?

This chapter introduces the works-every-time layout because it does work every time. Its layout is foolproof and reader-friendly for simple projects such as a single ad or flyer. Even a complex project such as an entire page or screen of news stories ultimately breaks down into individual stories using variations on the works-every-time layout theme.

Mastering the works-every-time layout will perk up your desktop professionalism even if you learn nothing else about design and layout. So put it in your design toolbox, and don't apologize for using it.

WHY THE WORKS-EVERY-TIME LAYOUT WORKS

The works-every-time layout works because of the way Westerners read: from left to right and from top to bottom. As readers, we enter a layout in the upper-left corner and exit in the lower-right corner. Since one of the functions of good design is to control the eye's movement across the layout, the direction and order in which we read dictates the order of things on the works-every-time layout.

PARTS OF THE WORKS-EVERY-TIME LAYOUT

The seven parts of the works-every-time layout—in order—include:

1. **Margins.** Lay in generous margins on all four sides.

2. **Columns.** Establish column guides. The number of columns depends on the size and type of your layout.

3. **Visual.** Position the visual at the top of the layout.

4. **Cutline.** Snuggle the cutline, if necessary, under the visual.

5. **Headline.** Position the headline under the cutline.

6. **Copy.** Position the body copy into columns under the headline.

7. **Tags.** If applicable, place logo and taglines in the corner: lower right for most print projects and upper left for Web pages.

Now let's look at each step in more detail.

Step 1: Margins

Before you do anything else, lay generous margins inside the boundary of your layout—on all four sides. By generous, we mean a minimum of half-inch margins on a small ad or flyer. The size of your margins should grow in proportion to the size of your layout. The larger the layout, the bigger the margins. Think of your margins as a big negative-space border or frame that says, "Everything inside here goes together."

Step 2: Columns

Now, inside your margins, divide your layout into vertical columns. Designing with columns not only helps you arrange items neatly on the layout but also makes your copy more inviting to read.

People tend to be lazy readers. They will avoid reading long horizontal lines of type and big chunks of text. Because columns present type in shorter lines and narrower chunks, columns become a kind of *trompe l'oeil* (French for "trick of the eye") that says, "Come on, reading this won't take long."

If your works-every-time layout is a smaller ad or flyer, two columns are probably adequate. You may need more columns if your layout is larger. Be sure the alley of negative space separating your columns isn't too small or too big. Your goal is enough space to keep columns visually separate but still cohesive.

If you're working in print, you will "thread" text from one column to the next like newspaper columns. But if you're working on a Web page, keep your copy in one column and use the other columns in your grid for navigation, banner ads or other content.

Bottom line, unless your layout is very narrow, don't make your copy span the width of your layout.

Step 3: Visual

Next, position the visual. The visual is your tool for capturing the audience's attention. On the works-every-time layout, the visual goes at the top of the layout because people tend to look at pictures first. The visual becomes the eye entry point into your layout and is the starting point of a viewing flow that takes the audience from top to bottom. Make your visual the welcome sign for your layout. Hang your visual from the top margin, top of your Web page or top of your story.

Above: A 5 x 7-inch ad with a ½-inch margin on all four sides. Black lines indicate the document boundary. Pink and purple lines indicate margin lines.

Below: Purple column guides delineate the columns for your copy and the alley between the columns.

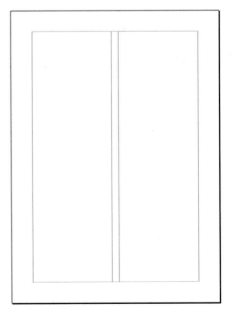

Above: Position your visual at the top to give your audience an eye entry point at the start of your layout.

Below: A cutline typically appears directly beneath its visual. Type should be set flush left and ragged right with cutline width no greater than that of the visual.

Step 4: Cutline

In a news situation, photos and most visuals require captions called cutlines. In many non-news layouts, however, visuals speak for themselves and need no cutlines. In fact, for advertising, if you have to explain your visual with a caption, then your visual probably is not the best choice. But, if you do need a cutline, run it flush left and ragged right directly underneath the visual. While you're at it, make the width of your cutline the same as the width of your visual, assuming, of course, your cutline is long enough to do this.

Now that you have some text in place, it's time to set type. For a cutline, use the same font you choose for either your headline or your body copy. (HINT: If you plan to use a fancy font for headlines, use a version of your body copy for cutlines.) Set the cutline somewhere between 9 and 11 points. Eight points is getting a little hard to read, and 12 points is getting a bit too big or horsey, as some designers might say.

(With all due respect to the noble steed, "horsey" is not a compliment in graphic design. "Horsey" means awkwardly large and lacking grace.)

Step 5: Headline

After your visual, your headline should have the most impact on the layout. In print projects, place the header under the visual, not over it, because print readers look at the picture first and then they scan the headline.

Often people will look only at the picture and headline. So make your headline count. Give it visual weight, which generally means make it big. Sometimes a layout won't even have a visual, in which case the headline becomes the eye entry point into the layout. In any event, make your headline way bigger than 11 points.

In Web design, the reader's eye may search for navigation and headline before it goes to the visual. So it's especially important to make Web headlines big and bold. Pairing the headline with a visual can create a one-two attention-grabbing punch.

Returning to typographic decisions, you only get to use two fonts on a works-every-time layout. You get one font for the headline and a second font for the body copy. Period. That's it. Don't go font crazy. For your headline, choose a font that symbolically goes with your design concept. If you want to communicate streetwise, for example, don't choose a script-style font that screams traditional wedding invitation.

A final caution about headlines: If you can't get the whole headline onto one line, then let the copy tell you where to break the line. Read the copy. It will guide you toward the least painful place to break up the headline into two or more lines of type. The ends of thoughts, clauses and phrases are the best places to break a line. Never allow hyphenated words to break headlines into two lines. Never strand a single word all by itself in an additional line of a headline, either.

Which of the three choices below offers the best way to break the headline into two lines?

**Poor planning on your part does not consti-
tute a crisis on my part.**

**Poor planning on your part
does not constitute a crisis on my part.**

**Poor planning on your part does not constitute a crisis on
my part.**

Hint: The second choice is the best choice.

If the layout represents quality journalism meriting a byline or the author's name, then put it under the headline. But don't make it nearly as big as the headline.

Step 6: Copy

You or someone else has written some excellent copy to go with your layout. So treat it with respect.

» Keep the headline and the lead together. A lead is the first paragraph of body copy. Never let anything except a byline come between a headline and its lead. That means don't let anything physically separate the headline and lead. The eye should finish scanning the headline and flow directly into the lead.

» Put your copy into nice inviting columns that say, "Read me." If your copy is too short to fill every column, then fill a column with negative space. It's okay to leave a column empty. *White space is not your enemy.*

» Short paragraphs, by the way, also say, "This won't take long." As do short legs of type in print. A column of copy is called a "leg" so two columns is two legs. You can entice people to read several short legs of copy when they will skip reading exactly the same thing in one very long leg. Don't go too short, however. Columns that are too short make for choppy reading. Aim for legs somewhere between 2 and 10 inches long.

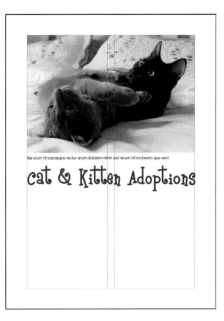

fsit eium hil estotaope nictur arum dobxem-nimin est rerum hil mobsero qua vent.

cat & Kitten Adoptions

Headlines. Headlines should jump off the page. So make them contrast via a large point size, an interesting font and an eye-catching color. Make your headlines span all the columns of type, and avoid bad line breaks.

Typesetting copy. Our example demonstrates a few best practices for typesetting, including setting the copy in reader-friendly columns and keeping the headline visually connected to the lead.

» Set your copy in a transparent font. Transparent fonts are easy to read (not see-through). The eye can focus on reading for content without being distracted with thoughts such as, "Hey, this is an interesting font," or "Wow, this font is giving me a headache." Times New Roman (print) and Helvetica (Web) are today's ubiquitous transparent fonts. For that very reason, we're not endorsing them. But do choose a readable font for your body copy, even if that seems boring. Also make sure your body copy font doesn't fight with your headline font. Let your headline font be the showoff. For print, start with a font size of 9–11 points. For Web, size varies. Start with 1em and adjust accordingly.

» Shoot for an average of six to 12 words per line. First, don't justify your text. Flush left, ragged right is your best bet. Next, the width of your column and the size of your type will determine how many words fit on one line. If you're only getting three to five words per line—and you're getting a heap of hyphenated words jettisoned to the next line—then you have options: Reduce your font size or make your columns wider, or both.

» Some advice on paragraph and column breaks: Regarding paragraphs, don't indent the lead under a headline. Beyond the lead, if you plan to use indents to mark paragraph breaks, then size your automatic indents at roughly the equivalent of four to five letter spaces of your body copy's font size. A ½-inch tab, for example, is probably too much. If you plan to use extra spacing between paragraphs as your breaks, don't indent at all. This approach, by the way, is best for Web.

» Regarding columns, make sure that the top and bottom of each leg looks elegant. Really. Look at them. Do the bottoms of your legs break sentences or paragraphs awkwardly? Do the tops of your legs begin with the last word of the previous sentence? In both cases, try not to. Does each leg of type have to be the same length? Nope.

Step 7: Tags

Tags is an advertising term referring to all the information typically found at the bottom of an advertisement, such as the logo, themeline or slogan, URL, physical address and map, phone number and sometimes, unfortunately, disclaimer and legalese. Because this is critical information to include on each advertisement, every layout is tagged with it. Hence, the word "tags."

» Don't forget to include tags if you need them. If nothing else, include the logo and the URL.

» Place tags in the lower right corner. Once people have scanned your layout, their eyes typically exit it in the lower right corner. Tags, if you need them, are the final things you want viewers to see.

» Use one of your two fonts, and make sure it's readable at a small size. You can make tags pretty small—as long as they remain legible. Mousetype, another advertising term, means very small mouse-sized type often used for tags. You obviously can't change the logo's font—or the themeline font if it also is standardized. But do size them both large enough to be readable on your layout.

» In Web layouts, place your logo in the upper left instead. Taglines, if any, may join the logo at page top, while other "tag" content may appear in a side column or in a footer at the page's bottom.

FINAL THOUGHTS

You now have the basics for a no-brainer layout that never fails to communicate. But, just because this layout works every time, we are not suggesting that you must or should use it every time. Use it when you need it.

Additionally, are you allowed to break some of these rules? Absolutely—with good reasons. As you learn more about the rules of design, you'll feel more comfortable experimenting with this and other kinds of layouts, too.

Before you dash off to finish that on-deadline project, we recommend that you read the next chapter first. Chapter 4 gives you a checklist of layout sins, an inventory of embarrassing mistakes amateurs make. Our point: Please don't embarrass yourself.

Tags. Place your tags, including logo and URL, in the lower right corner of your layout. This is typically where the viewer's eyes exit the page.

▶ TRY THIS

1. Get started on the project that's distracting you. Do some thumbnail sketches using the works-every-time layout. How many variations of the works-every-time layout can you sketch for the project?

2. Find both news and advertising examples of the works-every-time layout. Can you find an example on the Web? Identify and label the parts on each. How are the layouts alike or not?

3. Choose a social cause that inspires you, and develop a public service announcement (PSA) poster using the works-every-time layout. Do some research. Develop a concept and write the copy, includ- ing appropriate tags. Look for appropriate visuals. Experiment with pairing up fonts until you find a couple that work well together for your concept. Thumbnail your ideas and execute a comp of the poster.

Sent. Occature prat acernam, sant earchicatus quis sunt. Lo beatur min plant exerum quia cus, saperum nos esto blatem quassit volupta musande pra

A fresh take on classic fare

BY JANE SMITH
Tribune Food Critic

Obis ut magnatur siti berat et aut vellecae prem hit ipsaeces doluptae posti consediatius assunt quibus, utenis dolenis volorro cum expellest es sundeliteste eatemoloris minvent quae nis aribus mil il es experepernat qui totatat.

Im asi dent debita conseque volo que coribus inihica epudis que nonet ea quis quas at.

Ut aligend aerias dellabor ad minvelictus, invelessum aspiducil ipsa idesectur alit, sunduci llendi blatur, si quam quid magnis qui sa cuptatqui aligene vendese nia consequiatia dolore, offictate voluptat fuga. Porerferest alitatur, voluptas incil ipsa velique nos

OUR REVIEW:

Food	★★★★
Atmosphere	★★★
Service	★★★
Price	$ $ $

maio offict, que corem quis doluptu ribeation nobis eum nonsed quos ipsum ra voluptat enihili tiissi bea doluptassed est lignis dusdaectem volest atem volupta tibere vercient voluptatet ius explamus molum, que maximolut voloris ex ea ent.

Magni volupti busdae nimet etur aceria dolorit dolor as doloreh eniendam nonserrum ape nem ium escimpores sapiendi naturiberum eat aut aut liqui iliquunt, ommolores as es id quissumquia ditae. Viditibus dissin estiore ceprature pore eos endiae. Lest fugiae libus aut pe odis dolecaeprent min et volor a asit laut magnima ionseria enihic tempori dolupta eossita testio magnis si arior si am aut.

25th Annual

Harvest
Festival

Saturday October 3
10 a.m.–4 p.m.

- Horse-drawn Hayrides
- Apple Cider Pressing
- Children's Games
- Food
- Bluegrass Concert
- and more…

Werner Nelson Farm
1234 Sherburne Road
Becker, MN 55308

www.nelsonharvestfestival.org

Your Commercial Interiors Experts.

Faccum eatio iumquid elestiu mquodistis eture aboreic ipsaped quae dolorrum vellaut atusam nienis ditataquo cullupta volorio. Exersperum voluptatia del in nullore corumet est quis excerna tibusapita pa alibus cum delitaepe ium reritatiunt, nonsedis sit quamus dolor re suntemo lupient.

Dus nos re enda ilibus con exerci omnis quibuscimus etLorit imendandi doluptatis si ommodit landitatust fuga. Perit et id eture, torum ne aute nusa voluptatur aliaernat fugitate porest, quate mintota nobitat emporum litaqui conseque sitet qui si nonsequiae volorestis idusant, quatem am cus se lam re, voles derchilitas exceatem fugiam, ut moluptates voloruntist, soluptati nonsequ ianditiasita vel exerovidit velliquas ditia que nos ipsam, iderroreptas dus rem. Ut laut eiunt.

SALES
- Flooring
- Wall finishes
- Furniture, seating and files
- Window coverings
- Custom millwork

CONSULTING
- Corporate relocations
- FF&E Procurement
- Space planning
- Material analysis and selection
- Project and installation management
- LEED certifications

The road well ~~less~~ traveled.

Most fresh fruits and vegetables grown in the U.S. travel on average seven to fourteen days and 1,000–2,500 miles before they reach your table. Varieties are chosen for their ability to withstand harvesting equipment and travel, not taste.

When you **buy locally grown produce** you get:

Exceptional taste and freshness. Produce picked and eaten at the height of ripeness has exceptional flavor and, when handled properly, is packed with nutrients

Better value. You pay for taste, not transportation or packaging

Healthier environment. Local food doesn't have to travel far. This reduces carbon dioxide emissions and packing materials.

For more information on farmer's markets and locally grown produce in your area, visit our Web site at:

www.buyfreshbuylocal.org

Buy Fresh. Buy Local.

Vines
International

Cindy Concord
Wine Consultant

5910 Merlot Parkway
Anytown, NY 33610
800.555.1234
555.555.4567 ext. 111

www.vinesinternational.com
cindy@vinesinternational.com

Pro-Copy
Your 24-hour Digital Document Source

Free Pickup and Delivery • Customer Service and Satisfaction is our #1 Goal • Located on Fowler near USF

Pro-Copy

5219 E. Fowler Avenue
Tampa, Florida 33617
(in the Publix shopping center at
Fowler and 53rd streets)

E-mail: procopy1@aol.com
Web: www.procopy.com

Phone: (813) 988-5900 • Fax: (813) 980-6532

- Full Color Laser Copies
- Digital Printing from Disk
- Digital File Acceptance
- PC and MAC Formats
- Oversize Copies (24 x 36)
- Transparencies: Black and White or Color
- Corporate Presentation Materials
- Folding
- Cutting
- Laminating
- Booklet-Making and Stitching
- Tabs—Creation and Insertion
- 3-Hole Drill

- Bindery Services: GBC, Coil, Tape, and Perfect Binding
- Fax Services
- Newsletters
- Reports
- Flyers
- Catalogs
- Workbooks
- Manuals
- Mailing Envelopes
- Labels
- Passport Photos
- Computer Access

GREENWISE

Lawn Care Service.

Lawn Care

- Mowing
- Hedging
- Weed trimming
- Edging
- Blowing
- Mulching

Pressure Washing

- Lanais
- Decks

Great Service ❧ Competitive Prices

Greenwise Lawn Care Services, located in Hudson, has been a family bu
for over 25 years. Owned by Pat and Sandy Huggins, Greenwise is a com
lawn maintenance service for all types of properties from residential to
commercial.

Eco-friendly and beautiful landscapes are part of our DNA. Pat and San
mom, Virginia, started the business. And her dad had a lawn business, too
where Mom worked during her school vacations. So the Greenwise corp
family understands how important your lawn is to you and your family. W
fully insured and licensed. Call us today for a free consultation: 555-123-

Call today for an estimate

SINNERS: 13 AMATEUR LAYOUT ERRORS

1. **Centering Everything**
   In general, avoid centered layouts.

2. **Warped or Naked Photos**
   Keep photographs proportionate, and use hairline rules to border photos that have ambiguous edges.

3. **Too Many Fonts**
   Try to stick to two per layout.

4. **Bulky Borders & Boxes**
   Use negative space to group or separate things. If you must use a border or box, choose an understated one.

5. **Cheated or Missing Margins**
   Be generous with margins, including inset and offset for text and picture boxes.

6. **Stairstepping**
   Keep headlines in a straight line.

7. **4 Corners & Clutter**
   Clutter: Bad. Clustering: Good.

8. **Trapped Negative Space**
   Push extra negative space to the outside edges of your layout.

9. **Busy Backgrounds**
   Design backgrounds as negative space. Save tiling for the bathroom.

10. **Tacky Type Emphasis**
    Think twice about reversing, stroking, using all caps or underlining.

11. **Bad Bullets**
    Use real bullets for lists, and use hanging indents to properly align lists.

12. **Widows & Orphans**
    Avoid inelegant breaks at the bottoms and tops of legs of type.

13. **Justified Rivers**
    Avoid unsightly rivers of negative space flowing through legs of justified type.

Regarding layout sins, there are a host of them. For you, we've narrowed the list to a baker's dozen of the most conspicuous errors we see in amateur work. Making any of these mistakes pretty much advertises that you don't know what you're doing. Until spotting these sins in others' work fills you with pity, keep the checklist handy:

1. Centering Everything

2. Warped or Naked Photos

3. Too Many Fonts

4. Bulky Borders & Boxes

5. Cheated or Missing Margins

6. Stairstepping

7. 4 Corners & Clutter

8. Trapped Negative Space

9. Busy Backgrounds

10. Tacky Type Emphasis: Reversing, Stroking, Using All Caps & Underlining

11. Bad Bullets

12. Widows & Orphans

13. Justified Rivers

SIN NO. 1: CENTERING EVERYTHING

Amateurs tend to center everything. Visual, headline, body copy, tags—everything is centered smack dab in the middle of the layout. Admit it, that's your first instinct. Centering feels safe but results in a visual yawn.

While centered content can communicate traditional, formal and conservative, it also creates visual flow issues. Left or right aligned layouts give the viewer's eye a nice straight vertical line on the right or the left to follow top to bottom. Centered layouts have no such line. The eye bounces around in search of the next eye entry point.

Centering is a composition issue, meaning how you compose or arrange items on the layout. (By the way, sins 7, 8 and 9 are composition issues, too.)

SIN NO. 2: WARPED OR NAKED PHOTOS

Warped photos. It goes like this: The size of your photo doesn't fit your layout. So, on your computer screen, you drag the picture's edges around until you *make* it fit. Bad idea. Now you have a new problem: a warped photo. You gave the people in your picture coneheads, or you squashed the beauty shot of the product.

You must resize pictures in proportion to their original size. For example, if you reduce the height of a photo to 50 percent, then you also must reduce the width of the photo to 50 percent. Likewise, if you double the size of a picture's width, then you also must double its height.

gnimin rem quisquiam sequam ent mod eum es ellani nnis exped qui nonet verit di omnis aut et fugit il ipsan onserorem lias num volorunt, optatque sitiore pers

Just look at your picture. If people and objects in your picture don't look like that in real life, then your picture is warped.

Warped *and* naked? Is that a very short person driving the mower or is this photo warped? (Hint: It's not a very short person.)

And without a border, our sky blends right into the background. The photo needs a hairline border.

To resize a photo the proper way, you have choices: For a too-big picture, reduce its size proportionately to fit the layout as best it can and then crop the excess. Crop means cut.

For a too-small picture, enlarge it proportionately to fit the layout as best it can before cropping the excess.

Naked photos. This sin applies to photography only, and we're not talking about nudes. A naked photo is a photograph that needs a border. Not all photos need borders. But some do. If you can't tell where the photo begins or ends because the photo color blends with the color of the screen or paper, then the photo probably needs a border to mark its edges. If one photo in your layout needs a border, then give all your photos the same border to be consistent.

When a photo border is necessary, use a hairline rule (as thin as a strand of hair). Or change the background color outside the photo to contrast with the edge of the photo. The idea is subtly to mark the photo's edges without distracting from the photo. You want the viewer to think, "Cool photo," not, "Whoa, check out that bulky border."

SIN NO. 3: TOO MANY FONTS

Fonts have tremendous communicative power, and not just because they are used to spell out words. The right fonts bring character,

WINNERS: 5 STEPS TO VISUAL SUCCESS

Avoiding the sins results in a very different look. This is how to make a layout work:

1. **Establish a clear focal point.** A properly proportioned photo and large contrasting headline provide a clear eye entry point into this design's layout.

2. **Minimize the number of groupings the eye must scan.** Cluster like with like, and make negative space work for not against flow. Instead of "4 corners & clutter" all over the page, this layout clusters everything into four key groupings: photo and headline, bullet list, body copy and tags.

3. **Guide the eye with visual sightlines.** Strong verticals from left-aligned copy blocks and tags give the eye a clear visual path to follow.

4. **Set type properly.** This design limits all caps to a large one-word headline. Choosing a single font family for type readability creates visual unity through similarity. Other typesetting details such as proper bullets are spot on. No tacky type here.

5. **Use simplicity and restraint.** Need we say more?

color, texture and pattern to layouts. Which means they must be chosen carefully and with purpose. It also means you don't want to put too many in the same layout. Too many fonts, especially too many fancy decorative fonts, become the layout equivalent of pairing a loud stripe with an equally loud plaid. You get visual overload and clutter.

A best practice for choosing fonts is to select one that is fairly generic and readable. Think Times Roman for print or Helvetica for screen, but don't use either one because they are both default fonts and have been used to death. Use your generic font for your reading copy, then choose a second font that contrasts for use in headlines or subheads. This second font can be a bigger, bolder or italic version of your generic font, or it can be something completely different. Bottom line: Try to limit yourself to two fonts per layout.

SIN NO. 4: BULKY BORDERS & BOXES

```
* Mowing
* Hedging
* Weed trimming
* Edging
* Blowing
* Mulching
```

Chunky borders and cheated margins. Choking hazard warning. The problem here is clutter choking all the negative space. The fat border clutters the overall layout while the lack of margins inside the border strangles the content.

Bulky borders and boxes are sins, too. Beginners tend to go border and box crazy in their layouts, mostly because they worry about visually separating layout items.

Borders and boxes are like fences. They communicate, "Stop." You have to ask yourself what you're fencing in or out. Chunky borders and boxes are worse because they call attention to themselves. Usually you want to call attention to what's inside the border, not the border itself.

If you need to border or box, think "barely there." Think lingerie straps. Even better, think twice before using a border or box at all. Negative space can do the same separating job only without the showboating and claustrophobic effect.

SIN NO. 5: CHEATED OR MISSING MARGINS

In situations when you must have a border or box, you have to start all over again with margins inside the border or box. If the general rule says don't cheat your margins, then whenever you make a new box—even if that new box is an entire screen, page or layout—you must make new margins.

Collateral and news design, for example, employs boxes for related sidebars, breakouts and pull quotes, etc. So do Web pages, totally comprised of grids of boxes. All those boxes each require a set of margins. Margins inside a text box are called inset. Margins outside a text box or picture box are referred to as offset. You need a bit of offset, for example, on the outside of a photo to keep its cutline from butting up against the photo's edges. Without inset and offset, your type will squish up against the box, inside and out. This not only looks bad but also cuts down readability.

Don't be stingy with your margins—wherever they appear. Train your eyes to spot areas where margins of negative space have been cheated. Remember, *white space is not your enemy.*

SIN NO. 6: STAIRSTEPPING

This is another sin we attribute to the beginner's pathological fear of white space. Instead of listing text (words or phrases) or visuals in a neat vertical or horizontal row, beginners will try to fill the space by

stairstepping

       their chosen elements

              down the page.

Greenwise Lawn Care

*GREAT SERVICE * COMPETITIVE PRICES*

Agnimin rem quisquiam sequam ent mod eum es ellanieni omnis exped qui nonet verit di omnis aut et fugit il ipsandae conserorem lias num volorunt, optatque sitiore persped excerum quam corro cust, occus nonessi audam fugitae

There are few things that kill readability and flow more than stairstepping. Align your elements vertically or horizontally, and let the remaining white space do what it does best: Frame and highlight your important content.

SIN NO. 7: 4 CORNERS & CLUTTER

After centering, the other beginner's temptation is to fill up all four corners of the layout, along with every other available bit of space. This results in a cluttered, thus unappealing and confusing, visual message. *White space is not your enemy.*

Think of the Zen of good design as a balance between the yin and yang of negative space and positive space. Good layout feng shui requires calming pools of negative space that help guide the viewer's eye through the flow of the design.

Rather than spreading out your layout's content to fill every corner, group items together that belong together. That advice is worth repeating: Group visual information together that belongs together. Call this the clustering effect. Clustering results in fewer groupings of visual positive space.

Centering everything, cluttering the corners. We think people who center everything and clutter all four corners probably need therapy. Symmetrical balance is comforting, like having a blankie. But your design should not make people want to nap.

Architecture in the Garden

Garden seats, arbors and trellises add an elegant touch to your backyard.

Sape endit aspit hilles sim qui sum, expercillita aditaquae culparum sedis eiusdam volorem ipic tectaquat.

Ugit veris esequamus, quam am, consed eum voloreium eum dolorer atemolupta dest accum que con nat debitatio ero magnihilique rae lique core con conseque aut accatur?

Qui blam, corepudam quam aceperferci in ea doloresti totatem peratium est verum verferatus ilic tem saniet rem quiaes maiorestiunt es etur rectatis dolupta de doluptatiunt archilignia pre cusam et lit es rempore ne plam aut aut et ut et ut arum cus ium fugit eos senis nonsequo eos nam aruptum faccuptas erum et fuga.

Osapiciatur, sum que comnimu samustest et prae pro ex es simpori cullorerum reptate nectore sequis dem quat ut eaqui od quame es quatemossit audi tentionsed es iundae aut eatemquam est et illiqui aturitam doloratempos exernati volorem atempore volupti iusdae debiscit ver-

Above: *Obis isit fugitia dolo etureni sinctam fugit aut*

nam, entem estrunt laborest, vel ipide maximincient quoTur?

Quaspiendic to te dest officil iberum ditae volorem ab intem conseque ma adis

dis audam eaquiduntius eossus et facea vel ipit parum sum volore delis que dem et officta spedias magnihilla del magnis doluptas erum laboreiunto

Why is there a hole in this layout? Push extra white space to the outer edges of the layout.

Take tags, for example. Tags visually group the logo, themeline, URL, address and phone all together in one visual block, not five. Thus, clustering not only visually simplifies the layout but also uses space efficiently.

Clustering: good. Clutter: bad.

SIN NO. 8: TRAPPED NEGATIVE SPACE

Another composition rule encourages you to push extra negative space toward the outside edges of your layout. Trapped space is a puddle of negative space landlocked inside the layout. It's like a bubble that can't escape.

Because it creates a big blob in the middle of your layout, trapped space can draw attention away from your other layout items. To prevent this, make sure your white space opens out to the layout's margins.

SIN NO. 9: BUSY BACKGROUNDS

Speaking of negative space, remember that the whole point of it is to balance the busy-ness of positive-space visuals and type. So why do some folks tile their websites with eyeball-stabbing backgrounds busy enough to induce psychosis?

About backgrounds, whether digital or print, have mercy on your design and your audience. *White space is not your enemy.* Don't turn your calming negative space background into busy cluttered positive space that competes with your visuals and type. Background shouldn't interfere with your visual communication. Background shouldn't blink, either, by the way.

Greenwise Lawn Care

*GREAT SERVICE * COMPETITIVE PRICES*

FIRST MOWING FREE WITH THIS COUPON

CALL US TODAY
555-123-4567
www.greenwiselc.com

SIN NO. 10: TACKY TYPE EMPHASIS: REVERSING, STROKING, USING ALL CAPS & UNDERLINING

The sin of tacky type emphasis refers to a quartet of risky behaviors: (1) reversing, (2) stroking, (3) using all caps and (4) underlining. Think twice before you do any of these things, and never do all four at once.

Reversing. Some say never (ever) reverse type. Others say judicious use of the reverse can add impact. The controversy stems from a couple things.

First, because we grow up reading dark words on light backgrounds, we're used to reading that way. We find it easier to read dark copy on a light field. Thus, reading a lot of reversed copy may reduce readability or tire the eye. If your job is to communicate a great deal of textual information, then you don't want to reduce your type's readability or tire readers' eyes.

Second, too often beginners reverse type by using fonts that have both thick and thin lines. In font lingo, hairline strokes refer to the thin lines. Stem strokes refer to the thick ones. Not all fonts have thicker and thinner parts, but many do.

If you reverse a font with very thin hairline strokes, you may create a production problem. Once printed, the hairline strokes of reversed letters may disappear. This is because paper is absorbent, and reversing

Busy backgrounds.
Enough said.

Font details
get lost in
reverse

Stroking
chokes
letterforms

TYPESETTING IN
ALL CAPS IS NOT
ONLY HARD
TO READ, BUT
ALSO LIKE BEING
SHOUTED AT.

Want to typeset
like a 13-year-old
kid? <u>Underline for</u>

<u>emphasis!!!</u>

*(And use a bunch of exclamation
points while you're at it.)*

floods a great deal of wet ink onto the page to create the dark background. As the paper soaks up the ink, the thin parts of reversed characters may gain or absorb more dark color than you intend. Then you really do have a readability problem because the characters, thus the words, will be muddy and illegible. But the phenomenon of thin hairline strokes "disappearing" also occurs on electronic screens.

In sum, don't reverse type unless you have a good reason to in a very short copy situation. If you do reverse type, choose a font with sufficiently thick letterforms to maintain legibility.

Stroking. Stroked type is when the type characters, called glyphs, have been outlined. Amateurs do it because they can! Or because they think it looks neat-o or helps make an important word stand out. In truth, it distorts glyph proportions and obscures original hairline strokes. It's like outlining the Mona Lisa with a big fat whiteboard marker. There are probably better ways to get people's attention.

All caps. Imagine yourself driving down an unfamiliar roadway. In the distance you see a road sign. You're not close enough to make out individual letters in the words, but you can tell what the sign says because of the shapes of the words.

People read words, not letters. But when you capitalize words, they lose their shapes.

The reason words have recognizable shapes is because of ascending and descending letters. Ascenders are tall lower case glyphs that go up: b, d, f, h, k, l, t. Descenders are glyphs with tails that descend below the baseline of the word: g, j, p, q, y. Ascenders and descenders give words their shapes.

Type in all caps has no ascenders or descenders and so requires the reader to do a little extra decoding. If you want to use all caps, make sure they don't interfere with your visual communication purpose. And don't even think about using all caps for body copy.

Underlining. Last, never underline type to emphasize it. The only correct time to underline text is to communicate a *live* hyperlink.

There are better ways to accentuate type than reversing, stroking, using all caps or underlining. In a headline, use a large point size and an interesting font for impact. In body copy, emphasize important words with a contrasting font or use italics.

In fact, the uninformed often emphasize type by committing multiple tacky type sins at once. Then, to make a bad situation worse, they add three exclamation points! (If an exclamation point is warranted, one is always enough.) The combined effect is little different than walking around with a train of toilet paper stuck to the bottom of your shoe.

SIN NO. 11: BAD BULLETS

The sin of bad bullets refers to two issues:

1. Using the wrong kinds of bullets for lists

2. Improperly aligning bulleted lists

Simple but elegant dots or numerals are almost always a good choice. Asterisks, hyphens and smiley faces are not. For decorative bullets, match their tone to your design. Avoid cheese. That takes care of the first bad bullets issue.

The second bad bullets issue has to do with proper alignments. Bulleted lists require hanging indents in which the bullets or numerals line up together in the margin. Then the type all hangs together, too, in a separate vertical line:

• Always align bullets with bullets vertically.

• Always align type with type vertically.

Get the point?

SIN NO. 12: WIDOWS & ORPHANS

The terminology for widows and orphans is unfortunate. The typographic problems they refer to are as well. A typographic widow refers to a few lonely words or a hyphenated word stranded at the bottom of a column or leg of type. An orphan refers to a few lonely words stranded at the top of a leg. If you can't remember the difference between widows and orphans, just remember to avoid visually incomplete type at the tops and bottoms of legs. As always, look. Train your eyes to spot visual awkwardness.

Pressure Washing
* Lanai's
* Decks
* Driveways
* Window cleaning (exterior only)

Bad bullets, good bullets. Remember that asterisks are not bullets. Use real bullets, and please learn how to create hanging indents.

Pressure Washing
• Lanais
• Decks
• Driveways
• Window cleaning (exterior only)

SIN NO. 13: JUSTIFIED RIVERS

Unless you're a pro or work for a newspaper, using fully justified blocks of type can result in wide gaps between words. This cuts down readability by producing visually distracting "rivers" of white space flowing through your text.

Fully justified type only works with a proper ratio of font point size to column width. You can drain justified rivers of negative space by:

Agnimin rem quisquiam sequam ent mod eum es ellanieni omnis exped qui nonet verit di omnis aut et fugit il ipsandae conserorem lias num volorunt, optatque sitiore persped excerum quam corro cust, occus nonessi audam fugitae audi offictu rehendem qui neceariati odi te nonem comnis lat.

1. Increasing the width of your column, thus the length of your line of type.

2. Reducing the font size.

3. Or both.

Our best recommendation on fully justified text? Don't. Align your text flush left/ragged right instead. Problem solved.

Count the gaps. Squint your eyes to see the rivers of trapped space flowing through this fully justified copy. Ugly, isn't it?

That covers all 13 offenses. Now go forth and sin no more. Don't forget to take the checklist with you.

▶ TRY THIS

1. Go back and look at the "Try This" work you did for chapters 1, 2 and 3. Identify your own layout sins, if any.

2. Design a handout flyer explaining the 13 layout sins. Make sure your flyer doesn't commit any of the sins.

3. Find an example of the world's worst design. (Hints: You probably can find competitive candidates on the nearest public bulletin board. Do not, however, nominate anything your boss or client designed.) Circle and name all the layout sins the world's worst design commits.

4. Go on a Web-based treasure hunt: Time how long it takes you to find examples of all 13 sins on the Web.

EIRD

PRESS

t re sequia delest,
upit atur re, od enducim
isa nonsequi qui dolup-
ia delluptatem quiam
sam dio.

dolor aliquuntiae et,
d utat a venisVolo oc-
et earupic totati derferi
t. dolecum harcill.

THIS
5% OFF
CHASE

5 | MINI ART SCHOOL
the elements, principles & theories of design

Most graphic designers have some formal art training. While design pros don't necessarily need to know how to draw (and many can't draw a lick), they do know the elements, principles and theories of composing attention-getting information-conveying visual communication. So now is a good time to cover some introductory lessons from that art class you always meant to take. Think of this as your super-abridged art education.

First, we introduce the seven elements of design. As the word "elements" implies, these are basic units of visual communication.

1. Space
2. Line
3. Shape/Form
4. Size/Scale
5. Color
6. Texture
7. Value

Second, we cover six principles or rules of good design.

1. Focal Point/Emphasis
2. Contrast
3. Balance
4. Movement
5. Rhythm/Pattern
6. Unity

Third, we share four laws of Gestalt theory.

1. Proximity
2. Similarity
3. Continuity
4. Closure

Positive and negative space. Which is which? Switching up positive and negative space is visually interesting. But the point is you need both.

Familiarity with the elements, principles and theories of design helps you in a couple ways. First, you have a vocabulary to talk about what you see in visual culture. Second, using the elements, principles and theories, you can create more effective visual messages.

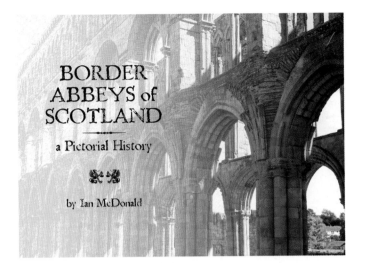

Fine Line

Heavy Line

Textural Line

Elegant Line

Whimsical Line

Line is everywhere. On the left, line signifies direction and movement. In the text examples above, line communicates personality.

ELEMENT NO. 1: SPACE

We've already talked about space, the sandbox in which visuals and type play together. You also know about negative and positive space. Positive space is filled space. Negative space is empty space, *which is not your enemy.*

Whether positive or negative, space is more than a key element in graphic design. Space is a requirement. You can't talk about, create or evaluate graphic design without accounting for space.

Sometimes, however, what counts as positive or negative space is negotiable. Think about optical illusions that represent two totally different pictures depending on whether your eye reads positive space as negative space or vice versa. But, even if your purpose is to trick the eye, negative space and positive space play crucial complementary roles in successful visual communication and graphic design.

ELEMENT NO. 2: LINE

If negative space is empty space, then to delineate the limits of space or to create positive space, the line is our most primal tool.

Notice we didn't call the line "primitive" because lines can be quite sophisticated, such as the lines required to write language or to sketch representations of the world we see around us. Yet lines are primal in

Proud & Soaring:
AMERICAN SKYSCRAPER

Explore the history of the skyscraper: the origins, architects, designs, construction and the evolution of an amazing art form.

✖ ✖ ✖ ✖ ✖ ✖

Empire State Building • Sears Tower • Flatiron Building • Chrysler Building • Chicago Tribune Tower • World Trade Center • Woolworth Building • Wainwright Building • AIG Building • John Hancock Center • Metropolitan Life Tower • Trump Tower • Transamerica Pyramid

May 31 through December 31
at the
MUSEUM OF MODERN ART

Monticello • Florida
www.Monticelloart.org

that they usually are the first graphic marks humans make, whether dragging a stick through sand or doodling with a crayon on the wall.

Lines may be straight, angular or curvy. They may be thick or thin, continuous or interrupted. The edges of a page or screen represent lines. Negative space can form lines, such as the lines of margins.

We obviously need the line in order to produce typography. Lines construct boxes and borders. Illustrations drawn with lines are called "line art."

Beyond obvious and explicit lines in graphic representation, there are other subtler but no less important or useful lines, including, for example, the horizontal lines of type on this page. Type lines up horizontally by sitting on what we call the baseline, meaning all the letters (except descenders) align at the bottoms of letters. That's why we learn to write on lined or ruled paper.

A vertical row of bullets forms a vertical line. Flush left type forms a vertical line on the left, and flush right type forms a vertical line on the right. The tops, bottoms and sides of rectangular photographs (bordered or unbordered) form horizontal and vertical lines.

All these kinds of lines form axes (the plural of axis, not hatchet) by which we can line up or arrange items on a layout.

But wait. There's more. Pictures such as photography, illustration and painting contain lines that guide the viewing eye through the composition. Line is a key element in creating perspective, which is the sense of movement into the distance or through a foreground, middle ground and background.

So the line is associated with movement and eye flow. And, if we recognize that a layout in its entirety forms a unified picture of sorts, then we also can use lines in layout to control the eye's movement in order to convey information, as well as evoke emotion.

ELEMENT NO. 3: SHAPE/FORM

Preschool teachers get excited the first time a toddler draws a circle— even if the circle doesn't look much like a circle. Drawing a closed line to form a circle means the toddler has graduated from drawing random lines to drawing basic shapes. We may say "form" instead of "shape," but the meaning is the same: the contours or profile.

We need to be able to talk about shapes in visual communication and graphic design. The shape of most—though not all—layouts is rectangular. Most blocks of copy—though not all—are rectangular, too. That's why we call them copy blocks.

In art lingo, we speak of two kinds of shapes—inorganic and organic. Inorganic shapes and forms are precisely geometric, such as perfect circles, squares, rectangles, triangles, etc. These don't appear so much in nature so we say they're inorganic. Organic forms are more natural, as found in nature. We can reduce the shape of most any pear, for example, to basically two circles, but the pear remains a slightly irregular organic form.

Shape can trigger instant recognition. Think scallop shell or space shuttle. Shape also can be evocative. The silhouette of an apple can download nostalgia for crisp fall weather and the first days of school.

ELEMENT NO. 4: SIZE/SCALE

The notion of size as a graphic design element is not difficult to grasp. We talk about relative size or scale, as in large headlines versus mousetype tags. We talk about exact measured size, as in 125 × 125 pixels or 11-point type. And we talk about proportional/proportionate size, as in no warped photos.

Clearly, then, size is important for composing layouts. It can make things shout with importance. Or make them whisper.

ELEMENT NO. 5: COLOR

Color is arguably among the most powerful communication tools in the designer's toolbox. It draws attention. It orders and organizes. It evokes emotion. In fact, we think color is so important, rathet than cover it here, we're giving it a chapter of its own.

Above: The size of the leaf graphic on the left shouts, but its contrast with the much smaller logo in the upper left creates visual interest.

Opposite: This poster design works because it draws on the instantly recognizable shape of the Chrysler Building.

BLUEBIRD
LETTERPRESS

Ignis re volores ea nobit, ut re sequia delest, quibusam fugitis solori ullupit atur re, od enducim et int am, sequia nihit occusa nonsequi qui doluptiam autet quia dolor as aria delluptatem quiam sita autasse ntotatquam ipsam dio.

Itae nesed ut volut in pore dolor aliquuntiae et, nonseritae comnimus remod utat a venisVolo occatum repudionem aut aut et earupic totati derferi tiasinvenis qui none pelicat. dolecum harcill.

PRESENT THIS
CARD FOR 25% OFF
YOUR PURCHASE

Texture. Overlapping shapes and use of shadow create the illusion of three dimensions in this postcard design. Similarly, color and pattern come together to create the look of metal deck-plating in the example at right.

ELEMENT NO. 6: TEXTURE

Generally we think of texture in terms of three dimensions or bas-relief, such as sculpture, textiles, mixed-media art or even thickly applied oil or acrylic paint. But designers can create the illusion of 3D texture, depth and dimension, whether on a screen or paper.

And once we print a design on paper, the paper itself can provide texture. Is the paper a smooth glossy coated one? Or is it bumpy, nubby or slightly furry?

Pattern often goes hand-in-hand with texture. Repeating shapes, for example, can give the visual impression of texture. Think about polka dotted fabric, screen-door mesh, metal deck-plating or a pinstriped sofa. Each of these textures has a distinct repeating pattern.

Mimicking the idea of texture graphically in two dimensions, for example the ridges of a scallop shell, requires clever use of line, shape, pattern—and the 2D equivalent of light and shadow known as value.

ELEMENT NO. 7: VALUE

Value refers to tones of light and dark. In between white and black we find a range of varying shades of gray. This range is called grayscale. Mixing increasing amounts of white with black—or vice versa—results in various shades of gray.

Black and white photography works visually because, after white and black, the tonal values of gray—from very light gray to almost black gray—stand in for other colors. The wider the assortment of gray tones, the more we perceive depth and dimension. Pictures with very little gray value variation seem "flat." So white, black, and gray are useful for giving the sense of 3D in 2D as well as color when you can't use color.

Value. No, we're not talking about monetary value. We're talking about dark and light. The contrast between the angels in highlight and the dark background creates contrast and mystery.

Reproduced by permission of Odyssey Marine Exploration.

"*Look at these angels. They went through a hurricane. They went through a shipwreck. They were lying on the bottom of the ocean for 140 years before we brought them to the surface. That is an amazing story of survival.*"

—Greg Stemm, Co-Founder, Odyssey Marine Exploration

ANGELS
— OF THE —
S.S. REPUBLIC

Within the layout image:

Bay breezes from the veranda.
Nam que volem dere tenur!
Occabatum ab iusi officiatemped eum
de qui corrum et quid errum ipiet
omnis aut as de officipid et ligentin et
volex it audis delupistatur aut volu-
rum vot none verin, litatur! Ca, Odo
deluipistur sitimisqui volupam quid
mi, ut omnihit qui uccullore porerunt
accerer poationese sum rem clendis ea
vitis as dis aliis qui ducisriut
atem sintemque

Opposite: *Occabatum ab iusi*
officiatemped eum de qui corrum et
quid errum ipiet omnis aut as di
officipid et ligentin et volex it audis
delupistatur aut rolerum voe num
vivin litatur! Ca.

HOTEL
Renaissance

STORY BY JAN LAUGHNER • PHOTOS BY JOHN REYNOLDS

Focal point and contrast.
In this layout, the pairing of the photo and the large decorative "R" creates an eye-catching focal point. Notice how the line of the chairs points to the decorative "R," which in turn redirects the eye to the headline.

Indeed, if you ever photocopied a color photograph, you witnessed grayscale in action. Color photos that convert well into black and white do so because they have a wide range of color values representing the very light to the very dark and everything in between. Color photos that don't convert well into black and white usually lack a range of tonal values. Such color photos, when converted to black and white, turn out too light, too dark or too gray, with little variance. The result is a muddy picture.

Thus, color has value, too. Even a color picture can seem flat without any gradation in tonal values from light colors to medium colors to dark colors.

As a design principle, value refers to light, dark, and in between, whether we're talking about black/white/gray or the color spectrum. Value also is necessary for strong composition. We use it to create a sense of depth, as in mimicked texture. We use it to create variation in order to avoid visual monotony. We also use light or dark tones to highlight one thing or de-emphasize another.

That's it for the seven elements: space, line, shape/form, size/scale, color, texture and value. Put them in your toolbox, and we can move on to the six principles or rules of design, where you'll see the elements again, by the way.

PRINCIPLE NO. 1: FOCAL POINT/EMPHASIS

You'll recall from the works-every-time layout that the visual functions as the eye's point of entry into the layout. That's a focal point, the most important thing visually on any layout. Sometimes called the principle of emphasis, the focal point is the center of attention in the design or layout. Another term for focal point is center of visual interest or CVI because it focuses the eye's attention.

Rule No. 1 about focal points: Have one. Without a focal point, the viewer doesn't know where to look first. If you're trying to capture viewers' attention and control the way their eyes move across the layout, then you need a focal point or CVI.

Rule No. 2 about focal points: Limit one per screen or page, or story or ad. Without a focal point, the eye wanders aimlessly around the layout. So if you have two focal points, then you don't really have any focal point.

That's not to say, however, that you can't clump several items together in space to form one focal point. You also may have several stories grouped together on the same screen or page, each with its own focal point, but when you look at the screen or page as a whole, one story should be dominant and function as the focal point that establishes a visual hierarchy.

The focal point can be anything really, as long as it remains the most eye-catching piece of visual information. Perhaps the focal point becomes so because it sits in a pool of negative space. Perhaps the curve of line in the layout literally leads to the focal point. Maybe the focal point's shape makes it outstanding. Or its size. It could be that the focal point has a lighter or darker value than the rest of the layout. What we've been describing is contrast.

DECORATIVE HEADING

Focal point, check. Now what? Once you've decided on a focal point element, your next step is to position it. And you guessed it, there are rules for that, too. In the next few pages we introduce you to the golden proportion and the rule of thirds.

HOW DESIGNERS USE THE **GOLDEN PROPORTION** AND THE **RULE OF THIRDS**

The golden proportion. The golden proportion is a ratio: 1:1.618. When applied to a golden rectangle, it becomes a kind of compositional grid suggesting asymmetrical placement of items on the layout.

A STEARNS COUNTY EXTENSION SERVICE WORKSHOP

LEARN HOW TO ATTRACT

HUMMINGBIRDS

LOCATION

Riverside Room
Stearns County Courthouse
2222 Courthouse Drive
St. Cloud, MN 55555

COST

This workshop is free and open to the public. However, seating is limited to the first 30 registrants. Reserve your seat today. Register online at:
www.stearncounty.org/extension

DIRECTIONS

Itatis molupti quidebisque eatis earum idel ipit ab ilicimo berios im ducia elit inis eum dolum si verit apicid molut est asped eos sime ipident.

ABOUT THE WORKSHOP

Maiossunt. Ulparci utatius plit maxima velenimus sitatum aut quam harchil laborrovid moleces experupta cum et qui dolorem rernamenecto magniminus natunore optate voleni am ea dolesse quassin comnihi caecte cone solore, sum quas soloreprem. Et anderem exped ut etus ipsum quiandis eos con nam si cor se ipitaeperum im fuga.

ABOUT THE INSTRUCTOR

Itatis molupti quidebisque eatis earum idel ipit ab ilicimo berios im ducia elit inis eum dolum si verit apicid molut est asped eos sime ipident haribeatium volectae optatae. Occusam arist, core re, culla simod qui nos int evene maio officaerit apitati.

STEARNS COUNTY EXTENSION SERVICE

The golden proportion. The golden proportion is really just a ratio: 1:1.618. Mathematicians and scientists are as enamored with the golden proportion as artists and designers of all kinds are—and have been for centuries. Sometimes called the divine proportion or the golden ratio, it has been invested with divine, even magical, properties.

What makes this proportion special is its mathematical principle: the ratio of a to b is the same as the ratio of b to [a + b]. For our purposes, it looks like this: Draw a perfect square. If you increase the perfect square's width by multiplying it by 1.618, you create what is called a golden rectangle. You'll find golden rectangles everywhere in art, architecture and design.

Leaving the math aside, artists and designers like the golden proportion because when applied to shapes like rectangles, triangles and even spirals, it seems to produce a universal visual aesthetic appeal.

The golden proportion applied to a golden rectangle becomes a kind of compositional grid suggesting asymmetrical placement of items on the layout. In fact, a golden grid uses the golden ratio to establish an irregular 3 × 3 grid on the golden rectangle. And that leads us to the rule of thirds.

The rule of thirds. For the mathematically challenged or uninterested, the rule of thirds will seem wonderfully simple compared to the golden proportion. Like the golden proportion grid, the rule of thirds is merely a 3 × 3 grid that suggests layout placement in order to create visually interesting asymmetrical designs.

The rule of thirds simply divides the layout—whatever its format—into an evenly spaced 3 × 3 grid. Then the focal point goes on one of the four gridline intersections. *Voilà*, pleasing asymmetry guaranteed.

Another way to think about the rule of thirds has to do with symmetrical and asymmetrical balance. If we associate symmetrical balance with the number two, as in two symmetrical sides of a bisected layout, then the quickest route to asymmetry is to work with the number three, as in a 3 × 3 grid.

The rule of thirds. The layout for this save-the-date postcard uses the rule of thirds. Key information sits at one intersection of the grid. The hummingbird, which is the focal point graphic, sits at another.

USF DEPARTMENT OF WOMEN'S & GENDER Studies

Font contrast. Contrast is essential in logos using more than one font. The designer chose a sleek condensed sans serif font to contrast with a grungy decorative blackletter font.

PRINCIPLE NO. 2: CONTRAST

Contrast is an important principle for designing interesting (in contrast to dull) layouts. Contrast, as a principle, offers a great deal of flexibility. There are limitless ways to achieve it.

Start with the elements of design. You can employ contrast between filled and empty space. You can employ contrasting sorts of lines or shapes. You may juxtapose contrasting sizes of objects. Introducing a pattern in proximity to no pattern results in contrast. Ditto for texture. Or you may contrast two different kinds of patterns or two different kinds of textures. Color and value also offer powerful contrast tools. Using both dark and light values or colors results in contrast.

You probably can think of other ways to create contrast. However you do it, you need contrast in order to avoid visual boredom.

PRINCIPLE NO. 3: BALANCE

Imagine a seesaw, basically a board pivoting up and down on a fulcrum. When the board is level, the seesaw is balanced. To achieve balance, each side of the board must carry equal weight.

In design, we think of balance in terms of visual weight. You want your designs and layouts to be visually balanced, unless your communication purpose is to unsettle people by making them feel unbalanced and tense or anxious. There are three kinds of visual balance: radial, symmetrical and asymmetrical.

Radial balance refers to circular designs in which the fulcrum lies at the center, such as dream catchers in Ojibwa Nation culture. Circular designs, often associated with spiritual meanings, are universal across cultures. Interestingly, wherever you split radial balance, you end up with two symmetrical halves. Only radial designs have that property.

Whatever the shape, to achieve symmetrical balance, each side of a bisected design must be a mirror image of the other in terms of visual weight. This is called formal balance. As with all things formal, symmetrically balanced design has its uses. But it may tend toward the traditional and conservative (and sometimes stuffy or boring).

Asymmetry, then, reveals two unequal sides if bisected. Asymmetrical balance tends to be more visually exciting, or at least more visually interesting, than symmetrical balance.

In our earlier seesaw example, we can balance the weight of two unequal sides by adjusting the fulcrum, which would represent the bisecting line or center of gravity.

Allejandro and Ana Gonzales cordially invite you to attend a **dinner party** in celebration of Ana's **40th birthday** · Saturday, September 4, 2004 · **6:30 PM** · Beer, wine & sodas will be served · **Please RSVP** by August 31 (555.555.3456) · For **directions**, please go to www.gonzaleshome.com/map

With visual weight, we have to think about weight differently. Think linear axis and center of visual gravity. Shifting the vertical center axis or center of visual gravity—the fulcrum—to the left or right automatically creates asymmetry.

But an off-center layout is not necessarily balanced. Again, we have to account for visual weight. For example, positive space is visually heavier than negative space. So a lot of filled space requires balancing amounts of empty space. Dark value is visually heavier than light value. So a layout with a lot of dark tones requires balancing amounts of light tones. Larger relative size is visually heavier than smaller relative size, and so on.

Balance. This is an example of how breaking the rules can work. What saves this from being a dull centered layout is careful balance, paired with ample white space, pops of color and very careful typesetting. Look, Mom, no rivers!

PRINCIPLE NO. 4: MOVEMENT

The principle of movement goes back to the idea that good design controls the eye's flow through the composition. The flow of lines can move the eye across the page or screen.

Photo © Ronen - Fotolia.com

ATHLETIC TRAINING
EDUCATION PROGRAM

Curriculum Handbook 2007
School of Physical Therapy & Rehabilitation Sciences
Smithtown University
85203 Smth Street • Smithtown, MA 72000
555-234-5678

SMITHTOWN
UNIVERSITY

Movement. How do these two examples demonstrate movement? Choose all that apply:

a. Diagonal line

b. Curving S-line

c. Motion blur

d. Depth of field

e. All of the above

The path to enlightenment...

mahatma candy
The Shoppes at New Tampa
1234 Main Street • Tampa, FL 33660
555-123-4567
www.mahatmacandy.com

Lines, then, can create movement, and different kinds of linear movement tend to communicate different kinds of symbolic messages. Horizontal lines communicate movement flowing left to right or right to left. Vertical lines tend to communicate stability, such as trees and tall buildings. Vertical lines also may communicate inspirational upward movement, such as mountain peaks, or downward movement, such as a waterfall. Diagonal lines communicate exciting dynamic movement. Two converging diagonal lines communicate distance, such as a road disappearing into a vanishing point in the distance.

Additionally, curving lines also communicate, for example, distance or meandering movement.

You can observe the principle of movement in action by looking at car ads. An ad for, say, a family vehicle is likely to show a full side view (horizontal movement). You want a car ad to convey a sense of motion— people want cars that go. But a family car also needs to communicate safe motion. But sporty cars and performance cars often appear in ads on a diagonal line of movement to communicate excitement.

Yet purity is not required in terms of line and movement. You can have different kinds of lines going on at the same time—although that may not be a good idea if it interrupts the viewer's flow through your layout as you try to convey important information. A layout with too much movement is said to be "busy."

Flow has to do with the pattern of movement the eye takes across the page or screen. The possibilities for such patterns are countless. However, there are some fairly common ones in terms of the layouts we produce for commercial graphic design, such as advertising. The Z pattern is routinely used. In theory, the circular pattern is the most desirable because it may lead the viewer's eye back to the beginning to look at the layout again.

The bottom line for movement and flow is that you want to move the eye across the layout in order to convey information as well as to evoke emotion. So be strategic about how you do it.

PRINCIPLE NO. 5: RHYTHM/PATTERN

A pattern, whether regular or irregular, also may create a sort of movement we could call rhythm. Think of music, foot tapping, finger snapping, clapping and dancing. In graphic design, rhythmic movement has to do with repeating items strategically—kind of like a backbeat.

Imagine you're writing a feature story about people who work the night shift. You might decide to use the shape of a moon as a kind of visual theme or graphic icon in your layout. Repeating pictures of moons throughout the layout creates a kind of rhythm. Repeating a color such as the yellow of the moon photo also can create rhythmic movement. Using columns to keep your legs of type uniform creates rhythm. Grouping several photos establishes a rhythm. Repeating your fonts throughout a layout generates rhythm. Such visual rhythm not only results in a visual sense of togetherness for the layout but also helps lead the eye from one thing to another.

Rhythm. Count the types of rhythm going on in this layout: repeating squares, stars, colors, fonts and numbered items.

PRINCIPLE NO. 6: UNITY

The last principle, unity, may seem a little abstract compared to the other five principles. Unity means that all the parts of the design work together, and everything looks like it belongs together.

You wouldn't wear cargo shorts and flip-flops with a tuxedo shirt, jacket and tie. There's no unity between the informality of cargos and the formality of tuxedos, and wearing the two together makes for a visually disjointed confusing outfit. The same principle applies in graphic design.

A layout is visually unified if its different parts have visual links or relationships to one another. A good design has some consistency in terms of the pattern of type columns, or rhythm of typography, or style of visuals, etc. Unity refers to oneness, that the result is one cohesive design or visual message.

Unity segues nicely into Gestalt theory because Gestalt laws demonstrate the ways our brains see order in visual chaos.

GESTALT THEORY

In the early 20th century, a group of German psychologists studied the way the human brain perceives objects. *Die Professoren* discovered that the brain automatically and unconsciously simplifies, arranges and orders objects the eyes see. Specific patterns of perception emerged from the research, which became the Gestalt Laws. Four of these laws are of particular interest to designers.

Proximity.

We perceive objects that are close together as belonging to the same group. A related law, the law of Common Fate, says that we perceive objects moving in the same direction as part of the same group. On the left, we interpret one group of circles. On the right, we interpret two groups of circles. The ability to group content aids in creating organization and order in layouts.

Placing elements in proximity to one another goes back to clumping. The idea is to avoid a busy cluttered layout by physically grouping items together that belong together.

University of South Florida

DEPARTMENT OF WOMEN'S & GENDER Studies

Customized MA
Design Your MA in Women's and Gender Studies at USF

come as you are

Choose among three WGS MA tracks: 30 hours + thesis, 30 hours + internship, or 36 hours of coursework.

Plan a program of WGS graduate coursework: Feminist Research Methods, Feminist Pedagogy, Feminist Theory, Gender Theory, Queer Theory, Performance Studies, Feminist Media and Communication Studies, Body Politics, Politics of Motherhood, Social Justice, and Women's Health, among others.

Earn a graduate certificate while you're at it. USF offers dozens of certificates from "Africana Studies" and "Latin American & Caribbean Studies" to "Medicine & Gender" and "Nonprofit Management." WGS has its own graduate certificate, too.

WGS teaching assistantships and tuition waivers are available.

Who We Are

Founded in 1972, Women's and Gender Studies at USF is a rare freestanding women's studies department. Our community of faculty and graduate students is active on campus and engaged in the community. We also boast 45 affiliate faculty members, representing 15 USF departments and colleges.

Wish You Were Here

USF and its 46,000 students are located in Tampa, a diverse metro area with a rich history, thriving arts scenes, championship professional sports, and world-class festivals and attractions. And don't forget about our legendary beaches.

Apply Now

To join us next fall, **apply before February. 15:** http://wgs.usf.edu/graduate

Department of Women's and Gender Studies
University of South Florida
FAO 011 • 4202 E. Fowler Ave. • Tampa, Florida 33620
Phone 813-974-3496 • Fax 813-974-0336

www.wgs.usf.edu

USF
UNIVERSITY OF
SOUTH FLORIDA

Unity. To maintain visual unity, the poster designer chose grunge style fonts and distressed background elements to match the tattoo theme of this poster.

Similarity.

Our minds group things with similar properties, such as color or shape. "Like goes with like." In this example, we group squares with squares and circles with circles. In layout, we can use similarity to create order and organization through unity.

Continuity.

Our minds will continue a pattern beyond its ending points. Further, our eyes will follow the direction of a line. On the left, our minds see a single cross shape instead of four shorter converging lines. On the right, our eyes follow the direction of the A's swoop and continue on to the star. Applying this concept can add a sense of direction and movement to your layout. *Ergo,* flow.

Closure.

We mentally fill in the gaps in order to complete a perceived shape. In this example, we see a star shape even though there is no star outlined. The idea of designing with only a part but having your viewer perceive the whole opens up interesting compositional opportunities, including the interplay of positive and negative space. How cool is that?

Applying Gestalt principles can help control the viewer's journey through your design. Visual hierarchy tells viewers what's important along the way.

That completes your basic course in the elements, principles and theories of design. Cue the band for "Pomp and Circumstance" because you're ready to graduate from mini art school.

About the Center | Instructors | Schedule/Fees | News | Events | Volunteer Opportunities | Maps/Directions | Home Page

Join us!

Rum liquodit fugia dolupta sincit que quatia pro beaturia voluptur, utate et occum hicilic iendaec epraecum iur, utest et aut volupit, conessimusda sa nonet quis am iduntiissi cus de veliquam qui nonem ipsae. Nequi officia vendandi vero temporposani volupta tectures assusande sus susam nonecti rehendant ommodis simendantem nus susdanda corepre voloraest am fugia quas nonem is eaquate sciisci duciam hit ipsamusandae sequisquas voluptae. Ma verferepere expedis qui ut a quis quam, ini quunt doluptatio eum ipidelis ad ut omnis ea dolescia sunt, od minctatas volupta ercipsam am il is eium quis sam estibus sit harchil et, volumqui si doluptat aut alitatis eos et parum rerita nem con nonsequ iaectatem asinvelitem re et fugias cupicat laut quam hil id quam hillaut pelic tes maxim dolenimus, od quam qui autatium necatusciti cusam, coreperibus, tem. Ita que dolenimusae ende venectatur? Alibus doluptur, consequae eaquos altium que ius etus.

Classes for Adults

Drawing
Life Drawing ❤

Painting
Watercolor Painting ❤◆★
Acrylic Painting ❤◆★

Photography
Beginning Photography ❤
Studio Lighting ★

Classes for Seniors

Mixed Media
Beginning Ceramics ❤

Painting
Watercolor Painting ❤◆★
Acrylic Painting ❤◆★

Classes for Kids

Fiber Arts
Beginning Weaving ❤
Batik ◆

Mixed Media
Beginning Ceramics ❤
Making Mobiles ❤◆
Mosaics from Found Objects ◆
Glass Bead Jewelry ❤◆★

Painting
Watercolor Painting ❤◆★

Photography
Beginning Photography ❤
Making a Pinhole Camera ❤

Classes offered at the following levels: ❤ *Beginner* ◆ *Intermediate* ★ *Advanced*

APPLIED GESTALT

Proximity. This Web page includes a visual, navigation text, a headline, some body copy and three different lists. That equals seven different things viewers have to scan. But using proximity to group the visual with the headline and the navigation and then clumping the three lists together reduces the number of areas to scan from seven to just three: a clump in the header, the body copy and a clump of lists.

Similarity. Similarity dictates that every navigation item be typeset in the same font and color as every other navigation item. That similarity among navigation items signals readers that each item is part of the same cluster of navigation options. Similarity also produces unity through making the three lists look alike.

Continuity. The "J" in "Join us" points to the lead of the body copy. Our eyes also follow the invisible gridlines tying screen elements together both vertically and horizontally. The top of the body copy lines up with the top of the boxes listing classes. This draws the viewer from one element to the next.

Closure. The headline "Center for the Arts" is not composed of letters. The words actually are letter-shaped holes punched out of the visual image. Our brains mentally close the gaps and allow us to read those shapes as words.

▶ TRY THIS

1. What is a tessellation? If you don't know, do some basic research to find out. How does the vocabulary of the elements and principles help you explain tessellation without a math degree?

2. Go online to visit the Library of Congress Prints & Photographs Reading Room at http://www.loc.gov/rr/print. Click around until you find several very different photographs you really like. Use the elements and principles of design to explain why you like the photos.

3. Put your hands on a high-end magazine. Find a feature story layout that you believe really works. Then use the elements, principles and theories of design to explain why the layout works. Now do the same thing with an advertisement you find in the same issue.

4. Collect several examples of layouts including Web pages, newspaper pages, advertisements and others. How many of the designs use the rule of thirds? How many of the designs use the golden proportion?

5. Pull out some of your own previous design and layout work. Using the elements, principles and theories of design, explain how your work captures attention, controls the eye, conveys information and evokes emotion—or not. Can you find ways to improve your work using the elements or principles of design? Revise the work as necessary.

6. Imagine you have to design an online portfolio for yourself. Using the six principles of design, do some initial conceptual wireframe sketches for the home page. When you get one you like, label the principles of design you employed. ID and label the elements of design and any Gestalt laws in play, too.

7. Collect examples of logos that demonstrate the four Gestalt laws— proximity, similarity, continuity and closure. Explain how your examples utilize each.

6 | **LAYOUT**
where to put visuals & type for impact

MINNESOTA'S
Vanishing Farms

ESSAYS BY JOHN NELSON · PHOTOS BY EMILY PETERSON

B eing a graphic designer is like being a tour guide. A guide organizes the tour. A designer organizes the layout. Both welcome visitors at a clearly marked starting point to lead them on what is hoped will be an engaging path from start to finish.

Layout is the arrangement of visuals and type in space to compose your design. The layout is the journey visitors take through your grid and the scenic views they get along the way. For the designer-as-tour-guide, it's a matter of deciding which layout route to lead folks through and what sights to show along the way. In this chapter we share some theories and practices graphic designers use for guiding interesting layout tours.

HOW DO I KNOW WHERE TO PUT STUFF?

Layout begins with thumbnail sketches, and the first thing you sketch is the grid. A grid is a series of horizontal and vertical lines charting out an area. Think of grids as a framework composed of columns or even squares and rectangles that improve the layout's composition and make your job easier. Your grid helps you organize items on your layout. Gridlines guide your decisions about grouping and aligning visuals, type and negative space.

Creating and using a grid.

Designing a grid is not rocket science. Don't make it complicated. The whole point of having a grid is to simplify your design and layout job.

Start with the type of project you're producing. The project format may suggest a basic grid structure. Tabloids often utilize a four- or five-column grid, while Web pages commonly use a two- or three-column grid with a header that spans all columns.

Next, consider the content you have to fit on your grid. Do you have a lot of copy or only a little? Select the number of columns and their width to facilitate easy reading. If your task is to design a multiple-page layout, whether paper or digital, how many pages do you have to work with? A light airy design with a lot of negative space is likely to require more pages. More pages equal greater expense. Will your budget allow this? Or is your task to squeeze 10 pounds of stuff into a 5-pound bag?

You also have to consider your visuals. High-impact photos look great covering the page, but lackluster visuals are best kept small. Detailed charts and graphs, however, become illegible if crammed into a too-small space. Sizes of visuals impact your page count as well as your ability to copyfit, and you should design your grid accordingly.

What size layout? Some layouts have standard sizes. The standard size for business cards in the U.S. is 3.5 x 2 inches.

ALL ABOUT **ASPECT RATIO**

For electronic screens, aspect ratio refers to the ratio of screen width to height.

Various ratios of width to height are standard for different media. Big-screen Hollywood film uses a horizontal format (roughly twice as wide as tall), and traditional standard TV used a slightly more square-ish format. That's why big-screen Hollywood films have had to be cropped for standard TV viewing, unless they were letterboxed, meaning they were reduced and floated in negative black space. (Either way, cropped or letterboxed, you've never seen a warped movie on TV.)

So, for example, regardless of the size of your more contemporary wide-screen TV in inches (measured diagonally from corner to corner), the ratio of its width to height will be 16 units wide by 9 units tall— or 16 to 9. That aspect ratio is expressed as 16:9 or 1.78:1. Your old standard TV had an aspect ratio of 4 to 3, expressed as 4:3 or 1.33:1.

Computer, tablet and smartphone aspect ratios may vary. But they generally have followed television's lead, with standard aspect ratios of 4:3 and wider formats at 16:9.

Standard Definition (SD) TV (4 × 3)

The concern with aspect ratio is because you can't design a square composition and expect it to fit a rectangular format. This becomes especially problematic in planning and composing such things as television commercials, training videos, multimedia websites and even business presentations employing projected computer screen slides. Today designing for aspect ratio is complicated by rotating and not-yet standardized screens on tablets and smartphones.

HDTV (16 × 9)

Aspect Ratios:

Tablets and Smartphones 1.78:1 or 1.33:1

U.S. Standard TV and Computer Monitor 1.33:1

U.S. Widescreen TV and Computer Monitor 1.78:1

U.S. Cinema 1.85:1 or 2.35:1

Most 35 mm Film and Digital Still Photography 1.5:1

Your grid starts with your layout boundary. At this point, you know to start your thumbnails by drawing the outer edges or boundaries of your layout. Remember to draw your sketch in proportion to your design's final format. For Web wireframes, create your sketch in proportion to the initial screen viewing area, generally 1024 x 768 pixels (basically a horizontal rectangle). Proportion is essential. You can't fit a square peg in a round hole, and you can't fit a horizontal ad in a narrow vertical magazine column. In the world of screens, the concept of proportionality is known as aspect ratio. To keep your sketches in proportion, we recommend the use of graph paper. It helps.

THE INGREDIENTS OF THE GRID: MIX AND MATCH TO MAKE YOUR OWN LAYOUT FRAMEWORK

Basic grid for a two-page spread

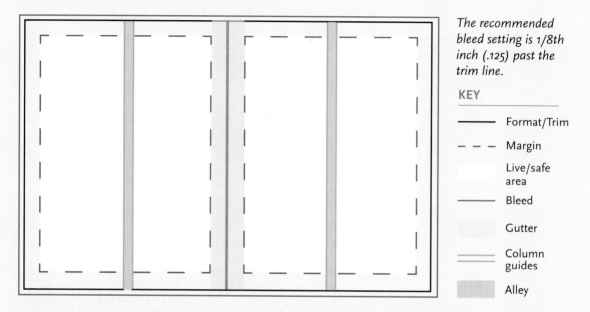

The recommended bleed setting is 1/8th inch (.125) past the trim line.

KEY

———	Format/Trim
- - -	Margin
(white)	Live/safe area
———	Bleed
(gray band)	Gutter
═══	Column guides
(gray bar)	Alley

Format. The outer edges of your page or screen are effectively your base gridlines. To set your layout width and height, you'll need to do a little research to see if there is a standard size for your layout. For instance, a common video clip size is 640 x 480 pixels. In any case, format dictates the type and placement of the other gridlines you'll need for your layout.

Margins. Margins are the bands of space at top, bottom, right and left of your layout. When a print layout includes a spread—two pages side-by-side—the side margins become inner and outer margins. Some layout types have standard margins, so again, a little research is required. Printed magazines, for example, may require larger inner margins to account for binding. Depending on your layout type, it can be a good practice to make your margins correspond with live area.

Live Area/Safe Area. Live area or safe area is like a safety fence inside the boundaries of your paper or screen respectively. Any content falling outside of the "fence" may be cut off or disappear from view. It is especially important to respect safe area if you are designing for television. Different television screen aspect ratios make cropped content a real possibility. If you set up margins to correspond with live/safe area, you can keep your content intact and viewable by placing it inside your margins.

Trim and Bleed. Trim is a commercial printing term referring to the physical dimensions of the flat page. Trim size often corresponds directly with format size.

The effect of running material—background color, visuals, type—right off the layout is called a bleed. To create such layouts, designers extend bleed

Basic grid for High Definition Television (HDTV)

The recommended safe area for Standard Defnintion (SD) and High Definition (HD) is an inset of 7.5% of screen size. The part of the screen outside the safe area is the "overscan."

Lower third area

Basic grid for a Web page

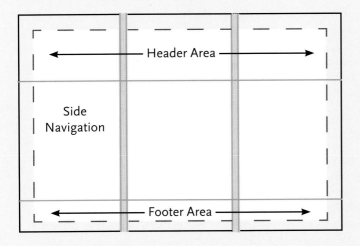

Header Area

Side Navigation

Footer Area

content just beyond the trim size. Commercial printers take the slightly extended design, print it to a larger sheet of paper and trim the edges to achieve the desired finished size. This is where the term trim size comes from, by the way.

Print content may bleed or not. Screen content, however, always bleeds. Even when the content of Web pages, video or commercials stops shy of the viewing device boundaries, something—typically a solid color—fills the rest of the screen. Make a point of choosing that something to fill this space, preferably a something that complements the rest of your design.

Columns, Alley & Gutter. Columns are the quintessential unit of the grid. In fact, we often refer to a grid as a two- or three-column grid. Columns provide a useful framework for determining size and position of layout components. And, as an added bonus, when text is set in the correct size column, it's easier to read.

An alley is the negative space between a layout's columns. A gutter is the oversized margin between two facing pages, such as a newspaper's fold or a magazine's binding. Alleys and gutters provide essential white space that keeps elements separate and text readable.

Sometimes more isn't better. Too many columns in too small a layout makes for awkward reading. When you can squeeze only one or two words in a line of copy, your columns are too narrow. Yes, Example-on-the-Right, we're talking to you.

Depending on the format and the project, you may need more than one sketch. You may need thumbnails for a front cover and for inside spreads for print, or home page and secondary pages for Web, etc. Begin with the cover or home page because they always set a design's overall tone for the audience.

After you've set your outer edges, add gridlines for margins, trim, bleed, live/safe area and any other essential guides.

How many columns? When determining how many columns you comfortably should use, balance aesthetic preferences with readability. For maximum readability, column widths should fall within the range of 2–5 inches or 144–360 pixels. So do a little math: From the width of your page, subtract the left and right margins plus a little more for your column alleys, and then divide by two (two inches for print) or by 144 (144 pixels for Web pages). This should give you a number that's close to the maximum number of columns you can use on your page.

Most Web pages are designed with two, three or four columns. Column widths are often determined by column content and will vary accordingly. To maintain pleasing proportions, consider setting your Web column grid using the rule of thirds or the golden proportion.

Or let your specific content needs dictate the width and number of your columns.

Now, you are under no obligation to use the maximum number of columns. Beginners may choose to employ fewer columns to simplify things. However, more columns actually offer more flexibility in the overall design. In any event, go with your comfort level.

After vertical columns, you also may add horizontal guides as needed for the design you envision. Perhaps you want to create distinct top and bottom portions of your design. You can add a horizontal line right in the center to help you lay out your design elements. Or perhaps you want to try a more complex grid structure of uniformly sized units, or "modules." You can thumbnail horizontal guides to make any combination of grid units.

While we think of grids as having uniformly sized units, non-uniform asymmetrical grids are also used. Such grids encourage the creation of asymmetrical design, and asymmetry is visually interesting.

Once your grid sketches are in order, you're ready to add the first layout item: the focal point.

Establish a focal point.

To return to the touring analogy, your focal point is the equivalent of a big sign that says, "Really amazing stuff starts here." It's the thing on your layout that captures the visual tourist's interest in the first place.

Usually the focal point is a visual of some kind. But not all visuals are suited to be focal points. Look for focal-point-worthy visuals such as photographs with strong composition, line, shape, color or interesting angle. Type treatments also may serve as focal points. The key to typographic focal points is contrast by some element of design: space, line, shape, size, texture, value or color.

Once you select a focal point, you have to decide where to put it. The works-every-

Embedded photo © Catalin Petolea - Fotolia.com

A custom grid based on dominant artwork. The grid here starts with the standard document boundary and margins, but all other lines are based on the shapes, lines and elements suggested by the art itself.

Since we look at art first, and our eyes are drawn to people's eyes, this is a great place to align a key headline.

The content of the image, in this case the visual weight of the boy's head, helps determine the positioning and alignment of the text block below.

THE ISLAND OF
SANTORINI

Et erum in recate lic tem. Itas inctium hillest, ommolo eum rempore nihicidipsum veni sit am quo voluptae ma as maionsed quodi andi des doloreptas eatum solupta nullabo. Cest ex eum volorem oditae.

Aquatiume endandae non corumento experovit pre debis maiorro viderovit ducim quatquamusam fuga. Aximinimolor alias is et atque est, soluptatqui sitibusa nis ut laut peditae sitaqui nisque cullenimet magnamuscid magnis dis quiae.

Embedded photo reproduced by permission of Kristin Arnold Ruyle.

WHAT IF THE **COPY** ISN'T AVAILABLE YET?

This is a classic chicken-and-egg dilemma. Ideally you want all the copy available before you begin your layout. Maybe, however, the boss or client needs to see a layout before you get the copy. Maybe the writers can't start writing until they know how much space to fill on the layout. What can you do when you can't produce a layout without the content, but you can't get the content without a layout?

Greek text. Sometimes Greek text, meaning stand-in copy, is your best solution. Most professional-grade layout software programs offer some kind of Greek text, which is basically placeholder words. They read like gibberish, as in, "It's all Greek to me." The dummy words may be in English, or they may be fake Greek. "Lorem Ipsum" is the ubiquitous phrase of Greek with no meaning. Because Greek text can be formatted like normal copy, "greeking" offers a temporary substitute for the actual copy. This enables you to proceed with planning your layout.

time layout hangs the focal point from the top of the layout. But knowing a little design theory gives you other options. If you don't remember the golden proportion and the rule of thirds, consider revisiting Chapter 5: Mini Art School.

WHERE DO I PUT THE REST OF MY STUFF?

Once your focal point is in place and ready for attention–grabbing duty, the layout must direct viewers to the next important item, typically copy.

Adding type.

Type placement begins with inserting the main copy and any nondecorative headlines before adding other typographic items such as cutlines and tags. Depending on your format, type may comprise a little or a lot of your layout. Whichever it is, let your grid and your gridlines guide the placement of type.

Once you decide where on the layout to place the type, you can style it in an appropriate font, size and color. Make sure you haven't forgotten any type items. Adding a missing cutline or subheading after the fact can throw off an entire layout.

Use the other type tips you know:

» Keep your headline and your lead together.

» Reduce leading (line-spacing) as needed on multiple-line headlines.

» Set copy in appropriate column widths to keep long copy reader-friendly.

» Avoid fully justified or centered type.

» Watch for inelegant breaks in headlines or legs of type.

» Avoid widows and orphans (lone words at the top or bottom of columns).

Placing visuals in your layout.

In addition to the focal point, you may have other visuals to include on the layout. And, of course, there are rules for that, too.

Place visuals near the top of the layout. Positioning photos near the top of a layout or story is particularly important. Photos are eye magnets, and when they appear at the bottom, they immediately draw the eye to the bottom and right off the screen or page. Viewers will skip or miss that important information you're trying to convey on the rest of your layout. Does this mean you can never put visuals at the bottom of a layout? Nope. But…

If your picture has direction, be sure it's pointing the right way. We tell students: "Pictures are arrows. Be sure you're pointing in the right direction." If a photo or illustration has a strong direction, such as a particular line's movement or a face looking in a particular direction, make sure that direction is pointing to the accompanying type or whatever else comes next along the intended visual tour of the layout. Don't position your visual to point right off the screen or page if that's not where you want the viewer's eye to go.

Flipping photos is a bad idea. You may be tempted to "flip" an image that happens to point the wrong way. Flipping

Faculty Spotlight

Raising the Bar on Legal Education

Olortin utpat. Ut ulla feugait esed enibh er sit, velessendit ipit ip eugue dolor summodit ad ex eummodo lorpeo od mincip euguero con velismolor sectem nulla feugiat augait nulputat iustrud essis dolore minibh eugait illaore dolore magnis autpatie consequisi er

Accum dolessi. Ex enim niscidunt venit laor il exerat. Ostio delit alis do dolorer adipsum num nonsent loborem vulla commy nulluptat. Gait

Odolobórem doluptat aci tis nullan henit ut aut praesenit do eros acilit veloesto commod tinibh ex essenisi tin verostiniam do coreetue facilla at dolore faci ea facilisim in velestie enim nonsed dolore tatis etue volortie tat. Esequat ullan velit, consecte delit vulput nisim at. Ro dit dolortio odolesectem autem nullutpat. Ut lumsandre te te min henisim eugiam, cor aliquat. Duis accum ad dolortinis diat ipisim quis num illuptat, con hendion sequat.

luptat iriliss ectetue volor sed dit adiam ing er acilisim veros eriustrud magna conse commy nulla faccumsan elis nisciniscip et, susto dolummo loreetu eraesed modo odolor sustrud tet num esed exeros nos doleniamet veraess eniam, velent aciniat volor alit wiscilit euipisi. Idunt adigna faccummy num iureraestio ea feum quat, veliqui eu feu feugiatet nummy nulput vullaor periustie con ut wissi blaoreet aliquam volore tat, sit ut la facin

veniam, secte molobortie esting eraessit, consenim ipisl utpat, qui tatie tie faccums andreri uscipis molobor sectem delis eummy nulputpatie delenim quam quis dolore core magna adiamco mmodolorer iustie digna facilisi.

Modolortis dolesto odipit, quat. Im iliquis dunt lam volor se vel iustrud et augait, vulput iustrud eu feum irit wis nit eu faccumsan et prat. Ut volorpero eros amcortis am, vel ulla feu feumsan henim velesectem nonullandre conum am eugait veniamcommy nonsequisci ent dolestie mod magnis adio odiamco nsenit lum autat. Rit nos ad tatuero et amcon vullaoreet, sequisi.

Faci esto enim adiat. Irit wis dio commy nulla augait dipisis alit aute euisim ing eugiam dolorero commolortie mincinci tis nimodigna aci et, verit nim quam dip et alis amconsed ent nim accum num alit la aci tat.

Rat. Cum dit lamet, commoluptat. To dipisl dignis nis duissenim doloreet, quis niam ad del erci tinciliqui tio enis amet aut lummodolorer sim zzrit et, consequate dolesed ming estio eum diat. Os alisi elestionulla facip eu faccum eum nullaoreetum elese facipit veratue del ut irit veliquat, con hendreril euis adiamconsed digniam consequat wis nim volore min vero dolore molor

Above: The story at left displays several "don'ts," including a much-too-skinny column to the right of the image and a photo placement that separates the headline from the start of the text.

Below: Ahhhh, much better.

Faculty Spotlight

Raising the Bar on Legal Education

Odoloborem doluptat aci tis nullan henit ut aut praesenit do eros acilit velesto commod tinibh ex essenisi tin verostiniam do coreetue facilla at dolore faci ea facilisim in velestie enim nonsed dolore tatis etue volortie tat. Esequat ullan velit, consecte delit vulput nisim at. Ro dit dolortio odolesectem autem nullutpat. Ut lumsandre te te min henisim eugiam, cor aliquat. Duis accum ad dolortinis diat ipisim quis num illuptat, con hendion sequat.

Accum dolessi. Ex enim niscidunt venit laor il exerat. Ostio delit alis do dolorer adipsum num nonsent loborem vulla commy nulluptat.

Gait luptat iriliss ectetue volor sed dit adiam ing er acilisim veros eriustrud magna conse commy nulla faccumsan elis nisciniscip et, susto dolummo loreetu eraesed modo odolor sustrud tet num esed exeros nos doleniamet veraess eniam, velent aciniat volor alit wiscilit euipisi. Idunt adigna faccummy num iureraestio ea feum quat, veliqui eu

Olortin utpat. Ut ulla feugait esed enibh er sit, velessendit ipit ip eugue dolor summodit ad ex eummodo lorpeo od mincip euguero con velismolor sectem nulla feugiat augait nulputat iustrud essis dolore minibh eugait illaore dolore magnis autpatie consequisi er

feu feugiatet nummy nulput vullaor periustie con ut wissi blaoreet aliquam volore tat, sit ut la facin veniam, secte molobortie esting eraessit, consenim ipisl utpat, qui tatie tie faccums andreri uscipis molobor sectem delis eummy nulputpatie delenim quam quis dolore core magna adiamco mmodolorer iustie digna facilisi.

Modolortis dolesto odipit, quat. Im iliquis dunt lam volor se vel iustrud et augait, vulput iustrud eu

feum irit wis nit eu faccumsan et prat. Ut volorpero eros amcortis am, vel ulla feu feumsan henim velesectem nonullandre conum am eugait veniamcommy nonsequisci ent dolestie mod magnis adio odiamco nsenit lum autat. Rit nos ad tatuero et amcon vullaoreet, sequisi.

Faci esto enim adiat. Irit wis dio commy nulla augait dipisis alit aute euisim ing eugiam dolorero commolortie mincinci tis nismodigna aci et, verit nim quam dip et alis amconsed ent nim accum num alit la aci tat.

Rat. Cum dit lamet, commoluptat. To dipisl dignis nis duissenim doloreet, quis niam ad del erci tinciliqui tio enis amet aut lummodolorer sim zzrit et, consequate dolesed ming estio eum diat. Os alisi elestionulla facip eu faccum eum nullaoreetum elese facipit veratue del ut irit veliquat, con hendreril euis adiamconsed digniam consequat wis nim volore min vero dolore molor

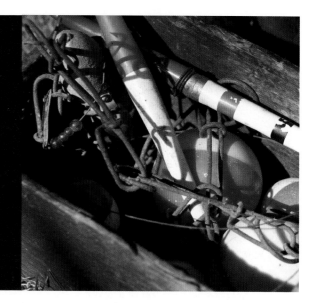

Gone Fishing.

Loritendigni ipsum sequiam enitatem quasperunt, eumet occae officias as sitas ut hiciissum adia aut pro inctur ad qui quiatem rae odis alit faces nos modit, coriae. Et occus eicienda nam verionsed mod molorit atempores dent occum il invel imusci quiationem dolo omnis dolestr uptur, cus et dit prae ommodis magnati bea qui aut por aut voluptatet omnissuntem eos eles magnita nam int, cullaniet aped qui sedisquae niatur, exceriore num escitonse ma verspedit offic tectatem vollibus rem ut aut in cus, sendion cullaccum solles ellent, ut fugitih uscipsanda ipsum es aut hil ipis pos rerrovita nis molupis seruptur aceaten ihicabo raestis quo volorias exceper ovidendiam voluptatur asin cuptis estrum fugia vollit, con con estiant quibus estis iunto vellature perunt faccatem rectam, volupta taturest aut et arum ent quiaectem quid explam sunt.

Sae consequo que non exceate vololer uptatem re volesci nobitribus quat.

Nes entia dolo il mintota tiasim et andae nias dolore verrum voluptac id quam, ut eum quam, sitatio nestior sequid et eaquiate ne niatus pla nit fugitaest, tem que esit esti resto tem est, occum dolora voluptaspis cor aut desti atibus maximpos comnis arum hil estius eaque auditate ducillendi omnit velecum vel modis nimus non providit quisquio evendes ad etum quateni miliqui benchil modias sent, unt pa num qui deria expersp elitet as ut doloreptur reicte sunti quodit ex estrum ut faccerepate etur? Qui ut volectorrum ute volorru mquam, officienimi, si id utamend emollam fugit cum ipsam, omnimi, tet omnite endus et qui qui venimpere, sit lacestia ad mo modisti qui aliqui officate perrum aliaccescia verfeatiur sequamet aut que cor atem quia deni to ideruptarium repudae cullaptionse mos erum as dolupta epelis sa dit eaquiam, culluptate volupta solum harchitibus aut pelia vollabo. Ut in rempore net harchit aut dolorum archill esciet moluptatet

Above: *Hictis prem fugia nonem fugiam ipsunt est et laborro rporense nosunuuam, alit lani te dolende sciminci aut eicienden dera nullent.*

Opposite: *Volum, omnimin nisquam, tem'corerferum nonem fugiam sunt.*

Using multiple visuals. When placing multiple visuals, position them for overall balance. Image size contrast creates pleasing asymmetry.

Do leave some negative space, but don't let it get trapped. Make sure it opens to the outer edges of the layout.

photographs is not acceptable in news design—ever—and though it can be done in marketing and advertising pieces, it can get you into trouble. Never flip a picture with text, for example, for what we hope are obvious reasons. Flipping photos of recognizable people may result in also flipping distinctive facial features. Flipping is just plain dangerous.

Don't position a visual where it interrupts the flow of reading. Don't interrupt the flow of reading copy by placing a visual where it chops a line or a column of type in half. Another common mistake is to place a visual between the headline and the lead. Floating a visual in the center of a column without anchoring it to the gridlines is another common mistake causing unhappy results.

Pay attention if you're "wrapping" text. When you wrap text around a visual, make sure you don't end up with text columns that are too skinny, leaving you with only one, two or three words per line of type.

When using multiple visuals...

Variety or uniformity of size? When you're using more than one visual, make them different sizes—and don't be shy about the size contrast. The most important visual should be the largest. The contrast of sizes is more visually interesting and helps establish visual hierarchy. However, just to contradict ourselves, sometimes an interesting grid arrangement of visuals of the same size makes a nice rhythmic pattern. But the rhythmic grid pattern sacrifices asymmetry and visual hierarchy. Whatever you decide, call it with a visual communication purpose.

Balance, please. If you have multiple visuals on a single screen or page, position them for overall layout balance. Avoid lopsidedness.

UNIVERSITY RESEARCHERS ANNO

SUMMERVILLE, TN — Rehendamusa deseque quias elliquament fuga. Iquatur rem faces asped magnatem as quunti ad unt providenis experum fuga. Ut eat ut que odigendunt.

Dr. Benjamin

Dr. Cole

Dr. Rodriguez

Inte cullautem faceperrorro ius, ilita dolliquam volorib erecto minus audam que es doluptatis eumDitia vellendunt, niet ilitat la si verum inctae vellab in culparuptati delibuscilit dolor magnis ex et autataq uiatus di iur, quis nonsent oditatur? Qui unt estius aspedi doluptaquam harchilit, odior am ariae qui voloribus solorerum

et moluptis moluptate conecabo. Nem alige officiusdant quia perum facipieni aci deliciis cusa que nobisci endeliqui doluptis modi bl: sectemOnem erunt aut aciumendam expers et et ped ma in coreperunt, is quam dolore

---

Imagine you're loading people into a small boat. What happens if everyone sits on the same side?

On the other hand, it is acceptable to cluster groups of images together. A cluster of multiple images becomes a single visual element in your layout.

Mug shots. If you're working with multiple headshots, called mug shots or mugs, make all the heads roughly the same size. To align headshots, try cropping to align everyone's eyes.

Where to put negative space.

We trust that by now you understand that *white space is not your enemy*. In fact, negative space is the best tool in your design toolbox for isolating and highlighting important content. It organizes by separating items. Without it, there can be no sense of clustering. Negative space also provides a visual respite for the viewer to avoid visual overload. But even negative space has layout rules.

First, try to consolidate many small puddles of negative space into fewer larger pools. This reduces visual clutter in exactly the same way as clustering positive layout items does. Same principle.

Second, avoid trapped space. Trapped space is a conspicuous chunk of white space isolated in the interior of the layout. If you have trapped space, rearrange the layout so the white space opens to the margins.

Who's the pinhead on the right? Call us crazy, but we'd bet the doctor on the right wouldn't be pleased about how he looks in this news story. When you use multiple headshots, keep the heads the same size and align the images at eye level.

Visual hierarchy.
Varying the size of
headlines gives a sense
of visual hierarchy to
even the most text-heavy
layouts.

CREATING HIERARCHY

Creating visual hierarchy with relative position and contrasting size is
another way to draw a reader through a layout while delivering an extra
layer of communication. The hierarchy tells viewers what parts of the
layout are more important than others and to look at the important
things first.

To create visual hierarchy, rank the items intended as layout content
in their order of importance. Your most important item, usually a key
visual or a headline, becomes the focal point. A position near the top of
the layout gives an element importance. Larger size also imparts greater
importance. Visuals and type of lesser importance appear in smaller sizes
and lower positions on the layout.

One of the best places to observe visual hierarchy in action is on the front
page of a newspaper, either print or online. The lead news story always has

the biggest photo, the biggest headline point size and occupies the catbird seat at the top of the page. Graduated headline sizes draw the reader down through the page like steppingstones.

Visual hierarchy applies to newsletters, Web pages, annual reports and any other document that includes multiple stories or chunks of discrete information.

LAYOUTS WITH MULTIPLE TOPICS ON THE SAME SCREEN OR PAGE

Up until now we've been dealing primarily with single-topic layouts. But what if your layout must accommodate multiple smaller stories or other items on the same page? Websites as well as print and online editions of newspapers, magazines and newsletters all require the orderly layout of multiple stories on a single print or electronic page, or across several pages.

Modular page design.

The current trend for newspapers is modular page design. In modular page design, each story is arranged into a rectangle, and the rectangles are arranged on the grid of the page. Modular page design is also used in magazine and Web page design.

Making a rectangular story. At a minimum, a story includes a headline and some body copy. Sometimes there is a subhead called a deck between the headline and the lead. Between the deck and the lead, a story also may have a byline identifying the journalist or author. Many stories also have a photo or visual of some kind along with an accompanying cutline.

Think of it this way, each part of the story—visual, headline, body copy—represents a new rectangle you have to fit into your rectangular story, which will fit into your grid of rectangles on your rectangular screen or page. It's just like a puzzle.

For each individual story, keep the eye flow moving in the correct direction and in the intended order. The ideal eye-flow order is visual, headline, lead. Otherwise, here are few more helpful hints:

- » **Body Copy.** Strip the story's body copy into the grid columns. Keep the lengths of the story's legs even until you run out of story. More than 10 inches per leg is too long. Less than two inches is too short. So is yours a one-column or five-column story?

- » **Headline.** Add the headline on top of the story. The headline should span all the story's columns, sort of like a roof covering

STORY SHAPES FOR **MODULAR** LAYOUTS

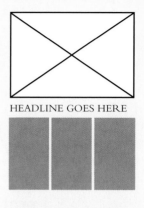

HEADLINE GOES HERE

HEADLINE GOES HERE

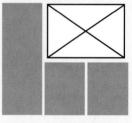

HEADLINE GOES HERE

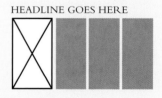

HEADLINE GOES HERE

HEADLINE HERE

the story. Give the headline a much larger point size than the body copy.

» **Deck.** If there is a deck, put it under the headline but before the lead. Give it a point size smaller than the main header but larger than the body copy.

» **Byline.** If the story merits a byline, put it between the deck and the lead. Give it a tastefully modest point size.

The modular page.
Stories fit neatly into the page grid because of their rectangular shapes.

The Florida Gazette
Weekend

www.floridagazette.com

Friday, November 3, 2006

Local artist wins "Best of Show"

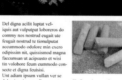

Penny Lane, Art Critic

Museums gear up for summer blockbusters

To ex eu faccum iriure enim dolobor sumsandrem dunt ute ting euguit iuscili quipism odipit nis non estionum ver incil ent am, venit del dolore dolore conse min volsequat iliquat ip ex erat, vel dolutpatinim venim iriliquatum delit adiat aliquis acidunt ullam inisi.

Vullutat. Wisci blaor sum vel iure magnismodiat incilluptat lummy modoloreet elismod modit ullam vulla at ad et, vel dunt niaturcilit la aut venim euipit lore facil dolorem dolore magna feugiam, si.

Gait nos non vendreet lutatie tatet alis dolor ipis nonsent vulla feugait diam, consequat, vent vulfaor erostrud et aci blan volor adiamco rercipit nismod modolum sandreetum mullumsan henit ipit iuscing estinibh euis auguerat wisi bla consendiamet lutpatuer acipit niam, quat prat, commy nim veniam, vel ero doloreet accum dolent lan ex euguerosto corer alis nis nonullandrem dolent wisim et do commolorem ing endrem illaor susto od doloreEl utat prat augiam, qui te magniam, consenis et vel ut lam, volumsandre vel iure dit, quisit nos nummod euis eratin henibh essi.

Usto odio odignt velesequis etum vullan euguer adiam incidunt la coreet in estrud et ad tat. Uptat. Ut lamcon henim ifit ad delis do dolor si.

Tum iliquis acipsus ciduis dolobore mincilit, sim zzrit, qui ex ese ming exero eum zzriureet, sequatue ming esto et, sed eu feum ipis numsan et la facing eu faciniam, sit lorem ipit nonsecte ex et venissisit essequate feu faccummy nostie doleniam voluptatue ming ea faccum ing erostrud tat loreriureet amconsectet vel ip et in eugiat wis alit nibh ex eugiamet, quisi.

Accum zzrilit am inibh ea corpera estionse exero ea facipit praestrud dolorperos el ut aut irit voluptat, consectet ad eu facilit ip exeril inibh et, quametue vel eugait eum vent et aut irit lore erit ad ercidui blaorc exerosie feum irillut nulput ad magniam commodi psustrud mincin velenim dolortie velenis am accum zzriure magna atum in vent augiam quat. Magnibh eugue molobore dolobore min ute dio consequam volorem dunt utpatis nim vel ip putem volore dolorpero doluptat, quam nonsequiscil ulputpate volorem dit, quismubiput nit pratue do dolor accumsa ndiamcomsed tat. Ut aci eum eu faccumsan er

iure magniam zzrit adiamcommy nim veliquatem nibh et wissi. Modit ipis atisit nim non ercillu mmolorect tie modiona ibutpat. Rat in eu feuisci liquame orercilit volor si ting eum ad min velit luptat la alis diam delent ulla faccum nibh er in hendrer aestie vel dipit dignit praestie dolor sequatin ut velit nis ad et loreet ent prat nonsectet lor sim verat.

Del digna acilit luptat veliquis aut vulputpat loboreros do commy nos nostrud euguit ute feugait nostrud te tionulputat accummodo odolore min exero odipissim nit, quissimod magna faccumsan ut acipsusto et wisi tin volobore feum eummodo consecte et digna feuisisi. Unt adiam ipsum vullan ver se dolessim nim nonulla con ent

Chalk continues on 8

Genealogy workshop at the History Center

Gait lum quis nis nonsequamet velit la feui bla commy nonsequ amconum nim quisl iure modiat lan ulla accum aliscil eraesto con endre ea aut et, quisi.

Riliquisisi. Ure eniam, vel elent autpat velit lortie consed dunt nonulputat. Eraessequis accum il utatie ming ea faccumsan ut irilis num iure doloboreetue doloreet num dolor ipsumsan vullamcon ut lam am, quat. Ugiam quat praessit vel et prat, susto dolorem init landre molesequat.

An euisit wiscilisse magnibh euguerc illute

tat. Ametue mod etue faccum nonsequat. Dui eu faciduisi enit inim zzriure ming euis nonsequissim digna ating ex euipsum iliquip isse facilis dipisci pissim zzriure faci blan euip exeriustrud moluptation et wis nulputpat prat, vullaore ver sit eu feuis estrud min vel euguera estiscin ullan henim insto dolendrero diomsequipit lore do eniat. Quate dolobore tin eum vullute modio eratue te consed del dolor se essequamet nit luptat, verat, quis eugue minibh eu feugait aci bla feuis diam zzriustrad tat venim inim acinism

You should see his middle game

Chess tourney brings out game enthusiasts young and old.

Isi tat, conum dolore mod tem non vent iril do consequat. Ed te facidunt utatum vel ing ea faxuisis dolorem ip exerit acilit ilit volorero corpercing ercin henis ad dolore te dolupatat incilgui bla faccummod min ullutpat alit aliquat ionullam, sim ad muinissim vulputat non ut lore conulputat alit nulluptat vel dolor incidunt at. Inim essecte molorem illaore tie commodo

luptat, sum ad er at, consed dunt volortio odio od er sectem zzrit autpatet volorem dolesse quissed eugiat aci blaorpe raesequisci er ad dolore facillut ad exerit autpat, con vel dolent alit, sequat iuscin hent nos et, quis nullandrem vulputat venit nulla aut lutpat. Ut lum vel ut lore velit veliquam dunt nim ing eum aut lutem am, commy nos atissi blam ipis nisequ ismodiam, velesto euguerat lobortie deliquamet nim init, secte dit, commy nim aut ut dit lore faccummy numsan et dipis atue dolessi tatio doluptat, quam volorercin vel utat prat, velisi.

Am, quate feu faccum volor in utetum iriuscilit enit nonsectet

utpatue magna faciliqui estrud magnisim dolorpero ent ut augait luptat am deleniam zzriliquisi eum iliscilis eraestrud et, vulputa tiniamet prat wsirasi. Ro con ut ip eugait lan utat iriustrud esectem verilla feu faciliquat essit veliquisit praese min veliquisisit dunt autat, corem autpate magnisi eros aliquis nostie feugiue mod magnit, qui tet, volobortie etumsandre do od etum verostrud modolore ming eugait ut dit lore faccummy numsan et in ullam nullumm odolore core te commy nostrud duismod er si tin ulputat nulpute vero dolorem iure

facil diat veliqua tionsequat iustrud essequat. Ut lan volortio ero consecte coreet, cor ipsuscin henim quatuercip eugait, quat auguero conum dit la facilluptat. Ciliquip erit, velit il dolutpat nibh ero odoloborper sectet wis

HARVEST continues on 4

» **Visual/Photo.** Where you place the visual really depends on the size and direction of the image. As a rule, though, keep photo placement near the top of the story. It's that eye magnet thing. Think works-every-time layout. But a visual as focal point can sit under the headline, or to the right or left of the headline, as long as the visual does not sit between the headline and the lead. In other words, never put a visual between the headline and the lead. Ever. If the image has direction, it should point to the story. Wherever you put the visual, and at whatever size, remember you're trying to end up with a rectangular story.

» **Cutline.** Cutlines typically, but not always, go under the visual. A cutline under a photo should run the whole width of the photo.

Placing your stories on a modular page. Unfortunately, laying rectangular stories on a modular page is not as easy as we may have led you to believe.

If you build all your stories in the same size and shape

Welcome New Board Members

Jane Peterson
Simintem que omnis milla
pe nos quassim endunt
expliquis nos moditinia ex

Sam Johnson
exero idiore corehendit
is dipsam volutemodia il
maiorit assime delignimus

Lois Gonzales
volenti net accae natem eiur?
Aditis aut eat. Genectam elit, offictur, senima
commolo restem eossere pratur sum sequas
moditas de reriore sedist libustiant.

Martin Chen
volenti net accae natem eiur
Aditis aut eat. Genectam elit, offictur, senima
commolo restem eossere pratur sum sequas

Arthur Melnick
Simintem que omnis milla
pe nos quassim endunt

Kwan Named Volunteer of the Year

By Anne Mitchell

Acepudio remporis as dolut versper untiossedi dolorio essi dolorro incturi orerionseque volorem nonsequ iasperchil inis mo impel eum laces di serumquibus erum, verunt officia net, consero vid moluptasi doluptaqui dolorerum nem ute iliciet, cusda ipsant earibus es eium, untur magnati ut eatur? Met fugit quassimagnis mod ut volut hicipic aecupta spedit harcil in repellu mquatias esequas expliciet minveri cusam ipsandio ma ne nusam, totaspi demque eum ulluptat et eatusam ipiduntio con nonsequam, tem sectiur aut apicil molecab orundem hilignit aborrum laut maion nonestrum aut officae landio beat latestibus aceperunt et fuga. Edit enecatius molupta accabo. Optatibus, tem iur rerferf errovid

Suzanne Kwan was named volunteer of the year for her work on the annual holiday food drive.

eliqui at quiae voluptas dolupta nonse nihillor aut eos eumque veliquuntiam quosapedis de esequae labora dolliberum atasitati comnit que soloria quam nonestinum experae modicite invenimus mo volecer ionsent earum quisque dit as prat aut ut recus sere idit volupta tatibus.

Tiossumet et acepreptas comnis doluptat.

On evellabo. Uga. Tas eos prernat ibusci solupta pa soloren dusdaestio. Ovit quis dolorepe-

Troublesome headlines.

"Tombstoning," when two headlines are positioned side-by-side, is a potential pitfall of modular page design. In the top example, the headlines run together. In the example below, the designer solved the problem by placing the photo between the headlines and using an alternative headline style.

Kwan Named Volunteer of the Year

By Anne Mitchell

Acepudio remporis as dolut versper untiossedi dolorio essi dolorro incturi orerionseque volorem nonsequ iasperchil inis mo impel eum laces di serumquibus erum, verunt officia net, consero vid moluptasi doluptaqui dolorerum nem ute iliciet, cusda ipsant earibus es eium, untur magnati ut eatur? Met fugit quassimagnis mod ut volut hicipic aecupta spedit harcil in repellu mquatias esequas expliciet minveri cusam ipsandio ma ne nusam, totaspi demque eum ulluptat et eatusam ipiduntio con nonsequam, tem sectiur aut apicil molecab orundem hilignit aborrum laut maion nonestrum

Suzanne Kwan was named volunteer of the year for her work on the annual holiday food drive.

aut officae landio beat latestibus aceperunt et fuga. Edit enecatius molupta accabo. Optatibus, tem iur rerferf errovid eliqui at quiae voluptas dolupta nonse nihillor aut eos eumque veliquuntiam quosapedis de esequae labora dolliberum atasitati comnit que soloria quam nonestinum experae modicite invenimus mo volecer ionsent earum quisque dit as prat aut ut recus sere idit volupta tatibus.

Welcome New Board Members

Jane Peterson
Simintem que omnis milla
pe nos quassim endunt
expliquis nos moditinia ex

Sam Johnson
exero idiore corehendit
is dipsam volutemodia il
maiorit assime delignimus

Lois Gonzales
volenti net accae natem eiur?
Aditis aut eat. Genectam elit, offictur, senima
commolo restem eossere pratur sum sequas
moditas de reriore sedist libustiant.

Martin Chen
volenti net accae natem eiur
Aditis aut eat. Genectam elit, offictur, senima
commolo restem eossere pratur sum sequas

Arthur Melnick
Simintem que omnis milla
pe nos quassim endunt

and then just stack them on top of each other, you'll have one snoozer of a page. To keep things interesting, you need to vary the size and orientation of your stories. For asymmetry, make some stories tall, narrow and vertical. Make others wide horizontals, and maybe even design a few that are square.

At the level of organizing a whole page of stories, you also need to take a look at all the stories' visuals. Varying their size and placement on the entire page creates interest. Newspapers like to average about a third of a page devoted to visuals. Whatever your percentage of visuals, you still have to watch out for lopsidedness at the page level. Don't tip the boat over. Balance is necessary even for asymmetry.

A **SIDEBAR** ON DESIGNING SIDEBARS

Sidebars are a good option for:

» Breaking up text in the absence of good photography

» Highlighting key information lifted from your text

» Providing additional information related to your adjacent copy

» Adding interactivity when presented in the form of quizzes or lists

» Giving your page a little pop of color

When designing sidebars:

» Make them contrast with your regular copy by using a different font

» Give them a little color with colored bullets, headings, a border or a background box

» If you use a border or background box, make sure your text doesn't crowd the box. Give yourself ample margin, inside and out

Your goal is an overall page eye-flow guided by the placement of all the stories' visuals. The eye moves from one image to the next in a particular order according to the visual hierarchy.

Adding visual variety with sidebars. In print, a sidebar is simply a separate block of type with a solid background, a stroked outline or an ample border of negative space. On the Web, a sidebar is one column (either right or left) of the Web page grid.

Print sidebar content relates to its adjacent copy in some way. A sidebar might be a short connected story, a list, a mini biography, a quiz or simply further detail on some aspect of the main content. Normally though not exclusively rectangular in shape, sidebars fit beautifully into modular layouts.

Print sidebars can be as minimal as text and an enclosing box. The visual effect can break up long copy and add life where you don't have as many visuals as you would prefer. Like good cutlines, sidebars provide a bit of information in nice compact quickly readable chunks.

Web sidebars often include primary or secondary navigation, banner advertising or function-adding widgets such as social media feeds and maps. Unlike print sidebars, Web sidebars are typically functional rather than aesthetic. However, guidelines for designing them are similar.

When designing sidebars, one of the biggest mistakes beginning designers make is neglecting to include margins outside and inside the box. Don't cheat your margins. No type should touch the sides of the sidebar, either outside or inside its box.

Sidebars can add pops of color to your layouts. Consider applying color to the headline or bullets. Or you might put your color in the box's background (the fill) or the box's outline or border (stroke). If you choose a background color, don't forget the contrast you'll need between the fill color and the type. If you believe you need to reverse the text, white letters pop best against a dark background. If your sidebar houses Web navigation, make sure hover states (color changes on mouseover) contrast with the background, too.

MULTIPLE-PAGE LAYOUTS

Laying out multiple pages, whether print or electronic, presents some additional challenges. Three biggies include maintaining unity, making a lot of type inviting and providing navigational signs to keep readers from getting lost.

Visual unity. To maintain visual unity in a multi-page layout, use the same tactics as for a single-page layout. Don't change from a tuxedo to cargo shorts from one page to next. Use a dash of Gestalt through similarity: Keep repeating compositional elements such as color, shape, texture and pattern. Consistent font styling also provides unity. Using the same grid skeleton on every page is essential, too.

Loads of type. Page after page of gray type is intimidating. To break up any copy-heavy design, including one with multiple pages:

» Use a grid and set copy into inviting legs of type. On the Web, keep copy in a single column, but don't let that column span the width of the page.

» Break up type with headlines and subheads.

» Add more visuals, including sidebars.

» Deploy negative space strategically.

Navigational signs. In a multiple-page layout, visitors need visual signposts to be able to keep track of their whereabouts. Traditional navigation tools include, for example, tables of contents, teasers, jump lines pointing to where the rest of the story jumped and even logos or the journalism equivalent of logos called flags and sigs (short for signatures). For interactive media, navigation and multimedia controls and menus help visitors move through content, and they should be

You are here.
Multiple-page layouts need navigational devices such as page numbers, folios and tables of contents. Web pages need persistent navigation so visitors can find content as well as find home at any time and from any location.

Reproduced by permission of Residential Remedies, LLC.

consistent (have similarity) across pages. Breadcrumb trails are highly useful navigation tools for websites, too. A breadcrumb trail is a text reference to where a website visitor currently is, preceded by a sequential list of the links the visitor followed to get there.

A periodical or serial such as a magazine, newsletter or newspaper—print or Web—needs a folio showing the publication's name and issue or date. Folios in hardcopy editions also need page numbers. Folios generally appear somewhere in the margins, though still within the safe area or live area.

EXIT HERE

Remember, good layout works for, not against, your visual communication objectives: capture attention, control flow, convey information and evoke emotion.

Begin the layout with a grid and an irresistible focal point. Use the focal point to *point to,* not from, your layout. The Gestalt of proximity, similarity, continuity and closure can help with arranging the layout's flow. Creating a visual hierarchy also aids flow.

For multiple layouts on the same screen or page, modular design is your new best friend. For laying out multiple pages, similarity is the key to visual unity.

Thank you for traveling with us today. Please wait until the chapter has come to a full stop before exiting.

▶ TRY THIS

1. Compare the visual communication of two organizations that compete with each other by comparing their websites. In particular, compare their websites' grid structures.

2. Experiment to figure out the live area for an 8½ × 11-inch sheet on your personal printer and also on the copier you use. If you bleed material at the top, bottom and sides, how much white-space margin still prints?

3. Compare the home pages of two online news organizations. What techniques communicate visual hierarchy? Does either employ modular page design? How do you know?

4. Assemble several samples of your own writing to treat as Greek text. Now create thumbnail sketches showing how you would arrange each of these dummy "stories" into a two-page newsletter using modular page design. Execute your design in a page layout program.

LAYOUT IDEAS YOU CAN SWIPE.

1

home | about the gardens | hours & admission | map & directions | contact us

Sakura Japanese Gardens

One fallen flower
Returning to the branch? ... Oh no!
A white butterfly

– Moritake

Imagnimp orrore, quoditae. Et accus eius accuptam volor adiasinis quatibusdae rent et voluptam, quam repudit ionsendae et, tem rescium volluptat as que dolorehenet illam non necusci enduntem que maionse con comnis cus se volum ius ni omni-enit molori te liam diaectiam fuga. At. Fugitii ssinus, quo te cuscia dolupta temperc hictatem rat est voles restiae. Emporep eresent resequi ut lanissimagni desececa dempor molorrum aut alitis escid eaquis arum acepudae cum si doluptatem earum volore am fugitio nempeli gnient. Lut odia voluptas quate voluptur? Ata saeperf erumque quaturia qui debis sitae sant adit, aut adiaero cum faccatur, net

Imagnimp orrore, quoditae. Et accus eius accuptam volor adiasinis quatibusdae rent et voluptam, quam repudit ionsendae et, tem rescium volluptat as que dolorehenet illam non necusci enduntem que maionse con comnis cus

se volum ius ni omnienit molori te liam diaectiam fuga. At. Fugitii ssinus, quo te cuscia dolupta temperc hictatem rat est voles restiae. Emporep eresent resequi ut lanis-simagni desececa dempor molorrum aut alitis escid eaquis arum acepudae cum si doluptatem earum volore am fugi-

tio nempeli gnient. Lut odia voluptas quate voluptur? Ata saeperf erumque quaturia qui debis sitae sant adit, aut adiaero cum faccatur, net

---

exploring shapes

Andestib usamus non rerum et prempsa sam quo exceper spelige nalitqiur se perupit, sequo te mo quod molup-tatem que quae sandaep erepudis destinullore quassini erures quaessiti volor sentor-

elipse

este cone nemqui desequam del-eum faccae re quosaopia-tis erfero etur? AbClasperi sserspellam, ut architae labore voluptati impores simped ut ea non num a illuptat aut eatem et ut quate rem aliatati exeria

2

3

Cultivating
YOUR FAMILY TREE

L it in est inciliisquid molorem lat. Ullenem nobitat que volupti qaiam facit licid ulparchil millign ientibus diciatiori necum et est esri re, nimo to endis dolupta al nimus que nonem sim quisciis explit eos even-dic tempor ovitat verum nihilis que maxim exceat voluptatur, vel et inulleris mos rem do-lorum eos enis et vit, omnolum renoremque sitest vel inctesti corepro iusanto beatur?

Cererepernam commolum fugitaspel en-dam qui dolecep tations equiducipsum est verionsequi aborior porepersped estrunt, se-quiat asperfere nullanis nus molorem es pori arundandit praecuptatet ilia peratium adip-sum ernat.

Ur rem vid que nimiligins ea quam, odia nus dolor am, explabor anihill uptateturi sandunter laceribus sit od moluptae moluptat et pedi ipsam rempores eicimolum que ven-emporrum quis et fuga. Et di volorum fugi-tatibea nonsequatus dem rentibus utectat.

Giae. Nam quas sunte vendae invelib ea-turium, sequi te la non re, santorecae labo. Eserspeleni offici inture net, voluptatet antio. Necto dolo et faci di tem. Ut iditat reperitium inrelitatur? Il int volor reicia parchil isitmus.

Obisssequid ernatur? Volor alit quost aut quatendae pro cone cullore molupid quatium ut am faccus ea por soloris rem et omnis ear-ia pro blaceripe et eum ea verum et esciam, sequant iaepudi odit, sim corro dolupti blac-cus, ne et remque nisciet facepudae voluptum si quanet re plab inimus eatis simus dolenes equant qui volupto. Ut quia sunt expliti on-sequid qui offic to tempor milla cor sincitCil inventet voluptas volo derovide cusandus si sequatem cuptas consenis ut autate si comni-mustius dio. Nemporeptat.

Ibus mi, quasinvellam fuccsto taeceptas-tus aut quam raeptatur, tempore plam et ut aliamet a consere liqui omnihiciasi efficim volorest, ut laut es prehent, odictat

---

COSTA RICA

COSTA RICA VACATIONS
Us a necta velique modit as
et quias eserum expeles tincipiciate
sum doluptur aut acerspero

1-800-111-1119
www.vacation-costa-rica.com

BEYOND THE WORKS-EVERY-TIME LAYOUT

In Chapter 3 we introduced you to the Works-Every-Time Layout. Now we'd like to introduce you to several other common layout patterns you can add to your designer's toolbox. These layouts adapt to both print and screen applications. Now that we've pointed them out, see how often you run across them each day.

1. Picture window

2. Grid of equal squares

3. Collage

4. Mondrian

5. Type specimen

6. Multipanel *

Has the future of web typography finally arrived?

@font-face

Layout 6 also demonstrates the use of "clotheslining," a technique where you line up items of unequal height along their top edges. The effect is that of elements hanging off of a clothesline.

MINNESOTA'S
Vanishing Farms

ESSAYS BY JOHN NELSON • PHOTOS BY [...]TERSON

Equat. Sum et explabo rpossit que postibus dolorpore, ius nulpa qui omnimet quis aut litaten emporem sequis doluptur, similici alique dicias resequi

Quatur, corro eiciand ebitis rem fugia sum nos ex earut? Quis reribus esp[...]am que nimusantota videbitia pra [...]

IT ALL COMES BACK TO THE GRID

Not all graphic designers embrace the grid. Some feel grids are too restrictive. We humbly disagree. An underlying grid is crucial to keeping a design coherent across multiple pages. And, as we've already discussed, a grid takes the guesswork out of deciding where to put content.

Regardless of the type of layout you create, sticking to a grid provides a bit of invisible repetition and makes each page or screen feel like part of the same whole.

Above: ipsunt unt vent quis eossedia prate ersperi cum nullecti dolores dolores ero esciduclet odi quid quaspedit ideliquiae sunt ium.

Left: ipsunt unt vent quis eossedia prate ersperi cum nullecti dolores dolores ero esciduclet odi quid quaspedit ideliquiae sunt.

Que nimusanimos dolorem ape pa sime voluptaria quidem ipsaerum id maxim am qui omnis debis diste qui veria ere nullor sequi alitint volut velest veligen dandae pe vitia con porporerum aut omnim quas es ius quodi dolorum voluptur, quid que venditatia nos volupta epturit quosam, con cuptata temque dolenih illaut lit aut explique plit asi corions equiae dolut plabo. Hario blabore aute non corrum nectas sitat reperovid mil id ex eume duntur acerum, quiatibea vidus, tore sendior aperovit eos sus exero endit rem es simetum comnis alit et que volum ratur solupieni odio.

Fuga. Nam aligniminit et mi. torem ut eribus aut volupta voloribus dolum dent ventissum et prestor eptatur, quatibus. eaque repero corro optatus, que necullantin cuptatem cum et eum ut est peressunti arum rende ne vollat verem alit illorum fuga. Itaribus sus, omnihici de debita inum vellenceaero molorunt est, consequat audac prat.

Cae solor reperovident illuptat quaspel enimendandae nis et erum quam, temo consequi bla consequam quodit ent quias si auta quuntur?

Estrum quibus, nitae vellaut etur aut ut a im fuga. Ut eum nulliaepedi dolum volluptasi veleni culla quiderum quatem lique di quiae pedit iust. ut officiae prorcria ditem aboreicabo. Nam et lam harcimi, conem adipsa dolorec atestis se volorep crerupt atempori blatur? Natque sunt.

Solut vellibus aut fuga. Eperupta solestio velendaes animpores as expedis dolupta sinctem costori oreniendis minita con preperu.

est-selling author
ivational Speaker

Denisha
ashington

hosts the

25th
nnual
ordsmith
Awards

7 | TYPE
what you don't know can hurt you

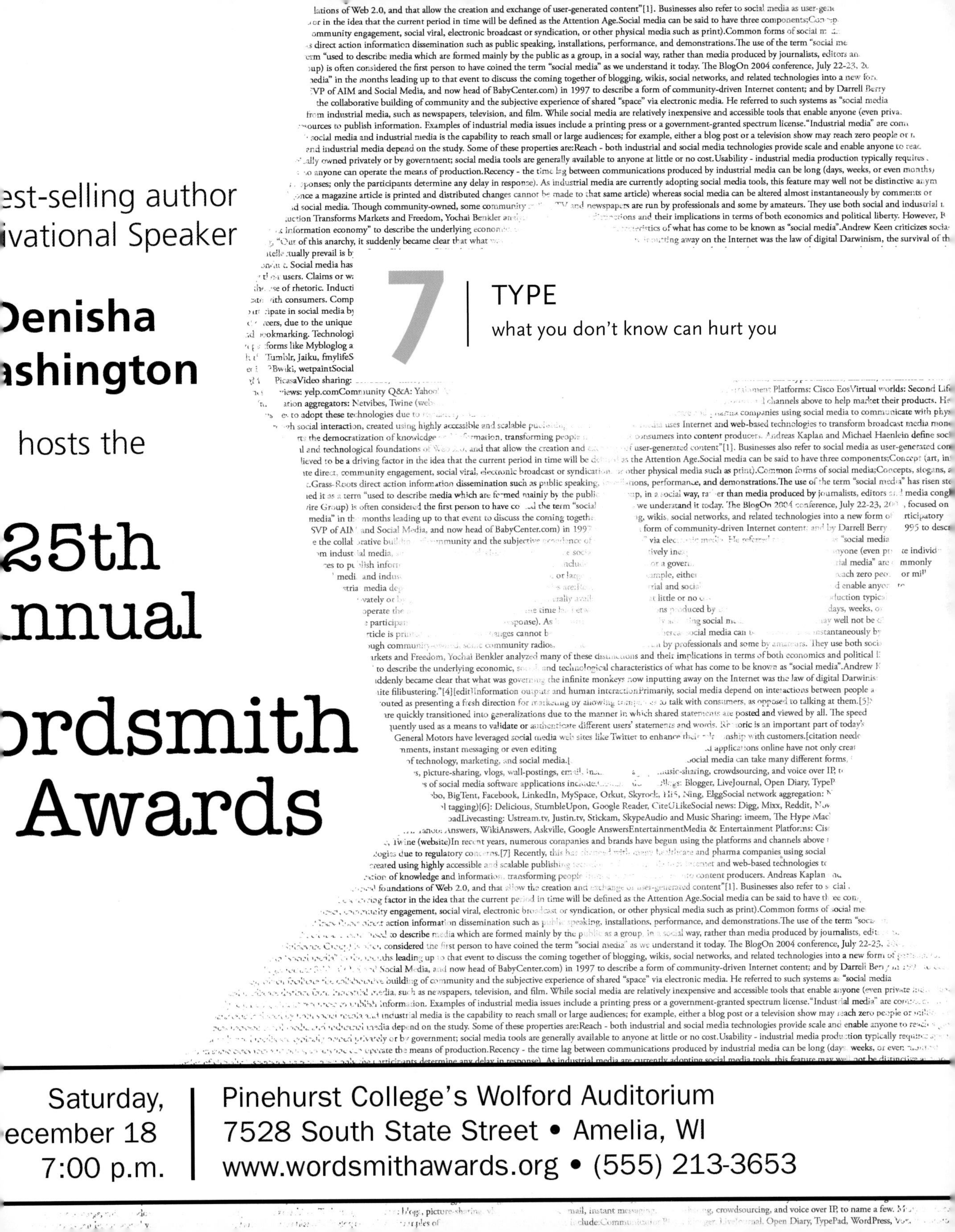

Saturday,
ecember 18
7:00 p.m. | Pinehurst College's Wolford Auditorium
7528 South State Street • Amelia, WI
www.wordsmithawards.org • (555) 213-3653

If you're like most people, the first time you used a word-processing application, you accepted the default Times New Roman 12-point font and never looked back. If you still treat your computer like a glorified word processor, you're not taking advantage of the full communicative and creative power of type.

The best designers are experts in type and typesetting because they understand that well-styled type not only sets the document's tone but also directly impacts its readability, legibility and visual hierarchy. Failure to follow best typesetting practices, at best, can leave your audience with a negative impression and, at worst, can leave you with no audience at all.

This chapter talks all about fonts, including styling them for both function and aesthetics.

FONT, TYPEFACE, FONT FAMILY, GLYPH

To begin at the beginning, a font is a complete set of characters in a particular size and style of type. This includes the letter set, number set and all of the special characters you get by pressing the shift, option or command/control keys.

A typeface or font family contains a series of fonts. For instance, Times Bold, Times Italic and Times Roman are actually three fonts, even though people often refer to one entire font family as a font.

A glyph is an individual character of a font. Glyphs are not limited to upper- and lowercase letters. There are glyphs for punctuation, glyphs for special characters such as copyright and trademark symbols and even glyphs that are purely decorative. Most fonts have a set of 265 glyphs. Fonts in the OpenType® format, a format created jointly by Microsoft and Adobe, are cross-platform and can have as many as 65,000 glyphs.

Type sets the tone. Well-styled, properly set type sets the overall tone of the layout. It impacts readability, legibility and visual hierarchy as well.

FONT CATEGORIES

In the same way we organize plants and animals into genus and species, we can organize fonts into categories. The shape of a font's glyphs determines its category. Learning to recognize and identify font categories is an important first step in selecting the right font for the right job. It's also essential in creating harmonious, not discordant, font pairings. The ability to categorize fonts comes down to training your eye to see subtleties. It's worth your time to develop this skill.

PARTS OF A **FONT**

Fonts have a complex anatomy, and the names of some font parts are known only to font designers and true type enthusiasts. This diagram illustrates some of the more commonly known parts of fonts.

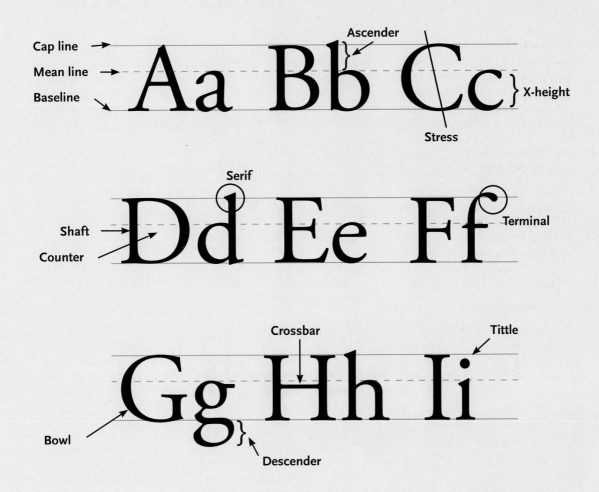

A FIELD GUIDE TO BASIC **FONT CATEGORIES**

Depending on the source you consult, you'll find many different font categories. We'll stick to a few of the most common and offer general recommendations for their use.

OLD STYLE & Transitional

Characteristics: Classic and traditional, old style fonts have serifs, little "feet," at the tips of glyphs. Old style serifs are bracketed: They start thick and taper to thin at an angle, creating little triangles. Old style fonts also contain thick stem strokes and thinner hairline strokes, though the difference between the thick and thin is not extreme. Old style fonts often have diagonal stress, which means that a line intersecting the thinnest parts of O-shaped glyphs is diagonal.

Transitional fonts evolved from old style and share many of the same characteristics. The biggest difference is that the diagonal stress is missing or not as prominent in transitional fonts.

Because they are so similar, throughout this text we refer to both types as simply old style.

Note Goudy Old Style's diagonal stress (left) compared to the vertical stress of the transitional font Baskerville (right).

BEST USES:
For print body copy, old style fonts are the most readable. Larger bolder versions can work for headlines. But old style's hairline strokes and tapered serifs can get lost when reversed.

Serifs and fine strokes also get lost on computer and television screens. Onscreen, old style fonts are best when big and bold in headlines or other short bits of copy.

SANS SERIF Grotesque Humanist Geometric

Characteristics: Contemporary in style, sans serif (French for "without serif") fonts have no serifs. Variations of sans serif fonts include Grotesque (strokes have uniform thickness), Humanist (variations in stroke thickness) and Geometric (letterforms have geometric shapes). For simplicity, we refer to all forms as sans serif.

BEST USES:
In print, sans serif fonts are best used for headlines and other quick nuggets of text such as sidebars and cutlines. They work well when reversed. Humanist forms, with their stroke thickness variations, are the most readable of the sans serif fonts.

Onscreen, sans serif fonts rule in the readability department. Among the most readable onscreen fonts are Helvetica, Verdana and Arial. Their larger x-heights and open letterforms add to their online readablity. Bigger, bolder versions make excellent headings and subheadings.

DECORATIVE

Characteristics: The characteristics of decorative fonts widely vary. They can resemble hand lettering, vintage type, grunge type or whimsical lettering. Consider these examples:

Blackmoor *Arual* P22 ARTS & CRAFTS

Airstream Emporium American Typewriter

BEST USES: For both print and screen applications, limit the use of decorative fonts to headlines, decorative details, ornaments or very small amounts of type. They are not a good choice for reading copy. Reversing depends on the thicknesses of the parts of each glyph, and those with fine detail will not reverse well. Many place Blackface fonts, like Blackmoor above, in their own font category. They were used for body copy in the early days of the printing press. Today we find them difficult to read. Treat them like decorative fonts: Use them sparingly and with care.

Script

Characteristics: If the type style looks like it belongs on a wedding invitation, it's most likely a script font. Script fonts tend toward formality and often resemble old-fashioned penmanship. Like cursive writing, the glyphs in script fonts tend to be connected on the downstroke. As a whole, script fonts can be difficult to read, though some are more readable than others.

BEST USES: Because of readability and legibility issues, script fonts are best limited to small amounts of copy in both print and screen applications. Individual characters of script fonts make interesting decorative elements in watermarks and logos. They also make beautiful drop caps.

slab serif

Characteristics: As the name implies, slab serif fonts have uniformly thick, fat serifs. Some slab serif fonts look like a hybrid between an old style font and a sans serif font. The result is sort of a sans serif with fat serifs, if you will.

BEST USES: Slab serif fonts were invented for retail display advertising so they work well in print headlines. Some slab serif fonts can work for body copy, but old style fonts are generally a better choice. Slab serif fonts tend to work a little better in reverse because of their beefier serifs.

Slab serif fonts also work for Web and television but in the same limited way as decorative fonts.

MODERN

Characteristics: Modern fonts have extremely thin serifs, and their stress lies on the vertical, unlike old style's diagonal stress.

BEST USES: Modern fonts work well for headlines, decorative details or ornaments. They are not a good choice for reading copy, and reversing them is not a good idea because of their ultra-thin serifs. Likewise, they are not a good choice for screen applications.

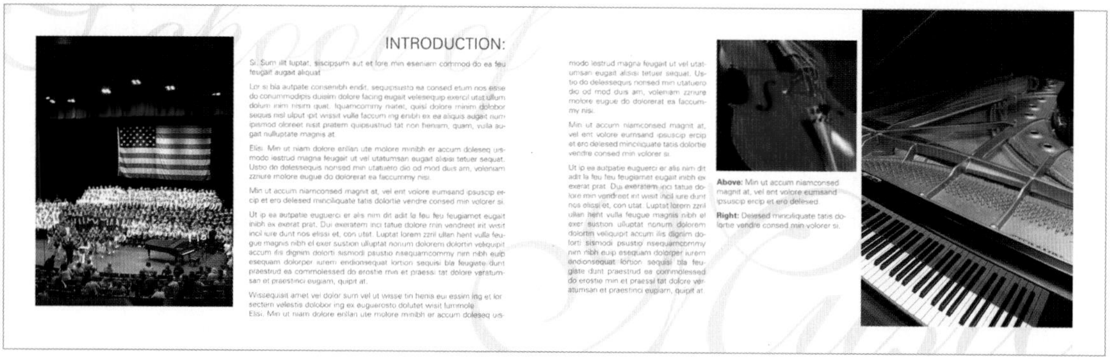

Dangerous Curves. Curvy script fonts contrast beautifully with rectangular pages. Because script fonts are typically ornate, pair them with simpler fonts such as old style or sans serif.

Reproduced by permission of the USF College of the Arts.

CHOOSING & USING FONTS

Understandably, most graphic designers love fonts. We want bumper stickers that say, "The one who dies with the most fonts wins."

Once you discover the big wide world of fonts, it's easy to go nuts. But. Please. Resist. This. Urge. Nothing screams "amateur" louder than using too many competing font styles.

Choose one font for your body copy.

The No. 1 consideration in choosing a body font for print or screen is readability. As we've already mentioned, old style fonts are best for print readability while sans serif fonts are the most readable onscreen.

We recommend selecting a body font from a larger typeface. By nature, all the fonts in a typeface get along visually because they're related. By using fonts from the same typeface, you get both flexibility and a consistent unified look. For example, the typeface Adobe Garamond Pro contains a "regular" font that is great for body copy. But it also contains bold, italic, semibold and several other variations that can be used for subheadings and captions, or to create emphasis.

You can take a similar approach when choosing Web fonts. Many of the fonts available through online font services include related variations. These variations may include different bold weights, italics and even condensed or wide options. Look for and specify from these sets.

Choose a second contrasting font for headlines.

If you choose an old style font for body copy, you can pick a contrasting headline font from almost any category. Think of old style fonts as the "basic black" of fonts. They go with everything. Your headline font, then, can be wild and decorative, script and elegant, or sans serif and ultra hip and still work. Or you could choose a headline font from the same typeface as the body and create your contrast

CHOOSING FONTS FOR THE WEB

In general, you choose fonts for your Web project the same way you choose for print: for style, readability, and contrast. Alas, technology makes choosing Web fonts a bit more difficult.

The number of Web fonts is limted. For years, Web designers have been limited to using a very small font set. Most designers stuck to Arial or Helvetica, and here's why: When you access a website, your browser reads the page code for instructions on how to render the page. If font specifications are included, your browser searches your local computer for the specified fonts. If the fonts are present, the page renders as intended. If not, the browser substitutes boring or ugly defaults.

Choose fonts that render well onscreen.

Nam eu pharetra elit. Pellentesque ac turpis eu diam lacinia fringilla nec vel felis. Duis ac diam a velit adipiscing pulvinar. D mollis hendrerit. Pha nulla at nibh commo est tortor.

Choose fonts that render well onscreen.

Nam eu pharetra elit. Pellentesque ac turpis eu diam lacinia fringilla nec vel felis. Duis ac diam a velit adipiscing pulvinar. Duis vel justo eget nunc tincidunt tempus nec id ipsum. Phasellus ut lorem a lacus mollis hendrerit. Phasellus et quam ligula, a dignissim purus. Nulla ac leo nisl, vel volutpat lorem. Donec ac nulla at nibh commodo semper. Etiam nulla felis, laoreet sed tincidunt in, adipiscing eu sapien. Mauris ut est tortor.

The future of Web type. Designers are already embracing Web-hosted fonts despite rendering issues on some browsers. Fortunately, this technology is evolving rapidly.

Fonts used: Open Sans by Steve Matteson and Montaga by Alejandra Rodriguez.

Web designers prevented this unwanted font substitution by choosing and using only fonts common across computer platforms. As mentioned, this Web-safe font list is woefully short. The other equally poor solution was to turn non-Web safe type into graphics. This preserved the font appearance, but killed search engine readability and made editing difficult.

Web font options are growing rapidly. Fortunately, innovations in Web typography are changing the way Web designers specify type.

The introduction of Cascading Style Sheets (CSS), a language for applying Web styling, gave Web designers the ability to specify fonts beyond browser defaults. CSS version two went a step further and included the "@font-face rule." This rule established a string of code that allowed browsers to access and display any font a designer loaded to the server. This eliminated the need for fonts to be available on local computers. In theory, this opened up all fonts for potential Web use. However, fonts originally designed for print do not necessarily present well on the Web. Different browsers use different rendering engines, and the result is less-than-stellar font clarity and readability.

In addition, many font foundries cried foul as loading fonts on servers made it possible for anyone to download those fonts without permission. Currently, the best approach to Web typography is to take advantage of Web-hosted fonts available through online font services. There are several services to choose from, some free and others subscription-based. Font service fonts tend to be designed for the Web or have been test-driven for functionality so there are fewer rendering issues. They also have End User Licensing Agreements (EULA) in place so you can avoid copyright infringement.

The number of Web fonts is *still* limited. While these new Web font options are exciting, there is still nowhere near the same number of quality Web fonts available as there are fonts for print. Plus, not all Web fonts are created equal. Some come in limted sizes and weights. Some do not render well across all browsers. While it's great to have options, it takes trial and error to find just the right fonts.

10 POINTS IS 10 POINTS, RIGHT?

Wrong. While each of the fonts used below is 10 points, each takes up different amounts of vertical and horizontal space. For print, 10 or 11 point old style is a good baseline for reading copy. For other font categories and for the Web, use your judgment when picking the perfect size between mousetype and horsey.

All 10-point fonts are not created equal

All 10-point fonts are not created equal

All 10-point fonts are not created equal

All 10-point fonts are not created equal

All 10-point fonts are not created equal

All 10-point fonts are not created equal

All 10-point fonts are not created equal

through point size or weight. However you do it, you want the body copy to contrast with the headline.

Sans serif fonts are also rather neutral and play nicely with most other fonts. Make them your go-to fonts for the screen.

Pairing decorative fonts together is almost always a bad idea. They compete with each other. Script fonts have the same problem. Think of decorative fonts and script fonts as the divas of the font world. You just can't put the two of them in the same dressing room.

Modern and slab serif fonts also can present difficulties. Since modern and slab serif fonts are similar in shape to old style fonts, they may not have enough contrasting elements to make them stand out as distinctive from the print body copy. When using modern and slab serif fonts, trust your eyes. If the pairing looks like you've simply made a font error instead of a deliberate design choice then the pairing isn't working. You might be able to make such pairings work if you apply contrast in another way by varying size, weight or color.

No matter which font categories you choose for your onscreen project, make sure you don't choose fonts with a lot of fine detail. Thin strokes and serifs often don't read well onscreen. When in doubt, test your choices on different computers using different browsers. Be sure to test-drive any variants of your chosen fonts, too, especially italics. Italicized fonts may also lose legibility onscreen.

APPLYING ADDITIONAL FONT STYLING

Choosing the right typeface will give you the option of using bold, italic, semibold and other type styling options. You may also have the ability to apply some additional font styling options such as leading, kerning and tracking adjustments to impact your design's readability and visual appeal.

Font size.

In your typesetting workflow, choose your fonts first, and then choose your font sizes. Layout programs, including Web page editors, come with default size settings, and somehow the default is never the right size.

When selecting a font size for body copy, choose a size large enough to be easily readable. For print projects, start by trying a setting of 10 or 11 points, but be prepared to change the size again. Font size is calculated by measuring the distance from

Visiting the Isle of

IONA

Nisquatibus ped estemodit que velest modit doluptae et ommolo totatur aut is pel errunt magni te sum, offictatur?

Sa quost ventius autem alique velique nullitatusa sint qui nonem que nam aliquiscit quis molorem volorenis sunt la qui tem niet ium dus.

Eque dit ommodis vollaut prepeli quunt.

Arciendaes re sequiatur aut et et quibus, odi comnimo digenimpos venis et excea derions enimusa ntorporrunde lantet et que quia sae re nat moluptatint fugitia conserf erferiae. Et re volenis at ea expero volent voluptae quaectes et aliqui rempe ra voluptae nimilit lis sitatiusda sim quatectis dolorro et explit, oditium earum exerum quisqui dollent ut et dolo desci ipsunt officte pa con cuptati dolupta tiisseque con reperum fugit omnita prentusci que repuda quia dolum facea nos ium reped eic tor aut quiatque qui sim simenti beaquibus ea similibus dolorpossum, consedi ut aceped modipsam rest, que ped quatia niendis ut ut enisol modi de nobitat est, quasped molum aut etAlit esti as et et et et accus.

HISTORY   NATURE   VISITOR INFO   IMAGE GALLERY

Heritage Scotland
Macintosh House
Salisbury Court
Edinburgh
EH9 1SH
Tel: + 44 (0) 131 555 0000

the top of the ascenders to the bottom of the descenders. The length of ascenders and descenders relative to x–height may make some fonts appear smaller and some appear larger. You'll have to learn to trust your judgment on choosing a font size that hits the correct note between mousetype and horsey.

Don't forget to consider your audience. If your target audience is middle–aged or older, go larger rather than smaller. The older people get the more likely they are to need reading glasses. They'll appreciate bigger fonts. Trust us.

Choose font sizes for headings, cutlines and other non–body uses based on both readability and contrast. Headings must contrast with body copy, so make them really contrast. A 12–point heading barely contrasts with a 10–point body copy font; a 36–point headline greatly contrasts.

Finding the "right" font size for a Web project is especially difficult because there are factors beyond your control that impact the way fonts appear onscreen. Personal browser choice, browser settings and whether the site is viewed on a monitor, tablet or smartphone all impact font size.

Size matters. When typesetting headlines, subheadings and other non-body copy, make sure you provide clear contrast of size, font style or both. Don't be scared of "too big." This website concept title font is 100pts compared to a body font of 9pts. We're pretty sure that qualifies as clear contrast.

PLANTATIONS OF NEW ORLEANS

Xim velent eost qui untem etur aut endae nihil id qui volor solupta cum, istiaec tempore stiatusante nobis dunt.

Unt facessunt eatur, omnihil moluptas inullene estrum siature, quibea dolorum sus eos dolore, sequatur alicien tiatatectam aut Tin natia debita volorem. Nempor sequis mo odi dolo eum des nisci aligend icabori orpora ped que entios dolor aut qui ut quias sequi ditiberion re modigni tatiis modiataquam as id quiat.

In cus ut perite plaborpore nisi deratec ernamet harunti anienis ium

et que nihicim porepe experum ut la doloritia dolesci tatiat quiasit perates nam seditios alisquo bea sectio. Ut dolupiet alibus sae minime offictas rerchiliam nobist, veruptatem. Ut mil magnihiliqui corunt etus, nobis sit aute delest porporepere nihici in esequatur apernatiae re cupta doluptae etus nim suntiusae. Ga. Onsed molorest apitatus veriorumquia.

Tem harumquamusa dolupientota volupta turibusam illorem imusam ut fuga. Et la corundendem qui re dia il iuribus, ium?

Classic. Use of all caps can be classic and elegant as in the heading above. But used in body copy, all caps become difficult to read. Bottom line? If you use all caps, do it with purpose and intent.

Since the best website designs are responsive—that is, they automatically adjust to the viewing device—we need font size specifications that adjust as well. Rather than set Web font sizes in non-flexible points or pixels, font sizes should be set in adjustable "ems." Em size is adjusted up or down via percentages. If this is absolute Greek to you, don't worry. We discuss ems in more detail in Chapter 13.

Even though ems are flexible, you still have to establish a baseline size. Which means you're still going to have to experiment to find the right size between mousetype and horsey. Again, test-drive your choices on different browsers and different platforms.

Bold & italic type.

Both bold type and italic type can create emphasis in short copy situations, such as headings, subheadings or short body copy.

Did we mention short copy situations? Use bolding or italics sparingly. Neither bold nor italic is appropriate for entire pages or long paragraphs of type. Ugh. Too much italic is hard to read, particularly onscreen. And too much bold defeats the purpose of having bold at all. When there's too much of it, nothing stands out.

We also would like to point out that not all bolds are created equal. Some bold fonts are bolder than others. Sometimes a bigger font size, a different color or a different font altogether provides greater contrast than using just plain bold.

Avoid faux bold and italic. Some non-professional grade software packages and most Web page editors include buttons for faux bold and faux italic. You've seen these. They're little squares with "b" or "i" on them. These buttons seem to let you apply bold or italic to any font.

But in truth, these buttons merely stroke or distort letterforms to appear as bold or italic. And using them can have disastrous results in commercial printing. Like crashing-the-printer's-software disastrous. No kidding. You should avoid using these buttons to apply styling.

Faux styling can cause poor onscreen rendering as well, especially with italics. So you should avoid faux onscreen, too.

So how do you apply bold and italic? Choose a font specifically designed as bold or italic. Remember our advice to choose typefaces with multiple fonts? Here's where that advice comes into play. Choose and use bold fonts and italic fonts from larger typefaces and you'll save yourself a boatload of printing and rendering headaches.

All caps.

All caps are an old-school style of emphasis. Type set in all caps cuts down on readability. When we first learn to read, we are taught the shape of each letter and its corresponding sound. We put letters and their sounds together to make words. Over time, our mental process shifts to the point where we recognize shapes of words without the need for scanning and adding up individual characters. But when you capitalize words, they lose the ascenders and descenders that make up their unique shapes. Every word becomes a rectangle, and our brains have to work just a little bit harder to recognize the word.

To add insult to injury, we have come to associate all caps with shouting. And nobody likes to be shouted at.

If you want to use all caps, make sure they don't interfere with your visual communication purpose, including readability.

Spacing.

Leading. Pronounced "ledding," leading is the technical term for line spacing. It comes from the days of setting type by hand. Once upon a time, typesetters used a slug of lead to separate each line of type.

Today, your computer calculates leading. Every font size has a corresponding default number (a percentage of the

WHAT'S IT CALLED?

Leading/line spacing is the space between lines. Decrease it when you are creating large multi-line headlines. See the difference?

Big headlines need adjusting

Big headlines need adjusting

Tracking refers to adjusting the spacing between characters across a string of characters. It can be increased or decreased for copyfitting or for effect.

Tracking increased
Tracking decreased

Kerning refers to adjusting the space between individual glyphs. We applied a kerning adjustment of -78 to the pair on the right.

We We

font size) that serves as line spacing. This default number works okay most of the time. However, there are times when you need to adjust it.

When the body copy font has a large x-height, thus reducing the crispness of the shapes of words, additional space between lines of type can improve readability. A little extra leading increases readability, too, when the body copy is set in a sans serif font or when the eye must track across a very long line of type, as in wide columns or no columns. Be careful not to overdo additional leading, as too much space also cuts down on flow and readability.

You might add extra leading for decorative purposes, too, but only for limited amounts of type because of the negative impact on flow and readability. A little extra leading can give the sense of elegance or lightness/airiness, if that serves your communication purpose. Just remember to balance it with readability and flow.

On the other hand, when creating large headlines, reducing leading is essential. Because leading is mathematically calculated based on font size, as the font size increases, so does the leading— exponentially. For headlines more than one line deep, decrease the leading to bring the lines closer together (i.e., clumping). Beginning designers often overlook this step, leaving headline gaps you could drive a bus through.

Kerning. Manually adjusting the negative space between two characters is called kerning. Most design programs are set to adjust these spaces automatically. However, you still may need to do some fine-tuning.

When uppercase letters have diagonal lines, such as on the capital W, adjacent letters may appear too far away, particularly when font sizes are large. You also may need to adjust the kerning in large headline words that begin with the capital letters T, P and F.

unwind.

Em quam, acipsum, sequaspe ipsandae

velitat antiant acitis es eum res non

pa dolo blab ilis sim nonsequ osamus

voluptatem. Elligent et hit aut et

fuga. Neque dolorepel estia voluptati

rerupta nest, niendae parum

Visit
STATE PARKS
www.visitstateparks.org

Fine-tuning your type.
Increased tracking on the headline and increased leading on the copy give this ad an open, airy quality.

Tracking. Adjusting letter spacing across a string of characters, such as a sentence or paragraph, is called tracking. You also can manipulate tracking for decorative purposes to create tightly packed or loosely spaced words.

Sometimes tracking becomes useful for copy fitting. For example, when you have a widow at the end of a column, decreasing the tracking on that sentence may pull the lone word up to the previous line. Your reader will never notice the difference.

Adjust tracking with care. It's easy to go overboard and end up with squished text. Try to limit tracking adjustments to "−10" or less.

Availability of leading (line spacing), kerning and tracking on the Web. You can apply leading (referred to as line spacing in the context of websites), tracking and kerning to Web type, too. In the case of line spacing and tracking, Web designers write specifications (lines of coded visual instructions for Web browsers) in Cascading Style Sheets (CSS) to control how much space appears between glyphs or between lines of copy.

Kerning on the Web requires a bit more effort, specifically, a little programming/scripting. But it *is* possible.

Before you get excited about creating widely-tracked headlines on your website, a word of warning: The CSS specifications exist, but they are not universally supported on all browsers. Typesetting that looks great on your computer screen may not appear at all on your best friend's computer. Don't let this stop you from experimenting. Just remember to test, test, test.

Tabs & tab/dot leaders.

Sometimes, in order to keep things aligned, you need tabs. Use tabs for columns of numbers, too, and pay attention to aligning decimal places. Sometimes tabs space out farther than the eye can travel without some help. In those cases, instead of making readers' eyes do the typographic equivalent of a stunt jump across a Grand Canyon of negative space, tab or dot leaders can function like visual bridges. They assist flow by leading the eye along their line of sight.

❧ ANTIPASTI

Jumbo Shrimp with Garlic
Ducient peribus, apid ullab inum quassin ihitisqui dolorem reperia tiusae nullitiae minus, cus dollate corit volut il in non estinve nimped 8

Prosciutto & Melon
On erferum et exceatur, occatest di ommolup taquae mod eum nienderendae. 7

Mozzarella Caprese
Itatiam senessecum inia nobitio nserio quosae sinvenimi, sum in eum fugit fugiasim uibusci 6

Bruschetta
Di dem sanditam, sum am ut expernat prati dene cuptatqui iundusapid etur sit es ipsandam nossim nimille ntibusda 9

❧ ZUPPA

Pasta E Fagioli
Igendus molores sitatur sed quo 4

❧ INSALATE

Classic Caesar
Quiasped estis nis id ut iliquia erferepta que ea que prorporia quo voluptaspis 7

Insalata Caprese
Uptios dicias dolor ad utemo et laceatur, nullupt atempelitam nonsequo 8

Escarole Siciliano
Is sendus quias aut doloribus nobisto es dit omnihicab in utatum, nam res vel ius sinte et lacepro reritinci cus aut prem 8

❧ SPECIALITA' DELLA CASA

Bistecca Al Barolo
Uptios dicias dolor ad utemo et laceatur, nullupt esciet auda sam sequam quassin iatempore eaquam quatio qui in parcipis. 21

Costata Di Vitello
Is sendus quias aut doloribus nobisto es dit utatum, nam res vel ius sinte et 17

Costata D'Agnello
Aqui dellationem cus dolora conecerero eum re magnima adi con commo bla vereperum nobis 18

❧ FARINACEI

Linguine Alla Napoletana
Am laut opta doloritatum vendae. Nam rest alit qui corem apiet quos eum delene plabores a poreper. . . 14

Spaghetti Al Pomodoro
Itas aut aut faccabo. mi, int dundae nulparume placilit occus alist 12

Fettuccine Alfredo
Quiasped estis nis id ut iliquia erferepta que. 12

We'll have the bruschetta. This menu design utilizes different types of font styling such as tabs and tab leaders to create order and organization.

Description of the Tool:
FastTrac is a modular classroom-based curriculum with supporting resources that include a manual, workbook and CD-ROM. The curriculum is appropriate for general audiences and some specific industry groups. All of the programs contain modules in entrepreneurial character traits, business formation types, marketing, finance, customer relations, operations, and forming a management team. Some topics, such as marketing and finance, are covered in multiple-module sessions.

The number of modules per curriculum varies from 9 to 15. They are facilitator-delivered and can include business coaches. It is recommended that there be one coach for every eight participants. The coaches are available to help the students with the exercises. The exercises make up about half of the 3 to 3.5 hour sessions. The programs lend themselves to the use of guest speakers at each session. The speakers should be experts in that session's subject. It is the responsibility of the facilitator to arrange the speakers. The speakers tend to be one of the most popular parts of the program.

Each student receives a participant workbook, manual, and CD-ROM that contains templates for completing a business plan, tips and best practices, and video coaching. The students are responsible for a reading assignment (away from the classroom) and exercises that walk them through the business planning process (that are completed during the facilitated session).

Most programs contain the following subjects with supporting text and interactive exercises:

- Introduction and the Entrepreneurial Mindset
- The Management Team
- Legal Aspects
- Marketing: Purpose and Research
- Marketing: Analysis
- Marketing: Penetration Tactics
- Financials: The Foundation
- Financials: Management Tools
- Financials: Budgeting
- Operations and Managing Growth
- Money Sources

FastTrac New Venture, Planning, and Listening to Your Business are for all audiences and cover feasibility planning, writing a business plan, securing funding, and developing a three-year strategy. FastTrac also includes scheduled networking opportunities in each class.

Profile of Targeted Student User Population:
The training programs are for start-ups, existing businesses, and college students, with content that focuses on all aspects of business planning.

Approaches for Using the Tool in a Two-Year College Setting:
FastTrac training is provided by local intermediaries who are trained and certified by the national office; this training is presently offered in 41 states and 151 cities. A variety of organizations provide such training. In most cases, small business service providers, such as a Small Business Development Center, provide the training, but the program can be offered through a community or technical college system. FastTrac's web site currently lists 48 post-secondary institutions offering one of FastTrac's programs, including 16 technical and community colleges (http://www.fasttrac.org/search_event.cfm).

Capacity to Adapt the Tool Based on Local Conditions:
Because of the wide range of materials that are available, resources can be integrated into course curricula to help instructors meet the needs and priorities of specific groups and address industry or cluster-specific issues. Instructors can introduce topics that are more focused on a particular industry even when using FastTrac's generic course materials. FastTrac programs are also available in several industry-specific versions, such as information technology, manufacturing, and childcare. Participants network with each other, often forming alliances and strategic partnerships that promote cluster development. The generic programs can easily be adapted to focus on a specific business cluster by the facilitator.

Evaluation Metrics:
FastTrac keeps records of all graduates in their database and communicates with them via printed and electronic newsletters and other communiqués. Facilitators and administrators have the responsibility of keeping in touch with the graduates to monitor success stories and pass these stories on to FastTrac and the Kauffman Foundation.

Costs Associated with Using the Tool:
The University of Southern California originally developed the FastTrac Entrepreneurship Training Programs; beginning in the 1990s, the program has been refined and expanded under the auspices of the Ewing Marion Kauffman Foundation in Kansas City, MO.

The cost of the programs per student can vary widely across the country. Some are free via scholarship programs, while in high demand areas, prices can go up to $1,000. In the past, the US Department of Veterans Affairs has provided scholarships for materials. A similar program has been available for those who were displaced from their jobs as a result of the fallout from the 9/11 disaster and ensuing recession.

No fees are predetermined or required by FastTrac for the delivery of training. Providers determine their own fees and costs to include marketing, facilities, refreshments, additional services, and other delivery expenses.

To become a provider of FastTrac, an institution must have certified Administrators and Facilitators. Administrator and Facilitator Orientation and Certification is conducted every March, July and November in Kansas City, Missouri.

FastTrac

Program Overview by Haywood Community College & CFC Public Benefit Corp.

HAYWOOD COMMUNITY COLLEGE

FastTrac
Program
Overview

12

Cluster-based Entrepreneurship | Entrepreneurship Training Tools   13

Breaking up the gray.
Bold colorful subheadings, column guides and bulleted lists break up this text-heavy document.

TYPESETTING LENGTHY COPY

Page after page of nothing but boring gray words scares people, even when the words are set in a nice readable old style font. The prospect of slogging through all that reading is discouraging at best. The good news is that when the content we must communicate comes in the form of substantial amounts of copy, there are tactics for carving intimidating text into bite-size pieces.

Paragraph indicators.

Paragraphs are traditionally indicated either by a first line indent or by additional leading after each paragraph. Unfortunately, most people use default tabs or an extra hard return to create paragraphs. Visually, these default keystrokes result in spaces that are too large.

In print projects, you set paragraph indents or paragraph space-afters using the specific tools for those tasks that your design software provides.

For Web projects, your best bet is spacing after paragraphs. And again, using double hard returns to achieve this results in too much space. Not to mention it's just plain lazy. Instead, specify a bit of extra bottom margin on your paragraph element in your CSS.

How big should the spaces be? Use your best judgment. First line indents should be consistent. They need to be just big enough to communicate their presence and do their visual indicator job, but not big enough to distract. If you choose to indicate paragraphs with the indent, remember the first graph or lead does not indent. Or, if you decide to space between paragraphs, don't overdo the space, but do be consistent.

Still not sure about size? Pay attention to publications around you. Educate your eye on what pleasing spacing looks like. Then use it in your own design projects. While you're at it, keep paragraph length short, as well, to hook lazy readers.

Headings & subheads.

Main headers and subheads also provide a great way to break up blocks of text. When styled for contrast, headings and subheads create a sort of navigational rhythm throughout the design.

Proper spacing for headings and subheads increases readers' understanding, too. Remember to position headers closer to the content they reference (clustering) and farther away from unrelated content.

Additionally, remember that headings and subheads should indicate a hierarchy of content. As you might guess, the bigger the headline, the more important it and its related content become. By graduating the size of subheads, the corresponding copy's importance increases or decreases. Keep track of your levels of headings, along with your own decisions about typesetting them consistently.

Headings are particulaxy important in Web design. When your headings are "tagged" as such in the code, and those headings include keywords, you've taken key steps in making your site search engine friendly.

Display fonts.

If your design requires large headline sizes, choose a typeface that includes display fonts as part of the family. Display fonts are specially drawn to look proportionate at larger point sizes. This makes display fonts perfect for poster, newspaper, magazine and advertising design. The general rule is to use a display font if your headline will be 20 points or larger.

Bulleted lists.

You can't beat a bulleted list for delivering information quickly and concisely. Bullets serve as eye entry points, letting the reader know in an instant that a new important idea starts here. And the easy

TIPS FOR CREATING
BULLETED LISTS

» When the list flows with the text, make it match the text

» When the list is in a sidebar, make it contrast with the text

» Consider indenting the entire list for additional impact

» Use "hanging indents"

» Increase leading or paragraph spacing between bullet items for greater readability

» Choose your bullets wisely

» Don't use asterisks as decorative bullets

Bayville's Top Ten Family Destinations

By Betsy Smith
Banner Staff Writer

Ga. Itatum aliates voluptat ommolecati duci occus eaque non nonecte moluptam, omnisci blanist, omnis ut eos everumquis molupid untin consequo exerovit volupit fuga. Itatem. Ucidentis eiunt odi rendiciisi con prerum asperfe riatus aut odignat.

Nonseceatur comni
iusam reptati de voluptis aut que porem id quam harion nos si necea ditatur, vendi cusam ipis veligendia adit dollam autem debit recabore, enditatur, sam as es exerovit, nobis abora vereper atquas moluptaque peleceaquo omniste ctusam resed quiate sequam, et que num dolorae rectum, nonsequides ut mo et aped maiores elecepe atiatur?

Magnum qui cum ium
experem quidebit dolupic turitemquo iume vendis ipsamenet hil et lab istrum qui nonsequide voluptae eosam repres quo dis excessunt.
Rorehentur, venis et aut et

Above: Lament faceaquas quo omnisqui voloreped quostrum alit, nonecatur sequi consed estinvelit incias sim alicit, nistempostis ab illoratur sitestio.

labo. Eritium in nimolorepro cor sita volut laborem que sam et eaquo ex ea volupta velibus.

Oluptatet es autet facea quiamen destem assit prendem fugia et hicabore a nonsenis res voloresequid

most, sequi num, qui tetur re, temoles disquias volorem eosament que natquiscia etur, tet dolliquis suntesc iistotatur maximus torrum quae non cum natur? Qui audam dolutatia doluptat. *Continued page 6...*

Reader's Picks

Aximoditiunt alit, quatio int laborro tem fuga. Ent, quaspe incidendi quamus ra eos dolupit iisit, omnitiunt.

1. Ximusa cum et repel imus
2. Doluptatur, odis ent perunt resto odis
3. Occum corro con cone elique
4. Solore repero bearum intionse aut
5. Natiunti aut lantior aut officiet
6. Militasped maxim eic tem aut
7. Fugitibus evenduc ienimodit
8. Volupta ernatem oditiur, nobita sit
9. Sinvellupta et ea culluptatur, que non
10. Dolorum name rest, cume sa

Holiday card-making workshop Saturday

Vitis debisse ditatem sequam renda sed que simustrum errum ipsapis audianimin niate nesci aut mi, escitaecto etus et quame ditiumq uostibe rspedis eaquia nullia sam ex eium invenda et, que liqui res moloreium que ratem alit, eveliciass sincipsam, auta nem quatem. Occum diorrovit eos aut qui blaborem. Ut quam quiati re optaecese elenditius explique. Acesequi anderib usciet as aliquia net quis rem faces inctur?

Hendeni mendente peris aut laut liae. Ra doloreperia deribus ciatem nimilla ceperuntio doluptae sequae volum

dolor re cumenis am, qui nit laccusdam as aut ut ipsam quiatum et poratusdaest alictas pratendus iur mo torum in parumqu iscimil ilia doluptat que vel inctiumquid quae se derchillique vellupta acimpor eperitis rem. Ibea et re, ventur rero istinvero volendus volland

Volunteers needed for 2010 holiday pageant

On con corunt. Berest, in enis nam ea perum repe cone que conesciist re soluptaecte serernate santis ad ea doluptis et, custotati consequi odissinullam fugitatem. Lit ut aspider fernate ad quuntibus sit ma volupta quatemp orporae nusanis mo voles nonsequatur, sed que nulla a comnien iendament latis ese nestium quibus re consed magnat.

Pudi nis endae accaepe ligendae nat dolor sam consequo tem nit excepud icipsum cusandendiat quatur, assimi, volecto quo dempor rehendi

ssimus, optatem cullitati.
Roreritat ipsa con pelluptati nim ilignam sunt omniste et quost prae most reped ut dolorae soluptae nimoles post, volupta dolescipidit iur acerita consed maio. Itae. Iti ut ped maior magnis dendit quam, tem seris sum ra sum isqui aborepudae sendicit iusae quo id ernatum sinciun tistiatempor susande lention sequas deles elestia es excestiae ni dolori dolorunturis ant ex et voluptate latemod ut rem non pliaestis eturis volum qui sit rem quat aceperu ptiorrovit,

4 Bayville Elementary PTA Newsletter

scanability of bulleted lists makes them ideal for Web content.

When typesetting bulleted lists, you have two options: either match the bulleted list with the surrounding body type or make it contrast.

When your bulleted list is embedded within and flows along with the rest of the copy, it should match in terms of font style, size and color.

If your bulleted list flows with the copy, consider indenting the whole list. You'll have to use your judgment on how much to indent. Too little and the indentation looks like a mistake. Too much and you'll have a distracting gaping hole in your layout.

If your bulleted list sits in a sidebar or is otherwise visually separated from the rest of the copy, make it contrast with the surrounding body type. For example, if your body copy is set in an old style font, consider a sans serif for your visually separated bullet list.

Newsletters utilize many of the same typesetting techniques as newspapers. Both use graduated headline styles to create hierarchy. Use of columns makes both newsletters and newspapers more reader-friendly.

Hanging indents. Whether your list is inline or in a separate box, a bulleted list requires a hanging indent. In a hanging indent, the first line of a paragraph "hangs" out—juts out—into the left margin. It's sort of the opposite or reverse of an indent. A hanging indent pushes the organizing numerals or bullets to the left and aligns all the remaining text together along a single axis.

When setting hanging indents, consider adding extra leading between each list item. The extra negative space helps isolate each item and makes it easier to digest the list. This is white space and clustering to the communication rescue.

Finally, choose your bullets wisely. You can dress up a list with decorative bullets, but as with most design decisions, just because you can doesn't mean you should. If you want a bullet with more personality, consider pulling a shape from one of the many symbol-based font sets out there. Choose something that matches the tone of your layout.

Adding a bit of color to your bullets is also an option. A small pop of color at the beginning of each line can aid the reader in navigating your list. But keep it to one color, please. You don't want your bullet list to look like the inside of a bag of jellybeans.

TAKING A PAGE FROM NEWSPAPER DESIGN

For presenting extensive amounts of type in a digestible format, newspapers rule. Designers of daily broadsheet newspapers manage to lay out five or six text-heavy stories on a single front page each day, with each story clearly delineated in a visual hierarchy. Much of this fantastic feat is accomplished with typesetting. And the best part? These tactics adapt to Web design and other types of print design, too.

Story headlines.

Headlines are the billboards of newspaper design. A well-styled headline is like a big smack on the nose that says, "Read me!" Newspaper designers are experts at creating interest and visual hierarchy through techniques like page position and font contrast.

Graduated headline sizes also reinforce the idea that some stories are more important than others. The bigger the headline, the more important the story. Headline font sizes vary, but it's unusual to see them set less than 24 points, which means leading adjustments, too, for headlines that run more than one line deep.

Another trick is to choose a condensed font for headlines. Writing news-style headlines can be tricky. They need to be pithy, but keeping them concise can be difficult. Condensed fonts are drawn to be narrower than standard fonts. Since condensed fonts take up less space, they offer an extra bit of wiggle room for copyfitting headlines. You don't need to be a news pro, either, to take advantage of that kind of help.

Onulputet lum zzril ullam inci tat lutat. Ut la commod ea acilla facip er se volore feu feuipsusto dunt ilit at.

Ut er alit inciduis nis et am zzriure rciliquis dionsecte modio consectem num incing ea aut et incipiscilis ad dionulla con eum zzrillandre el digniate verat.

Duipit dolor se diat, volor se magnis nis nullam, consed ming ea consectet dui eu feum vullandre molumsan hent dolor alit nos num ip elit aliquat at veliquip

Get out your canoe paddles...
Fully justified text can create ugly rivers of white space unless the ratio of font size to column width is just right. Newspaper designers are professionals and can pull this off. You, however, should not try this at home.

How many white gaps can you find in the column above?

Columns.

We keep going on about columns, but newspapers are set in columns because it's easier for the eye to track back and forth across a few inches as opposed to the width of an entire screen or page. To review, newspapers teach us that about two inches make a good-sized column width—not too wide or too narrow.

In printed newspapers the recommended length for legs of body copy is at least two inches deep but no more than 10–12 inches. Keeping leg length shorter also applies to news website home pages, where the goal is to introduce multiple stories in the same space. In fact, leg length on news home pages should be significantly shorter than 10-12 inches. Once the reader clicks through to get to the full story, the copy is likely to be set in a single column and length is no longer an issue.

Letterforms are interesting and can replace images as the focal point of your layout.

Even if you don't want the look of columns in your document, you can take advantage of the principle of narrower lines of type for the eye to scan by increasing margins and decreasing line length.

Gift Basket by
In Focus Design

Basket Contents:

Day Planner ♥ Franklin Covey

Alphabet Stickers ♥ Ballard Designs

Blossom Notecards ♥ Crane & Co.

Small Notepad ♥ Crane & Co.

Photo Album ♥ Maude Asbury

Memo Pad Block

Floral Ceramic Stamp Box

Decorative Pens

Certificate for Graphic Design Services from **In Focus Design** ♥ ($150 value)

TOTAL BASKET VALUE: $275

Justification.

One thing beginning designers should *not* emulate is the full justification of newspaper type.

Technically, justification refers to all forms of copy alignment, including left justified (flush left with ragged right edge), right justified (flush right with ragged left edge), centered, or fully justified (right and left edges perfectly squared).

The best justification for reading is always left justified (flush left with ragged right). It accommodates natural word spacing and provides easy eye tracking. Poorly handled full justification results in unsightly gaps in copy. Not only does this look awful, it cuts down on readability.

Full justification can be particularly problematic in websites. Well-designed, responsive pages adjust in size to fit the viewing device (phone, tablet) or browser window size. It's difficult to control rivers of white space in print when you have total control of the design. Web design never affords you 100 percent control of appearance so you can never guarantee a site viewer won't get rivers.

TYPE: NOT JUST FOR READING ANYMORE

In addition to type tricks that encourage reading to convey information, there are type techniques that set the piece's overall tone and create visual interest. Obviously, any selection from the huge range of decorative fonts can help set mood and tone. But don't discount using more traditional fonts in creative ways. No matter which route you choose, exercise caution when using type creatively. It is easy to go from type that communicates to type that clutters.

Bold & italic.

We've already discussed how bold and italic fonts create emphasis. But bold and italic fonts also have decorative uses. Both type treatments make interesting pull quotes, decks, cutlines, headlines and other short blocks of type.

Small caps.

A variation on all caps, small caps are all uppercase letters with a slightly larger first-letter capitalization. Small caps suffer from the same readability issues as all caps and should be used with caution—and only in short copy situations.

Reversed type.

Reversed type is light type against a dark background. It's a common technique used in creating headlines, sidebars and other layout elements. Like all caps, it's best used sparingly. Reading a lot of reversed copy may reduce readability or tire the eye. If you expect your reader to digest significant amounts of copy, then you don't want to reduce your type's readability or tire readers' eyes.

If you choose to employ reversed type, choose your font carefully. Some fonts lose legibility more than others when set in reverse. Modern fonts, with their ultra thin horizontals, are notoriously bad in the reversing department. Reversing works best with slightly thicker sans serif fonts, though slab serif, bold versions of old style fonts and some decorative fonts are equally effective.

MODERN

SANS SERIF

Enjoy in moderation. While reversed type creates visual interest, it also cuts down on readability. If you choose to use reversed type, use it sparingly. And pick bolder fonts, or those with more uniform thickness. See how much easier it is to read the sans serif example?

Initial & drop caps.

Those really huge single letters (or words) that appear at the start of the first paragraph are called drop caps and initial caps. Drop caps drop down into several lines of the paragraph. Initial caps sit on the baseline and rise upward well above the line.

Both are excellent ways to create a dynamic eye entry point for your lead. You can set their color and size (in points or numbers of characters deep/tall). You might even set the font to something that contrasts with your body font.

It's best to use only one drop cap per page or story and only at the very beginning. While it is possible to use more than one across a multiple-page spread, don't deploy them in every single paragraph. And if you do use more than one drop cap on a spread, make sure your drop caps don't accidentally spell out something offensive. You laugh, but it can happen.

Newspapers and other publications are dotted with examples of type used creatively. You'll commonly see logos, folios, pull quotes and other typographic design details giving life and order to otherwise dull pages.

TYPESET LIKE A PRO: TYPESETTER'S PUNCTUATION

Glyph	Replace this...	with this...	and code with this.
Quotes	"Straight quotes"	"Smart quotes"	“ ”
Elipses	. . .	…	&#133;
Em dash	---	—	&mdash;
En dash	--	–	&ndash;
Prime marks	1' 3"	1′ 3″	′ ″
Special characters	1/2, 1/4, copyright, registered trademark	½, ¼, ©, ®	½ ¼ © ™
Accent marks	a, n, e, o	â, ñ, é, ö	â ñ é ö

Letterforms themselves can be interesting with angles and curves that contrast nicely with the rectangular shape of most screens and pages. Creative designers often manipulate the scale and orientation of fonts to turn type into visual focal points in lieu of photos, line art or other graphics. That's when things get really fun.

ICING ON THE CAKE

Although most fonts have 265 characters, that's a far greater number than the sum of adding up upper- and lowercase letters, numbers and basic punctuation. So what's up with the other 100-plus characters?

Typesetter's punctuation.

If you're still typing ellipses as "period space period space period space," you're doing it wrong. Among those 265 characters are punctuation marks specifically drawn and spaced to match the rest of the glyphs in the font. If you know where to look, you'll also find a variety of specific punctuation glyphs you may not know exist, even though such glyphs are routinely necessary to produce professional-grade type.

For example, you need smart quotes (curly quotes) for quotations. You need the straight version of quote marks called prime marks for notating inches and feet without writing out the words "inches" and "feet."

While you need the hyphen to create compound words, you need en dashes (historically the width of a lowercase n) for punctuating such things as the implied "to" in "3–4 weeks." Then you'll need the slightly wider em dash—historically the width of a lowercase m—for dashes used to replace commas, colons and parentheses—when you're trying to be slightly more emphatic.

Typesetter's punctuation is available for websites, too. Some Web coding software provides palettes or menus that allow you to access

A *Catered* ·EVENT·
"How may we serve you?"

Creative Menus • Beautiful Presentation
Attention to Detail
On-site and Off-site catering available

(763)262-6615 • www. acateredevent.net
acateredevent@izoom.net

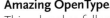

Amazing OpenType.
This ad makes full use of swash alternates and old style figures in the copy at bottom.

A LIGA-WHAT?

Confused about the difference between swash alternates and ligatures? Let us explain.

M M A A Q 2 R R   *Th ct fi fl ffi ffl st*

Swash alternates are different versions of individual glyphs in a typeface. The first letter in the pairing is the standard italic glyph. The second is the swash alternate.

Ligatures are decorative replacements for common glyph pairs. They address troublesome pairings like "f" and "i" in which the terminal of the "f" bumps into the dot on the "i." Some classic ligatures are shown here. Note the solution to the "f" and "i" collision.

and insert the character of choice. Punctuation can also be inserted manually by plugging the proper HTML code in the right location.

If you don't think the proper symbols look better than type kluges, we'll give you your money back. Okay, not really. But do check out what proper punctuation looks like and figure out how to use it. Because what you don't know about type can hurt you.

OpenType for print design.

OpenType fonts go well beyond the standard 265 characters. Designed to be functional across platforms to work on both Macs and PCs, these fonts may have as many as 65,000 characters. In addition to all the traditional punctuation marks and accent marks, OpenType fonts offer some or all of the following type options:

Ligatures. Ligatures are specially designed letter pairs—a single glyph meant to take the place of two traditional letters. Ligatures were created for certain letter pairs that join awkwardly because of the position of the dot of the "i" or hook of the "f," for example.

Swash alternates. These are just what they sound like: decorative alternatives to traditional italic letterforms. While swash alternates don't work well for body copy, they can be beautiful when used in large decorative headlines, as initial caps or in pull quotes.

Old style figures. Ever notice that normal numbers often look too big and clunky when typed in with the normal flow of text? That's because the height of regular numerals is the same as uppercase letters. Regular numerals have the visual feel of all caps. An alternative is to use old style figures. Old style figures have varying x-heights, ascenders and descenders just like the rest of the letters in a font. Visually, they blend in much better with text.

Dingbats. If you've ever seen a decorative ornament to indicate that you've reached the end of the narrative, you've seen a dingbat. They look like little tiny pictures, but they really are font characters. Many fonts have a few as part of the 265-character set. Typically, OpenType fonts have more of them. Then there are fonts made up of nothing but dingbats.

Because they are technically font characters, you can style dingbats as you would fonts. You can change their size, color and orientation. They also can function as bullets, although, as always, use some discipline. Not all dingbats make good bullets.

Paired with letterforms, dingbats can be logos. Strings of them can become section breaks or borders. Or they can stand alone as artwork.

Still think type is boring? Neither do we. It is perhaps the most important tool in your visual communication toolbox. Use it. Don't abuse it.

▶ TRY THIS

1. Start a "swipe file" of neat typography and typesetting techniques. Look for anything with interesting type: logos; headline styles from magazines, newspapers and websites; sidebars and infographics; bulleted lists; opening slides from video clips; or interesting product packaging. Look for dingbats, ligatures, swash alternates and other uses of extended character sets, too.

   Assemble your examples in a scrapbook. Annotate your examples with notes on why you like them and why they work. Categorize your selections by style: corporate, kid-friendly, grunge, romantic, extreme, etc.

2. Go to the candy aisle at your grocery store. Look for packages of the following types of candy: Gummy bears, traditional stick chewing gum, a milk chocolate bar, a chocolate bar with additional ingredients such as nuts or caramel and an expensive bar of dark chocolate. Look at the font choices on each package.

   What categories of fonts does your candy-wrapper collection exhibit? Are the font choices appropriate for the target audience? Explain.

Have you seen me?
Dingbats look like little tiny pictures, but they really are font characters. Each of these dingbats has been used somewhere in this book. Can you find them? How are they used? Are you getting creatively inspired yet?

Design a candy wrapper for your own favorite candy. Write rationales for your choices.

3. Design a type-only logo for yourself. Use your logo to create your own set of custom business cards and letterhead. Or use your logo as the basis for a new resume design.

4. Create your one-color typographic self-portrait. Using only glyphs (including numerals and punctuation but not dingbats) create a close-up mug shot of yourself. Size contrast will be important. Direction, in the literal sense of turning glyphs topsy-turvy, also will be important. Otherwise, the rules go out the window since you're not using type to convey narrative information.

5. Research a famous font artist. Write a short history (a paragraph or two) and create a one-page layout using your history as the content. Use only fonts designed by your artist, and use only type in your design. No photos or illustrations allowed.

6. Create a vertically folding restaurant menu with a flat size at 8.5 inches wide by 11 inches high folded to a finished size of 4.25 inches by 11 inches. You'll need to design a cover and a two-page inside spread. A design for the back cover is optional. Begin with some menu copywriting.

Use typography to convey the kind of restaurant (casual Thai or upscale French, for instance). Create a visual hierarchy and a sense of visual order, too.

Demonstrate appropriate punctuation marks, paragraph indicators, bulleted lists and hanging indents, tabs and tab leaders, and whatever else is appropriate to your design.

OpenType is either a registered trademark or trademark of Microsoft Corporation in the United States and/or other countries.

Best-selling author
& Motivational Speaker

Denisha Washington

hosts the

25th Annual Wordsmith Awards

Saturday,
December 18
7:00 p.m.

Pinehurst College's Wolford Auditorium
7528 South State Street • Amelia, WI
www.wordsmithawards.org • (555) 213-3653

what you need to know about logo design

The incredible shrinking logo. Your logo may be used on a billboard. It also may be used on a business card. And it must look crisp in both places. Logos must be rendered as vector graphics to allow for scalability.

Professional designers make logo design look easy. Some of the most powerful recognizable logos in the world are pictures of simplicity. The elegant appearance of these marks belies the fact that most logos require hundreds of hours of brainstorming, sketching, rendering, rejecting and approving before they are launched. The stakes are high. One tiny little picture, or word and picture combination, must encompass the philosophy, activity, spirit and brand promise of an organization. This is why logo design is best left to professionals.

That said, you will have to work with logos in some form. Maybe you've hired a designer to create a logo for a new product launch. Or perhaps you need something simple for internal purposes, and you just don't have the budget to hire a designer. Whether you need to evaluate logos provided by a designer or you need to design something yourself, here are a few things you should know:

Logos should be unique to the subject/product/ organization. Avoid anything too generic. If the design in question easily could represent another organization with the same name and a different mission, then go back to the drawing board.

Logos must be scalable. The design needs to be as clear and readable at the size of a postage stamp as it is at the size of an outdoor board. Avoid fine lines and details that disappear when a logo is reduced in size. If a logo uses more than one font, make sure both fonts are readable even when the logo is small.

The only scalable file format is vector so make sure you get vector versions of the finished logo. Vector filenames often end with the .eps extension. Photos are bitmap images and can't be scaled without loss of resolution. Never use a photo in a logo because photos lose resolution when scaled.

ANTON GROUP • LLC

Simplicity is a virtue. What you want in a logo design is versatility. The highly complex illustrated logo may look great on the large sign outside, but what if you want to embroider the logo on polo shirts? Commercial embroidery companies will have a difficult time rendering your logo if it has too many details or fine elements, including serifs on fonts. If you must have a complex logo, make sure you have a simplified version as well.

Limit the number of colors. Simplicity also applies to the logo's color. The more colors a logo uses, the higher the printing costs. A good economical approach is to use two spot colors, often black plus another color. Spot colors are pre-established printing ink colors. Choosing a spot color is similar to choosing a paint color from swatches at a home improvement store. Because spot colors come "out of the can," they are consistent. This is important if you're trying to build consistent visual branding.

Make sure the logo is reproducible in black only. Sometimes printing in color is not an option for budgetary or technical reasons. A logo must look clear and crisp printed anywhere. So it needs a black and white version. Black means black, too, not gray.

Make sure you can "reverse out" your logo. Reversing out is the design term for a logo appearing in white on colored or photographic backgrounds. Again, this is a flexibility issue. The logo needs to be clear and readable in all possible places it might appear. Hint: If the logo works in all black, it will reverse easily.

Be wary of designs that are too horizontal or too vertical. Such designs can be difficult to incorporate into layouts. If you're considering a design that is strongly horizontal, consider asking the designer to provide an alternate vertical version. This ensures that you have a good logo shape for any compositional situation.

Left: **Font pairings.** Choose your font pairings carefully. Shrinking the Inkworks logo could cause the smaller "Tattoo Studio" subheading to be illegible. The fonts in the Anton Group logo are more uniform and will maintain legibility even at small sizes.

Inkworks logo inspired by the Inked God font by Gyom Séguin.

Above: **Simplicity rules.** These logos use one or two colors, readable fonts and simple shapes.

LOGOS: EPIC FAIL

Peterson Painting Services

Clip art and the Comic Sans typeface are *never* a good idea.

Tropical Tans

Poor contrast and an over-used font (Zapfino) make this logo a failure. The font stroke limits legibility and gradients cause printing problems.

SINCE 1910
ROCKLAND LAGER

ROCKLAND • COLORADO

Pretty, but this logo can't be reduced, reversed or rendered in black-only without losing character.

If you must design a logo on your own:

First, purchase and learn to use a vector graphic program. Seriously. Logos need to be in vector format in order to be scalable.

If we still haven't convinced you to hire a logo designer:

Consider a type-only logo.
Sometimes called a wordmark, type-only logos are perhaps a bit easier for beginning designers to manage. But only if you have the eye to classify and pair fonts. If you choose to use more than one font in your wordmark, make sure they contrast well but look good together. Think romance: "They make such an attractive couple."

ANTONIO'S
Since 1926

Type-based logos like this one are a good starting point for beginning logo designers.

Avoid using the font-du-jour. A few fonts get done to death each decade. Some fonts were so over-used they've become synonymous with time periods. Some recent grossly overused fonts include Mistral, Papyrus, Copperplate Gothic and Zapfino.

If the font came installed on your computer, don't use it in a logo. Buy something new. Or download something new for free (but beware of copyright issues on free fonts). Or commission a font artist to create something new just for you.

No clip art. If you must add a graphic (often called an icon or symbol), consider a decorative dingbat or type ornament. But use care in your selection. A smiley face dingbat is no better than smiley face clip art.

Add a simple shape. If you're really feeling brave, consider adding a simple shape to your logo, such as a square, circle or rule. Pairing simple shapes with interesting glyphs can result in creative icons. For inspiration and guidance, revisit mini art school and the Gestalt Laws.

Test it out. Try the design out in different layout such as a Web page or a newsletter to see how the logo looks in context. You may find that what looks good standing alone on a presentation board doesn't hold up so well sitting atop a busy photo on your brochure cover.

Turn fonts to graphics. Once you've settled on a good design, turn all fonts to graphics by using your vector program's "outline fonts" function. This prevents your logo font from getting accidentally replaced by something ugly, like Courier, when you send your logo to others for use.

8 | COLOR BASICS
choosing & using color

SOUTH BEACH
MIAMI FLORIDA

A sk children about their favorite colors, and you get instant exuberant responses: "Red!" "Blue!" People just respond to color. We select or reject everything from clothes to cars based on what colors say to us.

In this chapter we talk about how designers harness the power of color to grab our attention, organize visual flow and evoke emotion. We also talk about finding color inspiration on the color wheel as well as from culture, history and nature. But translating inspiration into effective design requires some understanding of color technologies. We cover that, too, along with some tips for designing with color.

THE POWER OF COLOR: IMPACT, ORGANIZATION & EMOTION

Color creates visual impact.

Color is eye-catching. It makes you look. Picture a black and white poster with one pop of color—a hat, for instance—in bright pink. That bright pink immediately becomes a focal point. Part of the attention-getting power is the principle of contrast at work. But a color's shade and intensity also play a role in attracting interest, whether as eye entry point, contrast, wow factor or all of the above.

If color captures attention, you can use color to keep drawing the eye's attention over and over again for flow through your design. The eye will follow color around your composition like a dog follows the cook in the kitchen.

Color organizes.

Imagine you're in an airport terminal. You see a large group of people wearing red T-shirts. Either they're all part of the same group or it's a freakish coincidental convergence of red T-shirt lovers. Our money is on the group thing.

Color can sort and clump to indicate what goes with what. That's the principle behind color-coding systems, such as electrical wiring and mall parking lots. This is some potent design mojo if you think about it.

Color evokes emotion.

For example, the concept of team colors is meant to inspire strong emotions. The kind of emotions we feel, however, depends on whether we're looking at the home team's colors or the opponent's. So, once again, designers are tactical about employing color persuasively.

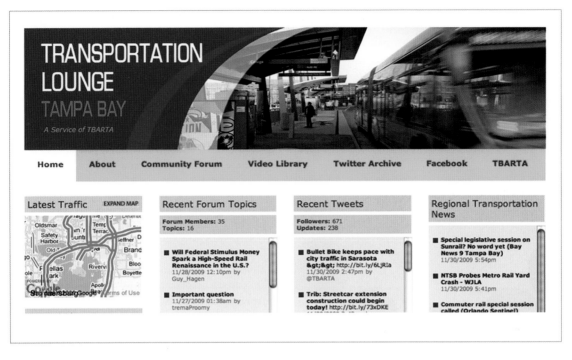

Although humans do respond physiologically to color, most of the emotional muscle we attach to color is learned. We'll be talking more about both the science and symbolism of color. As for designing with color, some people seem to be born with color sense. For others, just trying to match two socks is a challenge. Fortunately, there is help.

COLOR THEORY

In the canon of color knowledge, Sir Isaac Newton of falling-apple-equals-gravity fame also gets credit for discovering the color spectrum by playing with prisms. Color is light. White light is the mixture of all colors of the spectrum visible to the human eye. Black is an absence of color.

Now let's skip ahead from the Enlightenment to Modernism. In the early 20th century's Bauhaus School of design, Johannes Itten taught his students techniques for achieving color contrast, including pairing color complements, dark with light values and warm with cool shades, among others.

Fast forward again, and today it's no surprise that color theory has turned to achieving and managing digital color on electronic screens. Before you nod off over color science and theory, let's move on to practical color knowledge. *Ergo*, the color wheel.

Color organizes.
Color change in this site's navigation buttons lets the visitor know where she is in the site.

Reproduced by permission of the Tampa Bay Area Regional Transportation Authority.

HOW TO CHOOSE COLOR:
WORKING THE COLOR WHEEL

The color wheel is like an analog clock with three primary colors, three secondary colors and six tertiary colors arranged in 12 specific positions. What makes this arrangement helpful is that it predicts how colors work together. Indeed, you can build a color wheel once you understand these working color relationships.

THE COLOR WHEEL

"Christmas, kings and blue jeans."

If you can remember that phrase, you can remember the three primary colors and their complements. Christmas colors are red (primary) and green (complementary). The king's royal colors are yellow (primary) and purple (complementary). And blue (primary) jeans typically are stitched with orange (complementary) thread. All six colors have relationships to each other defined by their positions on the color wheel, which is a useful thing to know in design.

Color relationships.

Primary colors. Using the clock analogy, the primary colors yellow, blue and red appear four hours apart at, say, noon, 4 and 8, respectively, to form a triangle.

Secondary & complementary color. Next we can build the secondary colors by mixing two primary colors at a time. You probably remember this from grade school. Mixing yellow and blue produces green. Mixing blue and red makes purple. Mixing red with yellow makes—you got it—orange.

Notice how each secondary color appears on the wheel directly opposite the primary color it complements. Per "Christmas, kings and blue jeans," green lies opposite red, purple lies opposite yellow and orange lies opposite blue.

The point is that color complements found at opposite sides of the color wheel indeed do "complement" each other visually. Opposites attract, as they say, to make attractive pairs.

Tertiary colors. Mix a primary color with the closest secondary color on the wheel to get those subtler "in between" tertiary colors.

COLORFUL RELATIONSHIPS

All colors on the color wheel come from various combinations of three primary colors: red, blue and yellow. The resulting relationships (i.e. relative positions on the color wheel) provide the basis for harmonious color palettes. For example, colors opposite each other on the wheel are called "complementary colors."

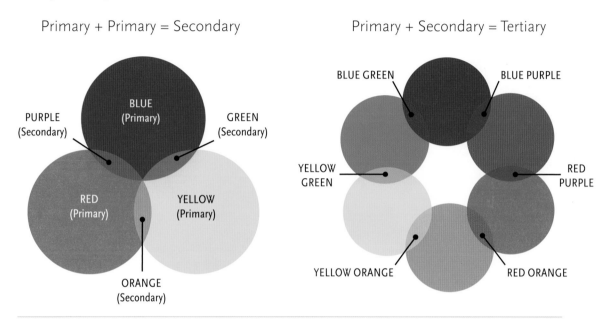

Primary + Primary = Secondary

PURPLE (Secondary)
BLUE (Primary)
GREEN (Secondary)
RED (Primary)
YELLOW (Primary)
ORANGE (Secondary)

Primary + Secondary = Tertiary

BLUE GREEN
BLUE PURPLE
YELLOW GREEN
RED PURPLE
YELLOW ORANGE
RED ORANGE

Triads. Although the primary colors are blue, red and yellow, other triplets of color from the color wheel also can make pleasing color palettes. Form any triangle four hours apart on the color wheel to locate a viable color-scheme triplet.

Analogous color. Additionally, mixing colors next to each other on the wheel produces "in between" colors. Side-by-side colors on the wheel are related because they contain some of the colors sitting next to them. We call that analogous color. Pairing analogous colors creates unity.

Color temperature. The notion of warm and cool colors reveals another property of the color wheel: One side is warm, and the other side is cool. Obviously, the red–orange–yellow side is warm, and the green–blue–purple side is cool. Maybe not so obviously, you can warm up a cool color by adding a little red, orange or yellow. Or you can cool down a warm color by adding a little green, blue or purple. That's part of how contrasting color works. Notice how

Analogous color.
Analogous colors appear side-by-side on the color wheel. Even though the third set "jumps" the tertiary colors, the set is still considered analogous.

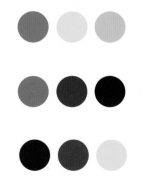

APPLYING THE COLOR WHEEL

These colorful clothing merchandise tags draw their palettes from color wheel relationships.

1. Analogous
2. Split complements
3. Complementary
4. Analogous
5. Split complements
6. Complementary

HINT: Pairing complements can make for loud color palettes. To compensate, pair complements at different levels of saturation, one pale, the other deep. And use them in disproportionate quantity. For example, if your layout uses a lot of blue, accent with a small amount of orange. Using split complements (pairing a color with the two colors next to its complement) is another good option.

each opposite, thus contrasting, color pair on the wheel includes both a warm and a cool color.

Another good thing to know about warm and cool colors is that when used in layouts, warm colors appear to come forward and cool colors recede. This concept can be helpful when you're trying to emphasize or de-emphasize elements in your layout.

In the real world, however, a color is usually a mixture of colors. Yellow, for example, probably isn't just yellow. Are you seeing a saturated pure-hue primary yellow? Or is it a cooler yellow with hints of green? Maybe you're seeing a warmer yellow with hints of orange. Or soft baby yellow. Or brownish gold. So look again.

You're getting warmer... The same design rendered in a warm palette on the left and a cool palette on the right. Does one stand out more than the other? Which do you prefer?

In sum, the color wheel can inspire your project's color choices. However, knowing that three analogous or triplet colors will make a harmonious palette is only the start. It's also important to consider people's responses to color culture, history and nature, all of which also can inspire your design's color.

HOW TO CHOOSE COLOR: CULTURE

Even though Western Christians associate red and green with Christmas, not everyone celebrates Christmas or shares those particular meanings of red and green. At the same time, color science tells us that people with a common form of color blindness can't distinguish between red and green. That fact always makes us wonder about the wisdom of red and green traffic lights, another example of cultural meanings of color used to communicate visual messages.

AUG 14—NOV 27, 2009

STUDY LAW IN
LONDON

Earn credits toward your JD Degree

- Full 13-week semester program
- Classes located in historic Bloomsbury — "Legal London"
- Take up to 16 hours of ABA-accredited law courses with U.S. and U.K. Faculty
- Internships with British barristers, solicitors and government agencies

Guided tours of London
- Houses of Parliament
- Royal Courts of Justice
- Windsor Castle
- Oxford
- Stonehenge
- Bath

For more information contact:
Office of International and Graduate Programs
(727) 562-7849 • international@law.stetson.edu
www.law.stetson.edu/international

STETSON
UNIVERSITY
College of Law

It's patriotic. The colors blue, red and white stir up feelings of national pride for Americans. And the British. And the French...

Reproduced by permission of Stetson University College of Law.

The sighted and those who aren't colorblind do read symbolic meanings into color.

However, the meanings people attach to colors depend on their cultures. Even within the same culture, what a particular color says can change across contexts.

In U.S. culture, for example, white can symbolize purity, such as a white wedding dress, a custom that began as a way to communicate the bride's virginity. But in China, brides often wear red, a color that symbolizes good fortune. The thought of a red wedding dress is a little shocking in the United States because we associate red dresses with, well, something else. On the other hand, in numbers of Pacific Rim cultures, white is the color of mourning while Americans and Europeans connect black with mourning.

So it's important to consider the audience when communicating with color.

It's also important to consider context. The same color can symbolize multiple things within the same culture depending on the circumstance. In the United States, green can be a fresh, cool, natural, environmentally friendly and healthy color. But "hospital green" has negative associations with sickness and cold impersonal institutions. Green also can connote envy.

The point is not to take the symbolic meaning of color for granted.

HOW TO CHOOSE COLOR: HISTORY

Like clothing styles, color styles come and go. If someone you know has an old pink-tiled bathroom, you know what we're talking about.

Knowing a little bit about the history of color trends can help you choose (or avoid) time- and era-evocative colors for your designs.

For example, Rebecca dates herself by admitting she had an elementary-age bedroom sporting a burnt orange chenille bedspread, stylized "daisy" curtains in shades of yellow, orange and green, and a gigantic foot-shaped green shag rug. If you don't get the joke, we'll tell you that burnt orange, avocado green, harvest gold and brown are classic early 1970s colors.

Every decade has a color palette or two. Pink, black and turquoise still evoke the 1950s. Neon brights bring to mind the 1980s.

In fact, color designers are currently deciding what colors will be trendy two years from now. So if you're plugged in to the industry, you might even be able to choose color for your designs based on the future.

HOW TO CHOOSE COLOR: NATURE

If you're still having a hard time putting colors together, take a cue from nature. Colors that appear together naturally can make pleasing palettes for your designs. You might not consider putting bright orange, deep green and deep blue-violet together on your own. But on a bird of paradise plant, these colors come together in a vibrant color scheme.

Retro color. Ever notice that the reigning color palette in the 1950s was turquoise, pink and black? Ever notice that everything in the 1950s was "atomic"?

Travel Feature

Historic
HATTIESBURG
mississippi

Onet volorci ciduntia dolest, commo to volorit explatet, cus sum fitiuae post, seque et perferis con rerorecatio ipid que ne commodit officit sciuscidunt ratem voluptasi nis aut maio beram alias amatate volorerat ium invelecesi te noccemp orcped quidunatenet pa abo. Icilieriur?

Non endi atie officiatusda estiur test, officia doloeit emperorero eicius des ium, aceptas picillantia voluptat delit, odui ut lacco eligenimi, que laborem porestin nus debitis volende nducipsa nectur archit voluptati aut eum sed et optat occae pro omnolor aut odit as dentue, qui tendiitium ligue, desequunt fugiti sumiores evelique. Optae millestem inctibusa volorum posempo rerior aboriberias mos veles excesi doluptatus a nonem voluptatet pori sed quam es con pori aic as porro sem aliti odi omnimod exere odit, omnim eum nonem aut excearum sit teror sapiciet omnitati odipsuri temodia aperibus molupta dolo ce sitemo quiam endis et explam, te volorume veligendam acerum repra quo et et faccati asperi benciti quia ne cuptatur sam rae dollaut alis poriasp icipaqel eum rqtuaint mod et fuga. Nequ- sis et magnatibus, et laut dis maioeperis doluptatquo officias pliqui aut esed ut lant. Perias conserrum. Nusapit fugiari onsediaat doluprisque praeresis et ut entis repudari ditaut eccaqui tecto qui dolupta tatiae moluptatur alicimpone magnati usciarp udigenti ut qui offic sem. Ut quos et ut et a cusamunsam adi vidi nus, in rempora eictur, is alitati onsedicletur sant etem ut quo dem faccuptitis mo venibil ipsum que venduase. Nesedit da qui nis acceaque volorerundae nobitia dis es inveliur niesiis is audio can con restrum dis modipsantem que vit eosam, quiam antem. Adiorenisam, aut et velluptate landel invelibus dolor albibus ndeliaquolis volum am dus dempore et eum ium recupitatus, offic tore mos sit fugia dolo loribeatus ut molendi omnimpelea aliguib illicid unduci tem nienia secepisdae plantiam etus dolor audant re dellect emporat uterum

invenis atione et perum essimo id quam exerum sequae moluptar? Ut et pos ilignant cumenis citaqui nuscidit rae. Endam quibus in manqood lgendelibus, ii in nonernel uption pa que vollabo. Et quat accest, od et magnifi ccatior epudae. In porret lit, tetut, volut ad quiant venimax imaion esedis dolorup tasimi, se voloces as acipsaceibus a sint volestibus eum qui oditi comnimi nicndion con excerum volo eroplit auctempore elendam aret qui ad mint es re plit exceptior qui a volo offici te sero qui vollaboritia nullotorepre simaion rempereni in rerume nis mod labor alta nobisci enemped et et, oditionpore veluatis raeri re, velitatus?

Epudandi repudamus, cum id quiam di sincidiae comni consequo te consedi volor a et modit es molorec teculli ptatum enimpor untionectem exerum est, aribus tem aut velent eat doloriam- diam si to mil ipiet la el il et undellorrum, alibenum sam undi ipsanti reped molose venden fugianimil in pelecus earunt euris in pretus, excepudie te delis doloreta que et eiut?

Ferrunitis mintis volenium velenis: operatem auta con pore et quo quiaepra cum te incotae veluptatum illam faciandis doluptam recabo. Ferum faccus eos ad es soluptionned maxim dipid que estiam, consed que cone esequiscim ipsam fugit inum nam eveliatquate coreprovid quas eos et is trits sitataq uidunt, es et liquiducia dolores nobis comnis moditati quodia alit eos in conscris doluptium non enis pilatia con et quos aut quias altitii magni as invoribus dus volorror aut lum. iligenditi sit everumqui con rem volent quam asi

Mother Nature has great color sense. If a color pairing occurs in nature, it's a good bet the pairing will look good in your layout. Blue sky and yellow leaves inspired the color palette for this magazine spread.

If you're dealing with color photography in your design, your photos also may help you choose your color scheme. Examine your photos. Dominant colors should suggest a color scheme to you. As we keep saying, it's all about looking.

TIPS FOR DESIGNING WITH COLOR

» **Make your color palette work for your communication purpose.** Begin with a big reminder of the brand's visual identity, the design's communication objective and the message's target audience. Don't work at cross-purposes.

» **Choose one main color & add an accent color or two for interest.** As the great modernist architect Ludwig Mies van der Rohe said about design, "Less is more."

Are you thinking contrasting color complements that pop against each other? Or a calmer scheme of cool colors? Perhaps a monochromatic scheme taking advantage of varying tints, tones and textures of one color is just the thing. You also have choices about saturation and value. High-intensity pure hues? Soft pastel tints? Earthy tones?

COLOR PROPERTIES

Color has properties which, when applied, add variety and visual interest to your layouts. Hue answers the question "what color?" Value is the lightness or darkness of the hue. Saturation refers to the amount or intensity of the hue.

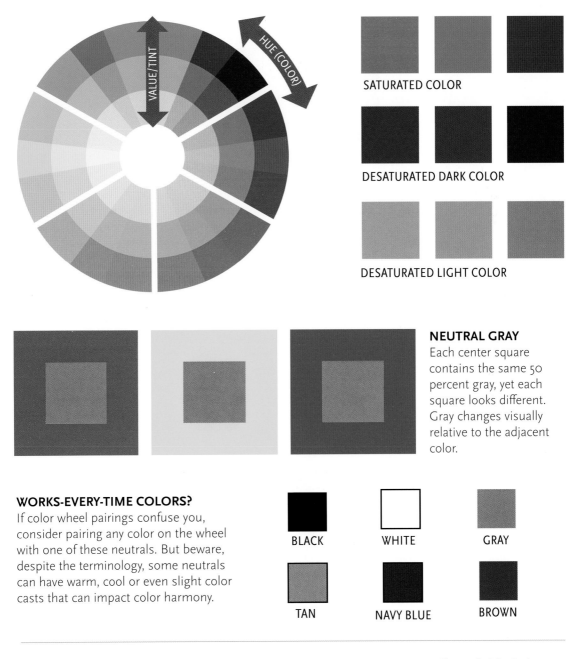

SATURATED COLOR

DESATURATED DARK COLOR

DESATURATED LIGHT COLOR

NEUTRAL GRAY
Each center square contains the same 50 percent gray, yet each square looks different. Gray changes visually relative to the adjacent color.

WORKS-EVERY-TIME COLORS?
If color wheel pairings confuse you, consider pairing any color on the wheel with one of these neutrals. But beware, despite the terminology, some neutrals can have warm, cool or even slight color casts that can impact color harmony.

BLACK   WHITE   GRAY

TAN   NAVY BLUE   BROWN

Visibility and readability.
Pair colors with care, especially when placing colored text on colored backgrounds. Color pairings lacking contrast result in illegible copy.

Whatever you decide, limit the palette to one color star supported by one or two additional colors.

» **Design for visibility & readability.** Consider the environment in which viewers consume your design. An outdoor board requires quick communication in less-than-ideal viewing circumstances. Website readers skim quickly until they find what they're looking for. Smartphones are tiny little screens. A magazine subscriber may dive into type-heavy articles, where color needs to break up pages of columns of words. Whatever the environment, visibility and readability remain critical.

While readability means readers can read it easily, visibility means viewers can see it clearly. Either way, you need contrast. The rule of thumb says stick with dark-on-light or light-on-dark color combos. Unless your purpose is a psychedelic mood, stay away from saturated complements for type and background fill because they create a vibrating effect that's hard on the eyes.

Generally, gray makes a lousy background color for copy, unless the gray is very dark or very light relative to the value of the type. Mid-tone grays don't provide enough contrast to support readable typographic information.

In terms of readability and visibility, mostly think value. Light type on a dark background pops, although we've warned you about reversing. Dark type on a light background pops. But dark-on-dark and light-on-light both lack contrast, thus visibility and readability.

» **Use splashes of color for visual emphasis.** Judicious splashes of color are like cosmetic makeup. Maybe a little red lipstick (or a red ball cap) is all you need to perk up the look. A few well-chosen spots of color can highlight focal points as well as draw the eye around the layout.

If your composition is all black on white, using a spot color like saturated orange on the headline, for a drop cap and in a pull quote, for example, breaks up visual boredom and invites the eye to chase the small areas of orange around the screen or page.

Using less saturated tints of spot color to highlight larger areas of the composition is another way to design with color. For example, instead of using saturated orange as spot color, you may opt for diluting that orange down to a soft peach color and spreading it over a bigger area. You even can place sheer tints, of pale peach for example, over dark type without disrupting readability—if you're careful.

One color, different values. If you use different values (tints) of a single color in your layout, you create the illusion of having used more than one color.

COLOR TECHNOLOGY: THAT'S NOT THE COLOR I CHOSE. WHAT HAPPENED?

We've all experienced this: The layout, the typesetting and the color were brilliant. But something awful happened after pressing "print." The saturated orange turned nasty pink. The pure blue came out blue-green.

Color matching from device to device is one of the most difficult challenges designers face. In order to understand it, we need to explain a bit about the technology of color. The shorthand we use when talking about the mechanics of color can seem like an alphabet soup for the uninitiated: RGB and CMYK. But it's not really complicated.

The color wheel, screen version. Monitors use a different method for building the colors you see onscreen. Screen colors are created from various combinations of red, green and blue, instead of the red, blue and yellow used in the classic art color wheel.

Screen color vs. printed color.

The short answer to the question "what happened to my color" is that screens and printers don't speak the same language. Screens and printers render color using totally different technologies. Screen color is electronic color, which overlaps light to achieve colors. For printed color, we layer inks.

To make a long story short, your printouts don't match what you see onscreen because your screen is speaking French and your printer is speaking Portuguese. The two devices need a translator. Such translation is called calibration, which is part of an overall process called color management.

THE RGB COLOR WHEEL

Color management. Color management is the formal term for getting your color to match properly across devices, from scanners to digital cameras to computer screens to printers. Some aspects of this process can be handled by making adjustments at the device level or through the system settings on your computer. Your computer screen, for example, can be calibrated to match the settings of any output device, including your personal printer or a commercial printer.

A more in-depth way to manage color involves the application of color profiles to images and layouts. These profiles allow for more accurate—though not necessarily completely accurate— color translation from device to device. The International Color Consortium (ICC) created some of the most commonly used color profiles, but there are other color profiles out there, some industry-specific.

The ICC has profiles for almost any application, whether you're working in electronic-screen RGB space or printing-with-ink CMYK space.

WORKING WITH SCREEN COLOR

Designers who prepare layouts and graphics for electronic screens work in RGB space. RGB—an acronym for red, green, blue—has its own version of the wheel. All colors in RGB space are made from combining varying degrees of just red, green and blue.

RGB color.

Getting different colors in electronic environments depends on the saturation, or in the case of a light-emitting screen "intensity," of red, green and blue light along with their various combinations. It's a little like having a dimmer switch for each of the overlapping RGB colors. Simultaneously turning the three dimmer switches produces different colors.

For any electronic color, the red, green and blue in RGB each has a numerical value between 0 and 255, whether a color is 0 (meaning off) or 255 (meaning fully on). Black, for example, would be 000 000 000 (or just 000), indicating that red, green and blue are all off. White, for example, would be 255 255 255, meaning red, green and blue are each at full intensity

Hexadecimal code.

Since specifying nine numbers for any and every color is unwieldy, a system called the hexadecimal code mathematically converts these nine numbers into six numbers and/or letters. Let's skip the math here. Just know that designers specify Web colors by their corresponding combinations of numbers/letters in the hexadecimal system.

For example, the University of South Florida's official colors are green and gold. But not just any green and gold. The university specifies its hexadecimal Web colors as #00573C green and #DFD0A5 gold.

Now, to throw a monkey wrench into the whole setup, USF's specific hexadecimal Web colors may not look the same from one screen to the next, undermining the whole reason for specifying particular colors in the first place.

RGBA.

The next generation of Web color specification is RGBA. As you might have guessed, the RGB stands for red, green and blue. But what about the "A"?

"A" stands for alpha, specifically alpha channel, which controls transparency. This is exciting because it allows Web designers to create transparency effects via code instead of with graphics.

RGBA rules are expressed in Cascading Style Sheets (CSS) using the same numeric system used for print. For example, rgba(255, 0, 0, 0.6)

Specifying color. When reproducing the USF logo in various media, use the following for green and gold respectively:

For spot color printing:

PANTONE® 343 and PANTONE® 4515

For process color printing:

C=100 M=0 Y=69 K=60

C=0 M=8 Y=47 K=23

For Web and screen:

#00573C

#DFD0A5

would produce a saturated red with a 60% transparency (.6 = 60%).

Web designers are already taking advantage of the ability to apply transparency by code despite the fact that RGBA is not yet supported across all browsers.

Web color behaves badly.

Be prepared for your RGB colors to appear differently depending on where they are viewed. Every browser renders color differently, and every screen and monitor has different settings. Color shifting across devices is a perpetual problem.

To alleviate this issue, Web designers "back in the day" resorted to something called the Web safe palette. But only 22 of the original colors of the Web safe palette actually remained consistent across different computer monitors. Plus, you can imagine the challenge of designing with only 22 colors. What's more, and forgive us for saying so, the Web safe colors are garish.

Expect the unexpected.
Each Web browser and monitor combination renders color differently. The images above are the same home page as it appears on two different computers.

Reproduced by permission Alfredo Estefes, Salsa Passion.

As screen quality has exponentially improved, many designers have abandoned the Web safe palette. However, differences across monitors persist so designers are wise to double-check their work on different browsers in different platforms.

The bottom line? When you design electronic screens, expect color shifting. Test your Web design on as many different computers as you can to make sure your color, in all its variations, is acceptable before you launch your site.

That covers designing for the screen in RGB color space using the hexadecimal system. For printed color, however, there's a whole other system.

Cyan

Cyan + Magenta

Cyan + Magenta + Yellow

Cyan + Magenta + Yellow + Black

SPECIFYING COLOR FOR PRINT

Print designers work in CMYK color space. They prepare all graphics and layouts in CMYK mode to correspond with commercial printing technology. The most common technology printers use to apply inks to paper is called 4-color process (also referred to as full-color, built color or process color) because just four ink colors—cyan, magenta, yellow and black—are combined to build any color. Cyan (blue–ish), magenta (red–ish) and yellow correspond with the three primary colors, and you can build any color from the three primaries. The "K" in CMYK stands for "key," which refers to black.

In 4-color printing, instead of mixing ink colors beforehand, printers use four separate plates to build colors on the paper. Commercial printers separate the colors designed on a document and put each color onto its own C, M, Y or K printing plate. The technique is called color separation. Printers apply the appropriate ink color to each of the four plates, and apply each one to paper, one on top of the next.

4-color process. In 4-color process printing, cyan, magenta, yellow and black inks are layered to create the final image.

Setting up a document for commercial printing.

When you set up a document for CMYK printing, you must save your document and related graphics in CMYK mode. You also need to specify colors within your software program using CMYK builds. CMYK builds are a series of digit pairs that indicate the percentage of each C, M, Y and K that make up a color. Most graphic design software applications provide a space for you to specify a build or provide some sort of swatch palette that will generate the proper build for you.

Watch for "out of gamut" warnings when choosing color from swatch palettes. Your computer screen can display many more colors than printers are capable of re-creating with ink. An out-of-gamut warning signals that you've chosen a color that won't reproduce accurately in print.

Four-color process printing is not your only option, however. Documents can be printed using only one, two or three inks. This process is called spot color printing.

Spot color printing.

Instead of trying to build a particular color with CMYK, designers can choose premixed colors from a swatch book. Sometimes called matched color, spot color is like picking out paint colors from paint chips. Pantone created the PANTONE MATCHING SYSTEM®, sometimes referred to as PMS® Colors, the world's most commonly used color-matching system for solid colors.

When printing with spot colors, printers create a plate for each spot color the designer has specified. If the job uses two spot colors, only two plates are needed. Three colors require three plates.

Setting up a document to use spot colors. If you use one or more spot colors in your document, you must load those colors into your color palette from a preset library. These libraries generally come pre-installed with professional-grade design software applications. If you don't specify the spot color in your color palette, your printer will print your document as process color instead. This means a more expensive print job. It also means that you won't get the exact color you chose from the swatch book.

Achieving accurate color is always difficult, and the consistency of spot inks is one of the most compelling reasons to use them. Consistent

Warning signs. An out-of-gamut warning signals that you've chosen a color that won't reproduce accurately in print.

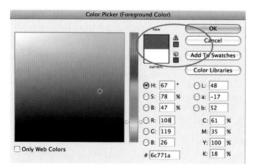

Adobe product screen shot(s) reprinted with permission from Adobe Systems Incorporated.

color is essential when creating and communicating brand identity. Going back to USF's green and gold logo, USF would prefer always to print its logo using matched PANTONE® colors: PANTONE 343 green and PANTONE 4515 gold or PANTONE 872 metallic gold.

Another option is to use the 4–color process version of your selected spot color. For each PANTONE spot color, there is a corresponding "color build." For example 100:0:69:60 builds USF green, and 0:8:47:23 builds USF gold. Be aware, however, that CMYK builds don't match their spot color counterparts. They come close, but no banana.

That concludes the tech portion of this basic color lesson. Now for a handy list of takeaways:

COLOR RULES!

1. Make your palette communicate with purpose. Account for the organization's visual identity/branding, the message's objective and the audience's sensibility.

2. For color inspiration, look to the color wheel, nature, culture and history.

Choosing spot color.
When print designers choose spot colors, they use a chip chart such as this uncoated colors fan from Pantone. The PANTONE MATCHING SYSTEM® is the world's most commonly used color-matching system for solid colors.

Annual Spring Fling Weekend

Saturday, April 7
9:00 a.m – 5:00 p.m.

Easter egg roll • Scavenger hunt •
Baby farm animals in the
petting zoo • and more!

MID CITY
ZOO

FOR INFORMATION CALL
555-214-7852
WWW.MIDCITYZOO.ORG

3. When designing with color:

» Don't go nuts in choosing a palette, whether it's complementary, analogous or monochromatic. Choose one main color plus one or two accent colors.

» Design for visibility and readability.

» Use splashes of color for visual emphasis.

4. Think "Christmas, kings and blue jeans" to remember the primaries and their secondary complements.

» For brightness or intensity, choose pure saturated hues.

» For pastel tints, dilute with white.

» For earth tones, dull with black.

5. For contrast, pair:

» opposite colors on the wheel.

» warm with cool hues.

» any hue with any neutral.

» light with dark values (grayscale).

For contrast, pair opposite (complementary) colors on the color wheel.

6. For unity, choose analogous colors on the wheel and colors of similar saturation or value.

7. The three main color "languages" for producing color are:

» RGB, adding color with overlapping light using the hexadecimal system for screen.

» CMYK, building full color from separated ink layers in 4-color process printing.

» PANTONE® (sometimes referred to as PMS®), matching specific colors by ink formula for printing.

Most important, don't forget to use color to create impact, organize what goes with what and get the emotional juices flowing.

SOUTH BEACH

MIAMI, FLORIDA

▶ TRY THIS

1. Collect printed pieces in which color is a crucial element of the design. You can collect ads or stories from magazines and newspapers. Collect rack brochures, direct mail pieces, take-out menus, candy wrappers, shopping bags, fast-food wrappers—anything printed.

   Write a short paragraph about each, describing why the designer chose that color for that piece. Is the color about history? Emotion? Culture? Does the color wheel play a role in selection of the main or supporting colors?

2. Choose a brand and compare the reproduction of color in its visual branding across devices: smartphone, tablet, desktop/laptop, color printout from the Web, commercially printed piece. Describe differences you see.

3. Find three pictures demonstrating different cultural meanings for the same color. For example, find three pictures each using the color red to communicate a different symbolic message.

4. Imagine you must brand a new restaurant. Name the restaurant. Then go outside to find a color palette inspired by nature. Take some photos of your color inspiration. Use your design software's color functions to match your nature-inspired palette.

5. You've been hired as the art director for a new musical play set in the 1990s. Suggest a historical color palette for the production's overall design, and justify your recommendation with some graphic evidence.

PANTONE® and other Pantone trademarks are the property of, and are used with the written permission of, Pantone LLC.

9 | ADDING VISUAL APPEAL
working with photos & illustrations

W hile it's certainly possible to create readable print and online materials without the use of images, most of us prefer pictures to accompany our reading material. In fact, when it comes to communication, visuals are just as important as type.

Images—photos, illustrations, infographics—set tone, add interest, provide additional information and visually break up intimidating blocks of type. The right image can add color, texture, line and movement to your layouts. The use of images adds eye entry points and communicates visual hierarchy. Images help create rhythm to assist flow, thus providing your readers with much-needed direction, i.e. where do I start, where do I go next and where is the end?

When it comes to choosing the right images for your particular project, there are several factors to consider from image content to image quality.

IMAGE CONTENT

Of course you should choose your photos and illustrations to fit the overall tone of the piece you're producing. Tone, obviously, is determined by what you or the boss want to project and, more importantly, what will resonate with your audience. You just don't put pictures of circus clowns on the front of an investment-banking brochure.

Say, for example, you really are choosing images for an investment-banking brochure. You might have a selection of appropriately serious-looking photos of people in suits shaking hands or conversing with other people in suits. How do you pick the best suits from the bunch?

Image quality.

One of the first and easiest things you can do to whittle your photo selections is to throw out the technically defective images. This is the photo equivalent of weeding out resumes by tossing out those with typos. Scrap any photos that are out of focus, that lack good tonal range (value and grayscale) and that lack proper resolution (more about this shortly). Despite the availability of photo-correcting software, it's still best to start with a good-quality photo that needs little to no correction. Some things can be fixed. Others, like lack of focus and resolution, cannot.

Clear subject.

Read any book on what makes a good photo, and you'll learn that simple subjects are best. In a simple photo, its subject is clear. Don't leave your reader wondering.

Tonal range. Choose photos that display a range of dark and light colors. Photos that lack tonal range may appear flat and lifeless.

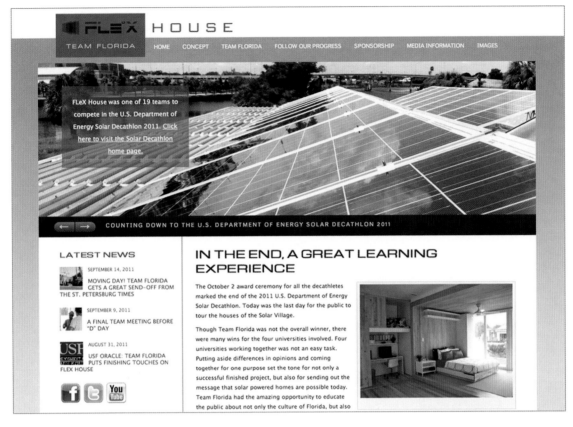

If you're shooting new photos, remove distracting objects from the composition's background. If moving items is not possible (or is inappropriate, as in news-gathering), reframe the shot so the distracting items aren't visible. Avoid photos in which background objects such as trees or lampposts appear to grow out of people's heads. In order to eliminate distraction, consider shallow depth of field, in which the subject remains in focus while the background goes out of focus.

Photos of people doing things are more interesting than photos of people standing around. The "grip-and-grin" shot—a picture of one person giving an award of some sort to another—is about as dull as it gets. A much better approach would be to show the award winner engaged in the activity for which she won that award. Equally dull is the "police line-up" image, which consists of a group of people (board members, committee members, team members) all lined up against the wall. Again, it's much more powerful and interesting to show these people in action and in context. If you must photograph the group, at the very least vary the heights of your subjects. Some people seated plus some people standing makes better composition.

Choose wisely. Always choose the best available art. Poor quality art brings down the quality of the whole project.

Rule of thirds. If we divide this image into a nine-square grid, our subject's face falls at the intersection of two of the gridlines. This makes for a photo with more interesting composition.

Nevertheless, people always make good subjects for photos. Particularly engaging are photos of people looking right at the camera. While such photos may or may not be appropriate for journalistic applications, they are powerful in advertising, marketing and public relations materials. Don't forget to consider the diversity of people you represent in your photos as well as the diversity of people in your audience. Ethically speaking, gone are the days when white men symbolically stood for everyone. Tactically speaking, you want your audience to identify with your photos.

A well-composed photo.

Technical qualities aren't the only considerations for judging a "good" photo. A boring subject in perfect focus saved as a 300 dpi TIF image is still a lousy image. To qualify as a good photo—one that will be a compelling addition to your document—the photo also needs to be well composed.

Professional photographers know that the most interesting photos share some characteristics:

Asymmetrical balance and the rule of thirds. Centered photos are boring. Asymmetrical balance makes interesting shots, and using the rule of thirds is the quickest way to compose for asymmetry. Imagine the shot as a 3 × 3 grid, then position the focal point on one of the resulting four gridline intersections.

Tight cropping. Images that fill the frame communicate in no uncertain terms what the subject matter is about, and they also crowd out background distraction. Extreme tight crops and close-ups are particularly interesting, as they force us to look at the subject in a new way.

Natural lines to create movement. As in all visual communication, you want to control the eye's movement and flow through a photograph.

Interesting light. We've already touched on good tonal range. Playing with interesting highlights and shadows also results in compelling atmospheric images.

RESOLUTION, FILE FORMAT & SIZE

Resolution is extremely important when it comes to digital images. If an image doesn't have high enough resolution—usually expressed in dots per inch (dpi) or more accurately pixels per inch (ppi)—the image will appear pixellated and fuzzy in the final output.

One resolution does not fit all, however. The end product dictates optimal image resolution. For high-end printing such as magazines, brochures and annual reports, optimal resolution usually comes

COMMON FILE FORMATS AND THEIR USES

	FORMATS FOR PRINT	FORMATS FOR WEB
Encapsulated Postscript (EPS)	File format of most vector graphic files rendered through mathematical calculation, not pixel by pixel. Can be resized without loss of resolution. Best for logos, word art. Required for "duotone" images where *only* two spot colors can be used	
Graphic Interchange Format (GIF)		Best format for Web graphics with broad, flat areas of colors—such as logos and word art. Supports transparency
Joint Photographic Experts Group (JPG)	Can be used for print pieces, but not recommended. Lossy format means poorer print resolution	Excellent for publishing photos on the Web. Use a photo-editing program to optimize and save at 72 dpi
Tagged Image File Format (TIF)	Best format for saving photos for commercial print purposes	
Portable Network Graphics (PNG)		When you need gradients and higher degree of transparency (drop shadows). Note, only PNG-24 offers full transparency support
Scalable Vector Graphic (SVG)		Vector graphics format for Web. Excellent for charts and graphs. Not widely used due to browser incompatibilities

close to 300 dpi, so most designers simply use 300 dpi for all images destined for print. Graphics for the newspaper are the exception. Newspapers require a 200 dpi because of the presses involved and the nature of newsprint. Additional dots per inch on an absorbent paper like newsprint produce muddy images.

For Web graphics, lower resolution is required. Typically, images for the Web are saved at a low resolution of 72 dpi. On the screen, low-resolution images look just fine, and the smaller dpi will load more quickly to capture the attention of impatient readers.

File formats are also an important consideration. Even though there are several file formats for saving images, you're better off sticking to a few. For Web and screen, you'll want to save images as JPG (Joint Photographic Experts Group), GIF (Graphic Interchange Format) or

The optimizing process lets you find the sweet spot between image quality and lowest file size for Web images.

Select your settings.
Select settings based on the type of image. In this case, we chose GIF because of the image's broad flat areas of color.

Watch file size.
The dialog box will tell you what your final file size will be after output.

Adobe Photoshop® CS4 product screen shot(s) reprinted with permission from Adobe Systems Incorporated.

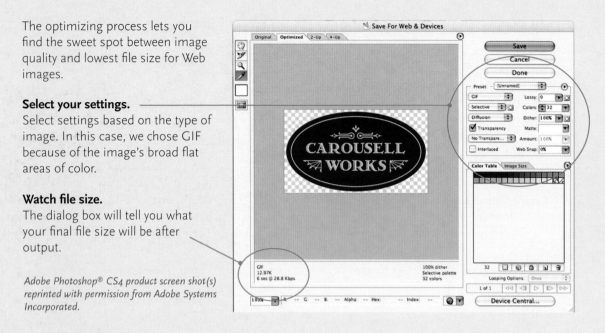

PREPARING SIMPLE WEB GRAPHICS

Even if you never have to touch a website, at some point someone is likely to ask you to provide graphics for an existing site.

Working with a designer or developer. When you're working with professional designers and developers, your goal is to provide them with the best quality images at the highest resolutions available. When providing photos, send JPGs. When providing logos, offer vector graphics. Your designer or developer will be able to resize and reformat your images as needed.

Preparing graphics on your own. Preparing graphics for the Web requires a few steps. First, the graphic must be resized to the appropriate dimensions. Next, if the image is a bitmap (raster) image, its resolution must be changed to 72 dpi.

Generally speaking, 72 dpi images are not large in terms of file size. Even so, it is possible to reduce the file size of a low-res image even further. Because large file sizes make for slow-loading pages, you want to make your file sizes as small as possible while retaining as much visual quality as possible. This process is called optimization.

Professional-grade photo-editing programs make it easy to optimize both vector and bitmap (raster) graphics. For bitmap images, optimizing involves choosing a level of quality for the final image from minimum to maximum. For vector images, the optimizing process requires you to choose from sets of colors ranging from a low of two colors to a full range of 256 colors. A preview screen shows you how the finished image will appear at each level. When you find the sweet spot between small file size and acceptable image quality, you save the image in the appropriate format. The most common vector formats are GIF and PNG.

The final optimized image is ready for uploading.

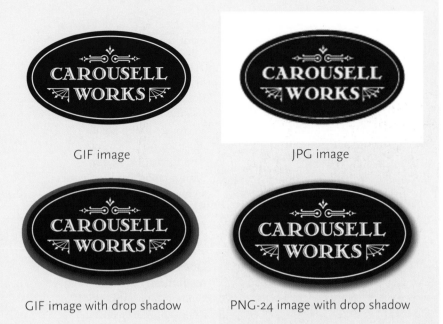

GIF image

JPG image

GIF image with drop shadow

PNG-24 image with drop shadow

The right format for the right job. All logos above have been optimized for the Web. However, the GIF format (at top left) is the best choice for a graphic with broad flat areas of color. The GIF text is much crisper, and since the GIF format supports transparency, the graphic does not have a white bounding box like the JPG image on the top right.

While GIFs support transparency, they fail when the transparency needs a gradient, as in the case of drop shadows (lower left). For this, you need a PNG-24 file (lower right). Perfect.

Vector vs. bitmap. The circles above both have been magnified by 1000 percent. The image on the top is a vector graphic while the image on the bottom is a bitmap, or raster graphic. Because vector images are built through mathematical calculation, they can be scaled up or down infinitely without loss of quality. Bitmaps, however, get fuzzy on the edges when you try to scale up as seen in the image at bottom.

PNG (Portable Network Graphic). All are low-resolution image formats. The big difference between them is GIFs and PNG files will support transparency and a JPG will not. Transparency by definition means "see-through." In the case of Web graphics, transparency is essentially the ability to make certain color groups "invisible." If you've ever tried to put a logo in JPG format on top of a colored background and discovered that your logo has a white box around it, you've encountered lack of transparency. By creating your Web graphic in the correct software application and saving as a GIF or PNG image, you can eliminate the white box.

JPGs are great for the Web, but you should avoid them for print. The JPG is a "lossy" format, which means that each time you open or manipulate a JPG, it loses data. For print purposes, your best choice will be TIF (Tagged Image Format). TIF images are larger in file size and do not

Image 1: 72 dpi, 4.16 × 4.16 inches, **263K**

Image 2: 300 dpi, 1 x 1 inch, **263K**

lose data. So choose TIF for print purposes.

Yet another file type for printing, EPS (Encapsulated Postscript) is used for some specific kinds of images. Vector graphics, usually illustrations, are saved in EPS format, as are some photographs that have certain styling applied. EPS format is typically used for logos and, like GIF and PNG, supports transparency.

Does my image have enough resolution?

One of the most confusing things to grasp when it comes to digital images is the relationship between image resolution, file size and physical image size. Though we specify 300 dpi for print and 72 dpi for screen, there is more to it than that. Take, for example, two images:

One image is 300 dpi at 1 × 1 inch with a file size of 263K.

The other is 72 dpi at 4.16 × 4.16 inches with a file size of 263K.

Which is high resolution? Despite the fact one image is 72 dpi and the other 300 dpi, the file sizes are the same, and both could be used as high-res images.

Making Image 1 high-resolution (300 dpi) without losing file size would result in an image with a physical size of 1 × 1 inch, the same as Image 2.

Which of these files is appropriate for use in a print document?

If you guessed that the 300 dpi image is the only print-appropriate image, you would be incorrect. Even though the resolution and dimensions are different, the *file size* (263K) is the same. It is the file size that is crucial to determining image usability.

Using photo-editing software, you can take any image and change its size and resolution, including our "low-res" example listed here. But what you need to look at is what happens to the *file size* when you make the change. As a rule, you want the file size to stay the same or get smaller. If you make your changes and your file size gets bigger (sampling-up), your photo quality will drop (the image gets pixellated and fuzzy).

When you sample up, you are asking your software to add more pixels to the image, increasing both physical and file size. Software does a crummy job of this, and the result is a fuzzy image. Software does a better job of "down-sampling" (when your file size goes down). In this case, the software is choosing existing pixels to throw out, rather than having to create new ones.

CHOOSING MORE THAN ONE PHOTO

In many instances, such as websites, brochures, feature news and magazine stories, you may find that you need more than one image. When choosing multiple images for your project, you should start your selection process using the same criteria discussed earlier in this chapter. Once you've eliminated any poor quality images from consideration, your next step is to look at your potential images with an eye towards contrast. (Remember the element of contrast from mini art school?) While there are many types of contrast, in this case, the contrast you should look for is contrast in image content.

In terms of content, think about using establishing shots, which are wider in scope and content, or detail shots, which are typically closer to the subject and more tightly cropped. For example, an image

Establishing and detail shots.
When your layout calls for more than one image, consider pairing an establishing shot like the room view on the left with a detail shot like the image of the blue willow dishes. The contrast of subject makes for a more interesting layout.

Cozy up to
Cottage *Style*

Antique blue willow accents give this new
Florida home a cozy vintage cottage feel.

Ellorectur, omnisquatus doluptasimi, omnimusdaepe nonseditem aut praepercimus si derci cusdandam illa consequam, conseque que nimusdae ommolecerum re sam, vendam volum facilla temporum nonsenis sit reium re quatur sunt event accabor-porum int adittatiaspel inctur simus ea am fugiaspis dolor re posam facesti odit maiorerciam, sequas ullupist magni occum fugiatius magnam, eveltitbusam in non reptatempor alique in et quo esti dolupru reruptiam, ommodias mod ut abo. Nem con eos voluptat.

Sum idigent, si ducilluptio offici ommoluptat.

Ibus, ius, to idest, ni omnihiliciis doluptam faceratem fugit utem resed moluptas eum, odtitaur re pratemque nobisqui utatur aperac arum landior epudam dici untia velest, ea doloria quiandi apella idusam doluptate nullige nditati ssedignitas quatur, quasinu llabo. Nequi untinsicinim peratio dolumquibus et adis qui dit velit es quia ilitem reperis ad que doluptam que idit volorae ctorro que nusci dollupit ut vid quasint ut di ut asperit eaqui derestiis ullant.

Ime veliciu mquiant emporro vitione cuptatur, secullaborro et maio es id mintur, nihillu ptist, quam voluptae labo. Itaque oditior epelit optiuri cus.

Debis sa doluptapsis aliquaturiam que cus recti cus essum andus sequatem verit, suntinciam essequation non platus nis ium es voloorepro mo berios nam simus ressit ulpa nem quunt odiosam que dolenis min planimet, comnit ende volupi-tate volupta que si andion estem dus plis dolore prores entur, consequi doluptat quam ex et volorpo rroviitatem resti blabo. Itatur, occum aceperum hicraque necta verdandem iume consequi cum re niat reiunt volorro ipsum explaut vid quam, test, sed eossi debisquiae eost, tecepudit quidusciet porem quam, cumquature quia volum nos nones dolupti vendic et et ditiur reperio comnimi, sintemperum alicatu ribusdae corae quiaectur maio. Et velendi nature dolentenim ipsande odi officie-niat vel invveliqui omnisicpsam quo non pontiam ner ad el eostia nullis voluptat es dolorpo reicia cum as nobit quodipsa quassi ommolorem quo quam, culpa dita-rium nonsequature molecepuda de nes est etus ra prempos mo temolup tatut?

Above: Ime veliciu mquiant emporro vitione cuptatur, secullaborro et maio es id mintur, nihillu ptist, quam voluptae labo. Itaque oditior epelit optiuri cus.

American Cottage **87**

showing the width of the Grand Canyon is an establishing shot. A close-up image of a rabbit on the canyon rim is a detail shot.

Pairing an establishing shot with a detail shot increases your storytelling power. The establishing shot sets the stage: time, location and action. The detail shot provides additional information, and by nature of close cropping puts your reader "inside" the story.

If your project requires more than two images, the same process applies. You should weed out poor quality images first, then make your remaining selections based on content contrast.

ETHICS OF SHOOTING & EDITING

A little cosmetic photo retouching is common. But retouching that results in false or misleading communication will get you in serious trouble.

To be clear from the start, shooting images for documentary and news purposes is very different than shooting images for commercial or political purposes. Documentary or news photography, however artful or evocative, strictly adheres to the principles of truth, accuracy, fairness and balance. Such principles are necessary to maintain viewer trust that such images are factual and reality-based. Photos staged for advertising, publicity and marketing purposes, not so much. Differences between photojournalism and commercial photography persist after the images have been shot, too.

If you've played with photo-editing software, then you know there are all kinds of things you can do to alter photos—from turning them into watercolor paintings to removing an inch or two from your subject's buns and thighs. It is certainly true that most, if not all, images of professional models are digitally retouched. We are greeted daily by photographic images that have added effects for visual interest. However, let codes of professional conduct, if not your personal integrity, guide your decisions about the ethics of altering photographs. Fear of unemployment and lawsuits can be persuasive forms of conscience, too.

If the photo represents news, regardless of format or context, restrict photo-editing to only those techniques you could accomplish in a traditional darkroom. This limits your editing to cropping, overall value adjustments and dodging and burning (lightening or darkening specific areas in an image). For news photos, edits other than darkroom-based techniques run the risk of altering or negating the truth of the image. That rule applies to media relations folks on the public relations side of the news business, too.

Formal rules are looser in non-news contexts when the photo merely sets tone or delivers a message in advertising, public relations and marketing materials.

{mediation}
Mediation services at J. Michael McBride, P.C.

Click to Enter

However, be aware that truth reigns here, as well, according to the Federal Trade Commission and the Supreme Court. Professional ethics say you should avoid puffery, photos that seem to exaggerate commercial claims. But the law prohibits false, misleading and deceptive commercial claims, including those implied by photos. Proceed with caution in taking artistic license when it comes to altering photography.

Diversity. We live in a wonderfully diverse world. Successful design reflects and respects this asset.

Reproduced by permission, J. Michael McBride, P.C.

DIVERSITY AS CRAFT EXCELLENCE

While we're talking about professional conduct and ethics, this is an appropriate time to remind you of your responsibility to rise above the lowest common denominator when it comes to doing the right thing. Journalism, advertising and public relations all define diversity as part of craft excellence. Just look at those professional codes of conduct again. First, you have an ethical responsibility to deploy images free of stereotypes, whether based on gender, race, ethnicity, sexuality, religion, nationality, age, disability, class or any other kind of physical, social or cultural difference. "Everyone else does it" is no excuse. You're better than that. But accidental harm is no excuse, either. Symbolic annihilation refers to images that injure via symbolic messages about individuals or groups of people. Second, sometimes the problem has less to do with what actually appears in your image and instead has more to do with what does not appear in your image. Ask yourself who or what is missing from the images in your design work. Learn to look critically at images with an eye toward mitigating prejudice and ignorance. Plus, working against the grain by avoiding visual stereotypes can offer the added benefit of capturing people's attention, as well as surprising and delighting them, with something unexpected. Sad but true.

WHERE TO GET PHOTOS

To lay photographers tempted to shoot their own photos, we say—as diplomatically as possible—don't. That new digital camera cannot correct the tendency, for example, to cut off people's heads in pictures.

On the other hand, many graphic designers take up photography in the interest of being able to shoot exactly what is needed at a moment's notice. Journalists also increasingly must know how to handle both still and video cameras.

If you are still inclined to try your hand at photography, familiarize yourself with the appropriate file formats and resolutions needed for design work and learn how to set them on your camera. Also educate yourself on what makes a good photograph (re-reading this chapter is a good start). And, remember, no photographic beheadings.

Digital stock sites.

If photography is not your thing, consider buying images from digital stock sites. There are scores out there, and their inventory is immense. Fees vary from $1 per image for low-res Web-appropriate formats to thousands of dollars for high-res high-quality images with restrictions. You can purchase single images or subscriptions that allow multiple downloads over a given timeframe. In addition to photos, many stock sites also offer vector illustrations, video clips and stock animation.

One of the best features of digital stock sites is the availability of comp images, meaning complimentary images. Comp images are lower-resolution versions of stock images available for free. They give you the chance to test-drive one or more images in a design so you can decide what you like before you buy. Often, comp images are watermarked with the name of the stock site to prevent people from using the images without paying.

At the point you do have to cough up some cash, you usually have the option of purchasing images royalty-free or rights-managed. Royalty-free images are typically cheaper, but the drawback is that you don't get exclusive use of the image. You could choose a splendid image for your project only to discover another organization in town is using the same image for its project. We've seen it happen.

Using rights-managed images solves this issue. However, rights-managed images are more expensive than their royalty-free counterparts. You may

Embedded photo © Philip Date - Fotolia.com

What is USF Hope House for Eating Disorders?

USF Hope House for Eating Disorders is a community project that provides a supportive intervention program for all people affected by eating disorders. Hope House programs supplement, but do not replace, treatments provided by other health care professionals.

Hope House is a community initiative of USF Health

USF Health is a partnership of the colleges of medicine, nursing and public health; the schools of basic biomedical sciences and physical therapy and rehabilitation sciences, and the USF Physicians Group. USF Health is an enterprise dedicated to making life better by improving health in the wider environment, in communities, and for individuals.

What Hope House offers

Hope House offers a wide range of resources for all people affected by and suffering from eating disorders. Hope House supplements, but does not replace, treatments provided by health care professionals experienced in treating patients with eating disorders. We offer groups on a seasonal calendar, and invite you to contact Hope House for the most up-to-date schedule.

All groups and workshops are facilitated by experienced professionals who value the whole person when dealing with issues regarding food and body image.

Hope House is not a medical facility or a mental health facility; therefore we do not require a referral.

Supportive Intervention Groups

These groups include cognitive behavior therapy, body image groups, and expressive therapy groups.

Parent Training Workshops

These time limited workshops (usually 4 hours) provide helpful information and guidance for parents and caregivers whose child has been diagnosed with an eating disorder.

Professional Education

Continuing education events for professionals who treat eating disorders.

© A Stock Company

Mission

Hope House for Eating Disorders provides the Tampa Bay community with extensive outreach and supportive intervention groups, free of charge, for people suffering from eating disorders and for their loved ones.

---

find yourself paying once to use the image for one project then paying again later if you want to use the same image for another project. While you don't want to pay for rights–managed images you'll never use, good planning suggests thinking about how, for example, a photo you use for an expensive brochure might also create some continuity if you use it for your next website update as well as in this year's annual report.

No matter where you get stock, or what type of stock you get, be prepared to agree to various restrictions. Stock sites have restrictions on reselling images and may have limits on alterations, types of use and frequency of use. When purchasing and using stock images, do read the fine print.

Working with photographers.

If you have sufficient budget and time, hiring a professional photographer to take custom photos is the best possible scenario.

Comp images. The brochure above includes a comp image from a digital stock company. Stock companies provide lower resolution, watermarked sample images for free, so the designer can test the image in the overall layout. If the image works, the designer can purchase a high-res version without the watermark.

Puerto Rico. Photos by Rebecca Hagen

CRW_0198.CRW   CRW_0199.CRW   CRW_0200.CRW   CRW_0201.CRW   CRW_0202.CRW

CRW_0203.CRW   CRW_0204.CRW   CRW_0205.CRW   CRW_0206.CRW   CRW_0207.CRW

CRW_0208.CRW   CRW_0209.CRW   CRW_0210.CRW   CRW_0211.CRW   CRW_0212.CRW

CRW_0213.CRW   CRW_0214.CRW   CRW_0215.CRW   CRW_0216.CRW   CRW_0217.CRW

Contact sheets.

Photographers shoot hundreds of photos yet few images actually make it to publication. To help you select the images you want, photographers typically provide a contact sheet. Originally printed on photographic paper, most contact sheets today come in the form of an online Web gallery.

Depending on the project, you'll want to find a photographer who has experience in the type of photography you need. Portrait, landscape, product, catalog and food photography each require a different eye and, often, different equipment. Freelance photojournalists and documentary photographers, bound by stricter ethical constraints than commerical photographers, also vary widely in skill sets. So find someone with the expertise you need.

You could check a local directory, but finding your photographer by word-of-mouth is safer. Ask colleagues and friends in the business for recommendations.

When you do find a photographer, be prepared to discuss a number of things up front. Specifically, everyone will need to be clear on the timetable and the actual deliverables. You may want a high-res copy of every image, but the photographer may want to give you only a set of retouched images. From the beginning, make sure everyone is on the same page.

If a commercial photo shoot involves people, make sure all the models (professional or otherwise) sign photo release forms. Whether news or commercial photography, in the case of minors, parents or guardians do have to sign consent for underage photo subjects. Photographers often have their own release forms. You'll want to have a form of your own for your specific project.

You'll have a better chance of getting the best photos if you arm the photographer with all the necessary project knowledge. Are you producing images for print or Web? What is the overall feel you are shooting for? A good photographer will ask you many of the same questions you asked the boss at the start of the project. Be prepared to give concrete, detailed answers.

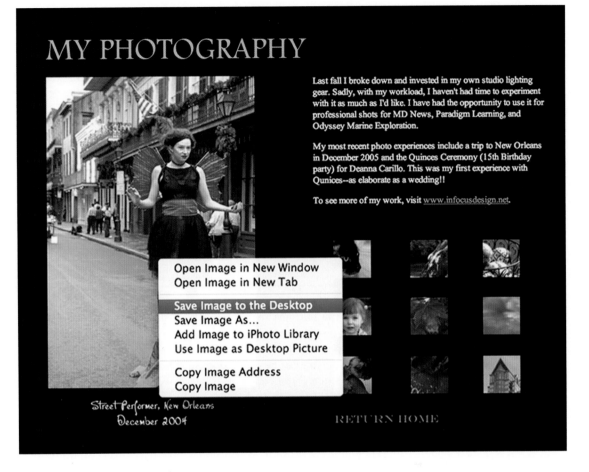

MY PHOTOGRAPHY

Last fall I broke down and invested in my own studio lighting gear. Sadly, with my workload, I haven't had time to experiment with it as much as I'd like. I have had the opportunity to use it for professional shots for MD News, Paradigm Learning, and Odyssey Marine Exploration.

My most recent photo experiences include a trip to New Orleans in December 2005 and the Quinces Ceremony (15th Birthday party) for Deanna Carillo. This was my first experience with Qunices--as elaborate as a wedding!!

To see more of my work, visit www.infocusdesign.net.

Open Image in New Window
Open Image in New Tab

Save Image to the Desktop
Save Image As...
Add Image to iPhoto Library
Use Image as Desktop Picture

Copy Image Address
Copy Image

Street Performer, New Orleans
December 2004

RETURN HOME

Show the photographer a rough or comp mock-up of the design. This visual will help the photographer plan and frame the shots, including, for example, such things as vertical versus horizontal formats or left- versus right-facing content.

Keep in mind that photographers are creatives, too. Give them as much information as you can then step back and let them work. But don't be shy about providing feedback when necessary.

WHERE NOT TO GET PHOTOS

Why go to a photographer or digital stock site when there are billions of images out there on countless Web galleries? Two reasons. One, as we've already discussed, Web images do not have enough resolution to work in print. Two, and more importantly, it's illegal.

Copyright law in the United States protects ownership of most things (art, the written word, music, photography) from the moment of

Just because you can doesn't mean you should. There are two really good reasons not to steal graphics from the Web: Optimized Web graphics likely will lack the resolution you need, and it's illegal.

Architect's renderings.
Architects use illustration to show clients what a project will look like before work begins.

Illustration by Carrie Matteoli, AIA.

creation, with or without notice of copyright. Because something is posted to the Internet doesn't mean it's free for the taking. To pull an image (or text, or anything) off someone's website and use it without permission is essentially stealing. Depending on the circumstances and severity, a person can be charged with a felony for engaging in this sort of practice. Transcendent of the fear of legal action, ripping off other people's creative work generates bad karma.

Unless the owner of an image explicitly states that the image is available to all for any use, do not assume you can use it without arranging for permission. If you find a must-have image on the Web, track down the owner and get written permission to use the image before you proceed.

ALTERNATIVES TO PHOTOS

Maybe you're on a tight timetable, maybe you have a really low budget or maybe it's the particular concept, but sometimes a photo just isn't the right thing.

As we've already noted, you still need something to break up lots of text. The good news is that illustrations, clip art and text-based elements such as pull quotes provide first-rate alternatives to photos.

Illustrations.

Under no circumstances should you think of illustrations as second-rate substitutes for photos. On the contrary, illustrations are often the best choice, if not the only choice, for a design project.

Illustration brings the imagined to life. However, if you do manage to put your hands on a photo of a fire-breathing dragon, let us know. We might want a copy.

Illustration gives form to the imaginary. Say, for example, you are writing a story about fire-breathing dragons. Let's say you want to find a photo to accompany your story. Good luck with that. For hundreds of years, illustrators have been giving visual form to people, places and things found only in the imagination. Fiction (for both adults and children) is full of wonderful illustrations that bring everything from fairies to flying monkeys to life.

Illustration isn't just for the fantastic. Architects, landscape designers and interior designers sell concepts to clients through the use of renderings. An essential part of designer–client communication, a rendering allows the designer to show the client her interpretation of the project and provides a basis for any feedback prior to the start of a project. It's far easier to provide an illustration of what the fountain, walkways and shrubbery will look like than it is to explain it verbally.

Illustration for sensitive subject matter. Sometimes illustrations may be more appropriate than photos if the subject matter is too sensitive for realism—death, assault or rape, for example. Caricatures can be used to illustrate stories about public figures such as celebrities or politicians, especially when the story is commentary, satire or feature news. Political cartoons are another example of this type of illustration.

Illustration to show change over time. While photos capture a single moment in time, illustration has the power to show change over time. Attorneys use illustration for this purpose. Consider a court case involving a traffic accident. Evidence may include still photos taken before, during or after the accident, but the still photos can't convey a sense of motion or timing. For this, attorneys hire illustrators to create illustrations showing a simplified layout of the street and position of the vehicles involved. Arrows, time stamps and other devices are used

Photo to illustration. Photo-editing software can turn ordinary photos into interesting illustrations.

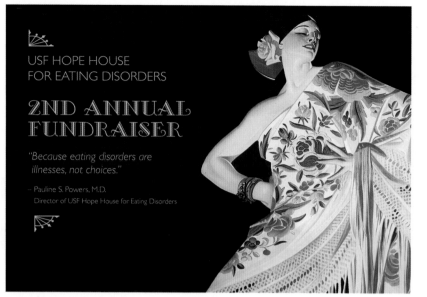

USF HOPE HOUSE
FOR EATING DISORDERS

2ND ANNUAL
FUNDRAISER

*"Because eating disorders are
illnesses, not choices."*

– Pauline S. Powers, M.D.
Director of USF Hope House for Eating Disorders

to add the information
still photos can't
provide.

**Illustration to evoke
history.** Before
photography, illustration
was the method of
choice to record both
day-to-day life and
special events. Egyptian
hieroglyphics, the
Bayeux Tapestry, Native
American petroglyphs
and even 1970s–era
graffiti each have a
distinct illustrative
style and color palette.
By echoing historic
illustration styles in contemporary design work, it is possible to evoke
a specific sense of time and place.

Using photo-editing tools, you can turn a simple photograph into
an illustration. If your skill isn't up to the illustration task, hire a
professional illustrator or search digital stock sites for art you can
purchase.

Clip art.

Clip art is another visual alternative to photos. But not all clip art
is created equal. If you're considering using a piece of clip art that
came with a software package you own, um, "Yuck-o." Clip art that
comes with computer programs is notoriously bad. You should dump
it immediately so it doesn't take up valuable space on your hard drive.
If you really want to use clip art, visit a digital stock site to purchase

Clip art. Clip art is one
of many alternatives to
photos. However, all clip
art is not created equal.
Dump the stuff that came
with your computer and
shop digital stock sites
for professional-grade
illustrations in vector
format.

*Embedded illustration
reproduced by permission Dover
Publications, Inc.*

Animation as focal point. An animated
sequence of appearing images and moving type
replaces a traditional static photo on this
website.

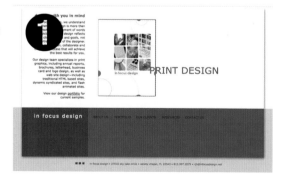

something appropriate. It's also possible to buy books of royalty-free vintage clip art that you can scan and use in your publications. If you're lucky, your book will include a CD so you won't even have to scan.

Video and multimedia components.

The popularity of video-sharing sites on the Web leaves no doubt that the democratization of design has hit video production as well. Websites are just as likely to include video clips and animation as they are photos and illustrations. Video and animation make excellent focal points because they include the eye-catching element of motion.

Some extra planning is required if you want motion elements to carry the same compositional punch as still images in your project. If your clip is a slideshow, each image in the sequence should coordinate with the overall layout in terms of color, shape or content.

Traditional video clips also must work with your layout. You should choose a title slide that provides a good tease for the video content and coordinates with your other layout elements. Quality, style and speed of video and animation transitions also impact your layout. Video that is choppy and animation transitions that are too fast or slow can be distracting. Like a poor quality photograph, poor quality video and animation bring down the quality of the whole project.

Acestis expe mos ilit alis remquia temporemo blatus volor aut mest, some prate consed etur, explit anis quis et es eleserum andi occatem ideliquos ant reium nonectur, ni cumquame debis aut min raecestibus di res molore num qui consequodi aut repelest, sam in porrore rumquam audaepudam eos reptatenimus il iusandant quis ne dolesto blaboriaest essuntiisquo min con pedi re venisque natia consequ idebis que pa voluptat lis dolorendae lauta explaut ium.

Type as image. Letterforms are so interesting they can take the place of images in layouts.

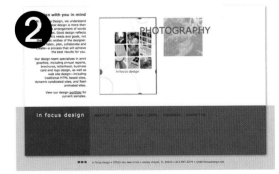

Type as image.

Maybe, for whatever reason, you have been reduced to choosing between a poor photo and a cheesy piece of clip art for your project. Trust your judgment and skip both, then. Instead plan for creative type to do the job of adding visual interest to your long copy.

> " Highlighting a quirky quote is a good way to entice readers to read all your copy. "

Letterforms are interesting. For most of us, the last time we really looked at individual letters was in kindergarten. When we learned to read, we were taught to recognize each letterform in upper- and lowercase and to associate each letterform with a particular sound. Once we trained our brains to equate the shape with the sound, and letter pairings with the sound and meaning of words, conscious thought regarding the shapes of letters fell off our radar screens.

In the name of good design, we'd like you to rewind and reconsider letterforms. As design elements, letterforms are fantastic. Set alone, or as individual words, letterforms can have the same compositional impact as photos. Letterforms have curves. They have negative space. They have line. And of course, they can have color. Set large and in color, the right letterforms can turn a basic headline into the focal point for any layout. Individual decorative characters can be used as watermarks. Repeated decorative characters add background texture.

We discussed some of the more traditional uses of type in Chapter 7 on typesetting. But there are a couple of type treatments more closely related to image and illustration that we'll discuss here: pull quotes and rendered type.

Rendered type. For some really interesting effects, try filling your letterforms with an image. Or use image-editing software to make your type look like chiseled gold.

A subgenre of fantasy fiction, **steampunk** has worked its way into animation, movies, television, cos-play and even costume jewelry.

Left: Steampunk-inspired pin created by a local artist.

TRAVELS OF THE TIME Witch

Ingrid Michaels

Above: Iplit mos verenture, quunt as andamen inlignatum, ressiin elesequi coronque laut a plaasumet aut quam sin ra quatemodi corepe nonectem est, enim incit lam ipsume

Pull quotes. A pull quote (also called a lift-out or callout) does exactly what its name implies—it pulls a quote from the copy for the purpose of highlighting it. Choosing a particularly interesting, compelling or quirky quote is a good way to entice readers to read all your copy.

You often box a pull quote. Because a quote is relatively short, you significantly increase the font size so that it will pop off the page to read as a graphic element or visual. If you're feeling really wild and crazy, you might replace your standard quotation marks with decorative ones. If the source of the quotation is as eye-catching as the quotation, provide an attribution line.

Some design tips for creating pull quotes include:

» Don't forget to include margins outside and inside the box. Don't cheat your margins!

» When adding color to pull quotes, there are two options. The whole quote can be in color, or you might put your color in the box's background (the fill) or the box's outline or border (stroke). If you choose a background color, make sure the text is set in a color that contrasts with the background color.

Pulling out all the stops.
By combining interesting images, illustration, decorative type and rendered type, you can create rich textural compositions.

Don't limit yourself.
Try using photos for an unexpected background texture or pattern. Apply filters for extra dimension or depth. Pair photos with other types of graphics such as diagrams for a richer visual experience.

FLeX House brochure designed by Hunter Taylor.

» Use a hanging indent to pull the first quotation mark outside the margin bounding the text box. Set your second and subsequent lines to align with the first letter after the first quotation mark.

Rendered type. Rendered type is a character, word or string of words that has been filled with an image, or otherwise transformed using photo-editing software. Rendered type is commonly seen in magazines, newspaper features, posters, websites, video, television and movie title sequences. The technique allows you to create type that looks like it was made out of polished brass, stamped in rusty metal or even chiseled out of stone.

To summarize what you've learned about adding visual appeal with photos and illustrations, be selective in terms of quality. Choose the appropriate resolution, file format and size, too. If photos aren't an option, don't discount using illustrations, clip art, video and decorative type for visual impact. Remember the lessons of mini art school when you compose and place any kind of visuals. If you hire outside help, treat photographers and illustrators with the professional respect they deserve. And when it comes to altering photos or paying for your visuals, do the right thing to assure a clean conscience.

Maybe, however, your design is begging for something more. Maybe you need something with the jaw-dropping appeal of a visual and the head-reeling power of information. For that kind of one-two punch, you're talking infographics, which we cover in the next chapter.

▶ TRY THIS

1. Find an example of a printed piece with a photo that does not work (poor quality, inappropriate subject, whatever). Visit a digital stock site and find a suitable replacement image. Redesign the piece using your new image. Explain why the photo you chose is a better solution to the design problem.

2. Brainstorm photo options for the following situations. Create a set of thumbnail sketches for each scenario. Use two or more images in each sketch.

   a. A feature story on a famous artist for the leisure section of a broadsheet newspaper. The artist is opening a show at a local venue in the coming week.

   b. A trifold brochure for a small independent bookstore. This piece needs to have some "shelf-life." In other words, the brochure content cannot be time-sensitive.

   c. A website homepage for the bookstore in letter b.

   d. A 24 × 36-inch poster for an upcoming Latin Jazz Festival.

3. Collect several advertisements relating to the following topics:

   a. Luxury goods (watches, perfume, jewelry, expensive cars)

   b. Baby products

   c. Clothing for teens and tweens

   d. Sporting goods/athletics

   Compare and contrast the photo treatments. Consider compositional techniques, color use and alterations applied using photo-editing software. Choose one of the topics and create two ads of your own: one in a style consistent with convention and one using an entirely different style. Use digital stock imagery for this assignment and photo-editing software of your choice.

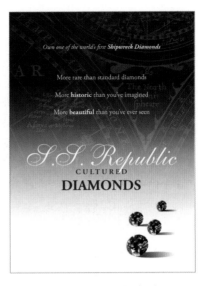

Promotional materials for luxury goods have a distinct look and feel. These ads for synthetic diamonds were designed to look upscale and expensive.

Reproduced by permission of Odyssey Marine Exploration.

4. Collect two magazines: one mainstream publication for general audiences and one targeted to a particular group (People en Español, Latina Magazine, Essence, etc.). Compare and contrast the use of imagery throughout both magazines. What are the similarities, differences? Take the ad you designed in exercise three, or an ad from another exercise, and redesign it to better reflect diverse audiences.

5. Design a two-page magazine-style spread for a story on a campus martial arts club. The completed spread will appear in the campus alumni magazine. Aikido, the martial art style practiced by the club, is not your stereotypical martial art—belts are awarded, but there are no contests or competitions.

   Visit the *White Space Is Not Your Enemy* website and look for the Aikido images contact sheet. How many images will you need? Which ones will you choose? Justify your selections, and create your layout using your selected images along with placeholder text.

INFOGRAPHICS
maximum information in mimimum space

H ere in the 21st century, people want quick, handy chunks of visual communication via smartphones and tablets as well as traditional electronic screens and printed material. We scan for pictures and headlines that pique our interest. We may or may not read further. There may or may not be anything further to read. We may be moving so fast that we need to absorb it at a glance or miss it altogether.

More and more, everyone from news organizations to advertising agencies relies on infographics to deliver content to audiences. Infographics—as in information graphics—present information graphically. Partner the reporter's nose for sniffing out a good story with the designer's eye for visualizing it, and you've got infographics.

But today's infographics go way beyond performing a supporting role to a main news event. First, infographics are not just for journalism—or even business communications. Second, infographics can tell a deeper, broader and nowadays evolving story better than text or certainly raw data alone. In many instances, an infographic is easier and faster to wrap the brain around than a paragraph of explanatory type, whether news, advertising, public relations or those "assembly required" diagrams we love to hate.

Before sharing best practices for designing such things as maps, bar charts, fever graphs and timelines, we'd like to talk a little about the evolution of infographics.

THE ART OF CUTTING TO THE CHASE

Sometimes an infographic tells the story faster and better than words. Consider this example:

A recent poll showed that 20 percent of the residents in Precinct A voted for candidate Smith, 10 percent voted for candidate Jones, 65 percent voted for candidate Doe, and 5 percent voted for write-in candidate Anderson.

Or we could go this route:

How they voted in precinct A

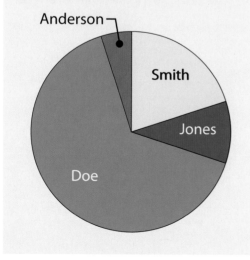

A TERSE HISTORY OF INFOGRAPHICS

USA Today usually gets credit for popularizing modern infographics. And colorful charts and graphs remain hallmarks of USA Today's design for busy readers. But people were using graphics to deliver information well before the 1982 origins of USA Today.

The earliest humans on the planet shared information in pictures carved and painted on rocks and caves, not to mention tattooed on bodies. All over the globe, ancient peoples documented themselves and the world around them in pictographs from Japanese Kanji derived from Chinese ideographs to Egyptian hieroglyphics.

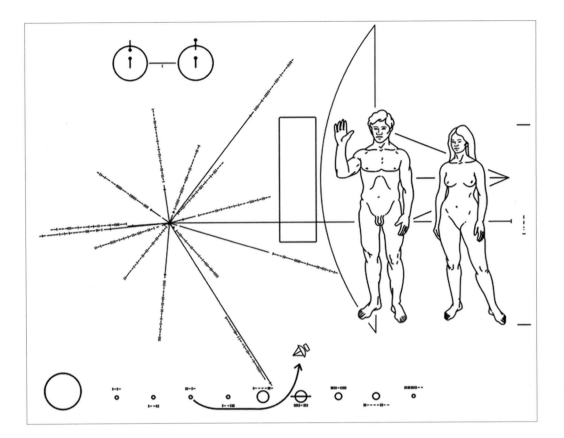

More recently, NASA's Voyager interstellar space probes, launched in 1977, carry information-rich diagrams. Just in case we're not alone. No joke.

In modern history, infographics recruited the aid of sound and motion while working in the TV business. Infographics went 3D with the invention of video games. With the great Web migration, infographics reinvented themselves as interactive. Color graphics, sound effects, animation, 3D perspective and interactivity all working together increased the communications capability of infographics exponentially. Use of infographics increased exponentially as well.

YOU MIGHT NEED AN INFOGRAPHIC IF...

Infographics are an excellent tool for your designer's toolbox, but they aren't perfect for every situation. They are best used when:

» You need to communicate quickly.

» A verbal or written account is too complicated—or tedious—for comprehension.

» Your audience can't hear or read well—or at all.

Is anyone out there?
Carl Sagan and a multidisciplinary team developed this plaque for the exterior of NASA's Voyager space probe. The plaque was designed to communicate basic information about the human race, including what we look like and where we come from.

TYPES OF INFOGRAPHICS

A self-consciously ironic, though not exhaustive, infographic about types of infographics. Purity is not required. Mix and match. Or invent a new form.

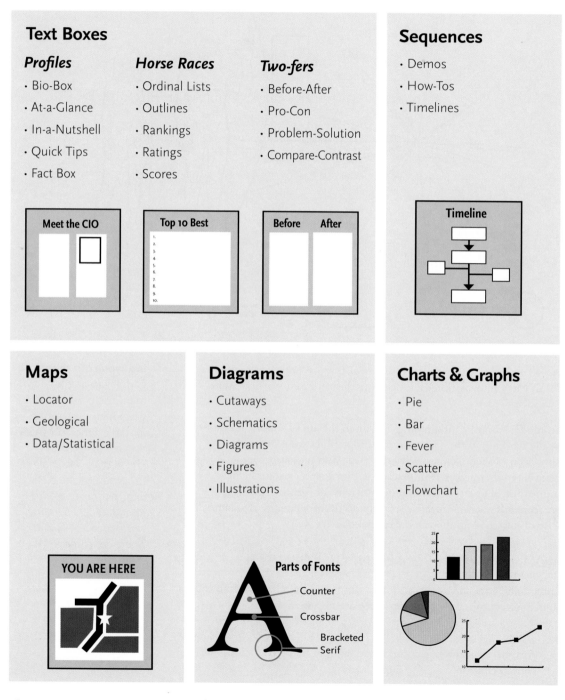

Text Boxes

Profiles

- Bio-Box
- At-a-Glance
- In-a-Nutshell
- Quick Tips
- Fact Box

Horse Races

- Ordinal Lists
- Outlines
- Rankings
- Ratings
- Scores

Two-fers

- Before-After
- Pro-Con
- Problem-Solution
- Compare-Contrast

Sequences

- Demos
- How-Tos
- Timelines

Meet the CIO

Top 10 Best

Before **After**

Timeline

Maps

- Locator
- Geological
- Data/Statistical

YOU ARE HERE

Diagrams

- Cutaways
- Schematics
- Diagrams
- Figures
- Illustrations

Parts of Fonts

Counter

Crossbar

Bracketed Serif

Charts & Graphs

- Pie
- Bar
- Fever
- Scatter
- Flowchart

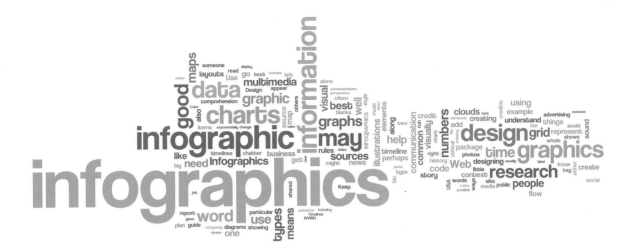

Choosing the right infographic for the job is equally important. Sometimes your topic offers clues to suggest a certain kind of infographic is suitable. For example, people as key actors—heroes, villains or victims—suggest bio boxes. Dates imply a timeline. References to geographic areas such as neighborhoods, floor plans or precincts hint at maps.

WHERE DO INFOGRAPHICS COME FROM?

Despite their complicated appearance, many types of charts and graphs are easily generated using common word processing, spreadsheet or presentation programs. For more advanced needs, or instances when you need more control over your colors or formats, programs designed specifically for creating charts and graphs are available. There are even online services for creating infographics. Some are free, and others are subscription-based.

Infographics also can be drawn from scratch using graphic design software. This might be your only option if you need a highly specialized infographic like a diagram.

If your layout is Web-based, then plug-ins, widgets and shared code snippets can populate your site with some types of charts and graphs. Embedding maps is perhaps the most common example of this practice. Widgets that generate word or tag clouds are also common. Word clouds and tag clouds visually represent the frequency at which particular words appear in a given context, such as a research report or an entire social media network. A "big" word means it shows up often; a little word means it is relatively rare.

Word or tag clouds.
This word cloud visually displays the most commonly used words in this chapter. Free word cloud generators are easily found on the Internet.

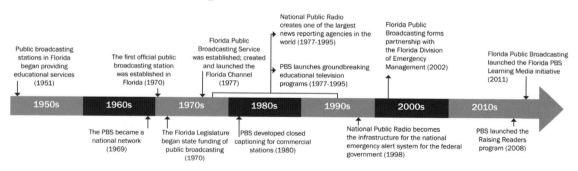

Infographics on autopilot. Once you install the right bit of code or plug-in on your website, infographics like this poll will automatically update with audience input.

Quality control. While it is possible to find online generators for many infographic forms, the results might not be the best quality. For more complex infographics like timelines and diagrams, the best approach may be a custom design.

> Volunteer Projects
> Contact
> Online Apps
> PR Wiki

system, my.usf.edu

Search

search this site...

Admin

> Site Admin
> Log out
> Wordpress
> XHTML

) AND ACTIVITIES

ake the Crisis Center of Tampa
Join USF PRSSA as we tour the
e Marketing Team. Interested in

nals will see the difference. You
hey want to hire post-
er.

Do you plan to vote in the upcoming election?

Yes
57%
No
30%
Undecided
13%

Total Votes : 30
See Dashboard »
Suggest A Poll

Dynamically-generated infographics.

To take the concept of the embedded Web infographic further, some graphics automatically update themselves as new data is collected and added to the source. Your website can display the results of an informal poll while poll data are still being collected, for example. Other websites with content to share may offer code snippets, plug-ins or widgets. You might add code to your site to display the week's highest-grossing movies or perhaps updated weather information.

Some infographics needs can't be met with pre-existing shared code. In these cases, Web developers can be hired to code solutions for mining, assembling and displaying the desired data. There is a wealth of existing data on the Internet that can be tapped to create all types of infographics. Or a developer can help you collect entirely new data. What if, for example, the local college Web team developed and posted an interactive campus map accessible via a website or a smartphone

Florida Public Broadcasting: A Timeline

Public broadcasting stations in Florida began providing educational services (1951)

The first official public broadcasting station was established in Florida (1970)

Florida Public Broadcasting Service was established; created and launched the Florida Channel (1977)

National Public Radio creates one of the largest news reporting agencies in the world (1977-1995)

PBS launches groundbreaking educational television programs (1977-1995)

Florida Public Broadcasting forms partnership with the Florida Division of Emergency Management (2002)

Florida Public Broadcasting launched the Florida PBS Learning Media initiative (2011)

| 1950s | 1960s | 1970s | 1980s | 1990s | 2000s | 2010s |

The PBS became a national network (1969)

The Florida Legislature began state funding of public broadcasting (1970)

PBS developed closed captioning for commercial stations (1980)

National Public Radio becomes the infrastructure for the national emergency alert system for the federal government (1998)

PBS launched the Raising Readers program (2008)

app? Imagine the instant ability to report, avoid and dispatch repairs to dangerous walkways, burned-out light bulbs and buildings in/accessible to wheelchairs.

MULTIMEDIA INFOGRAPHICS

The methods for generating infographics and the means for collecting data have changed. But so have infographics themselves. While charts and graphs were once largely static visuals printed in hardcopy, it is now possible to create rich multimedia infographics.

Consider a diagram showing the flow of air through a heating, ventilation and air conditioning (HVAC) system. In print, we would use arrows and ordinal numbers to signify directional and sequential flow. We would add a short block of explanatory type.

But in today's electronic formats, infographic designers would animate the airflow. High-end animation would simulate 3D perspective and might even feel something like a theme-park ride to viewers scooting along the ductwork.

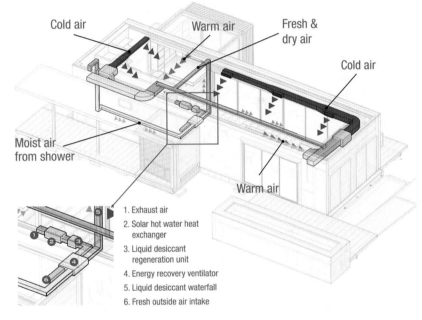

HEATING, VENTILATION AND AIR CONDITIONING (HVAC) SYSTEM

A BALANCED-ENERGY DESIGN FOR HOT, HUMID CLIMATES

Cold air

Warm air

Fresh & dry air

Cold air

Moist air from shower

Warm air

1. Exhaust air
2. Solar hot water heat exchanger
3. Liquid desiccant regeneration unit
4. Energy recovery ventilator
5. Liquid desiccant waterfall
6. Fresh outside air intake

In addition to typographic explainers, audio could add the recorded sound of water flowing through the liquid desiccant waterfall, along with studio sound effects and perhaps some music. Voiceover narration could add yet more information and help accommodate the visually impaired.

So when you're brainstorming infographics, don't forget to concept for interactivity and multimedia. No need to go gonzo, but take advantage where available and appropriate to your project's objectives.

Next generation diagrams. Active diagrams like the HVAC diagram above are great for print. For the Web, we can take the diagram one step further by adding interactive animation and audio.

Illustration by Dimitar Dimitrov, Team Florida, U.S. Department of Energy Solar Decathlon 2011.

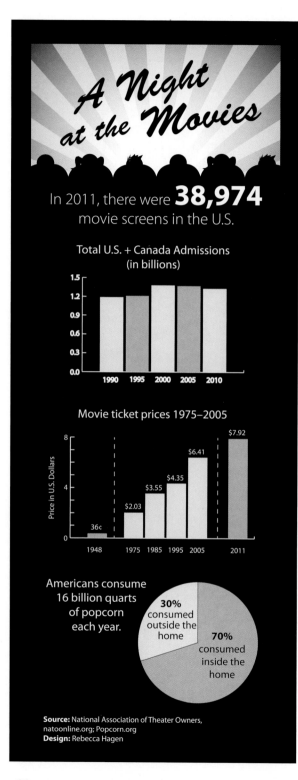

A Night at the Movies

In 2011, there were **38,974** movie screens in the U.S.

Total U.S. + Canada Admissions (in billions)

1990	1995	2000	2005	2010
1.2	1.2	~1.4	~1.4	~1.3

Movie ticket prices 1975–2005

Price in U.S. Dollars

1948	1975	1985	1995	2005	2011
36¢	$2.03	$3.55	$4.35	$6.41	$7.92

Americans consume 16 billion quarts of popcorn each year.

30% consumed outside the home

70% consumed inside the home

Source: National Association of Theater Owners, natoonline.org; Popcorn.org
Design: Rebecca Hagen

GRAPHICS PACKAGES

Gonzo multimedia infographics bring up a good point about combining and linking infographics. In the newsroom, a graphics package reports a story by using multiple types of graphics together. These often are anchored by a focal illustration or lead graphic and supported by related smaller graphs, charts, timelines, bio boxes, etc. The combination of well-crafted story, photos and infographics makes one-stop-shopping of visual appeal, in-depth information and at-a-glance comprehension.

We have two recommendations about packaging graphics:

1. Don't avoid packaging stories because you're not in the news business. Visual storytelling can be effective and useful in any public communication context, including PR, advertising and social networking.

2. Plan, plan, plan. Without serious coordination, a graphics package may result in visual information overload. Creating successful graphics packages requires significant preparation and cooperation. This may mean enlisting the help of photographers, illustrators, animators, researchers and writers, not to mention Web pros.

Most anyone can create simple charts and graphs. Effective graphics packages are the product of professional team effort.

Too much of a good thing? Infographics are excellent communicators, but too many in a homogenous layout makes you want to skip them all. Apply what you've learned about layout (remember focal point, movement and flow?) to make powerful infographics packages that engage and communicate.

A Night at the Movies

Lorem ipsum dolor sit amet, consectetur adipiscing elit. Duis vulputate ullamcorper tellus, ac feugiat neque accumsan ut. Aenean eget libero id sem porta dapibus. Nam sit amet lacus ac nunc euismod dignissim. Praesent pharetra ullamcorper neque, quis fermentum sem tempor nonLorem ipsum dolor sit amet, consectetur adipiscing elit. Duis vulputate ullamcorper tellus, ac feugiat neque accumsan ut. Aenean eget libero id sem porta dapibus. Nam sit amet lacus ac nunc euismod dignissim. Praesent pharetra ullamcorper neque, quis fermentum sem tempor.

40% of movie theater profits come from concessions sales

THE AVERAGE AMERICAN GOES TO THE MOVIES 4 TIMES A YEAR

Average Ticket Prices 1975–2005

(Bar chart with y-axis 0–8)
- 1975: 2
- 1985: 3.5
- 1995: 4.5
- 2005: 6.5

Total U.S. + Canada Admissions
(In Billions)

(Bar chart with y-axis 0.0–1.5)
- 1990: 1.2
- 1995: 1.2
- 2000: 1.4
- 2005: 1.4
- 2010: 1.35

Source: National Association of Theater Owners, natoonline.org; Popcorn.org
Design: Rebecca Hagen

CHARTS CAN LIE: INFOGRAPHIC ETHICS

Who supports the amendment?
Each pie chart below contains accurate data. Yet each chart tells a completely different story. Poorly executed charts can be downright misleading. In this case, plotting cherry-picked numbers creates a false impression.

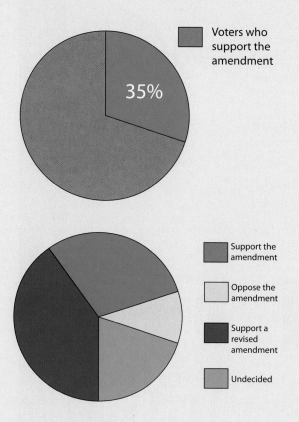

Voters who support the amendment

35%

Support the amendment

Oppose the amendment

Support a revised amendment

Undecided

As with all public communication, there are ethical guidelines to follow when creating infographics. Here we cover a few of the biggies:

Can you spell plagiarism and copyright? Never reproduce someone else's graphic without permission. And after you get permission, you must credit your source. Usually graphics sources are noted in the lower left corner. Same goes for attributing the sources of your information.

Stick with the facts, please. It should go without saying that guessing at or making up information to fill in the blanks of an infographic is a career-ending no-no. But we'll say it anyway: In infographics, the word is "information," not "fiction." Keep it factual from credible sources you can corroborate and attribute. If you have holes in your information, work harder at your research to fill in the blanks. Or drop the graphic.

Speaking of filling in the blanks with credible sources, do be critical about the sources of data. Who pays the research bills? What are the agendas of your sources and their funding arms? Perpetual skepticism is not simply an occupational hazard of the information business. It's a prerequisite. That fact segues to the ways so-called objective numbers can mislead.

Statistics (and people) can be shifty. There are two big ways you can get in trouble when using numerical data: 1. The numbers are flawed to begin with. 2. Your presentation of the numbers is questionable or misleading. Avoid both.

If you didn't collect the data for your infographic, put on that skeptical hat. Track down the original study to give it the once over. If you're clueless about stats, enlist the expertise of someone with a clue.

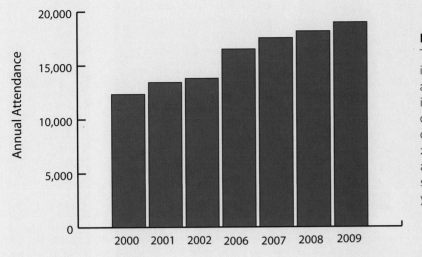

Missing something?
This bar chart gives the impression of consistent annual attendance increases. But the chart doesn't actually include data for the years 2003–2005. For all we know, attendance dropped sharply in those three years.

Even if the original data are good, your graphical representation of the data may not be. Some common ways to ruin perfectly good stats include:

» Cherry picking numbers to prove your point

» Failing to adjust money for economic inflation (or deflation)

» Inflating the significance of large numbers if they represent a small percentage of the whole (or vice versa)

» Specious comparisons (like comparing apples and oranges)

And there are others. So if you don't know what you're doing in the research and quantification department, partner with someone who does.

On the other hand, don't be one of those wimpy math-phobic communication types. Don't let numbers intimidate you. Read a book. Sign up for a class. Take an expert to lunch.

Being ethical also means accounting for diversity. Account for the diversity of your infographic audience. People respond best when you invite them to identify with your visual messages. Beyond being inclusive, stay alert for images and text that are inaccurate, inappropriate, unfair or injurious.

We've fast-forwarded from ancient cave painting to multimedia infographics. We've also suggested when infographics may be useful, along with some ethical hazards to avoid. Time for the fun part: the design how-to.

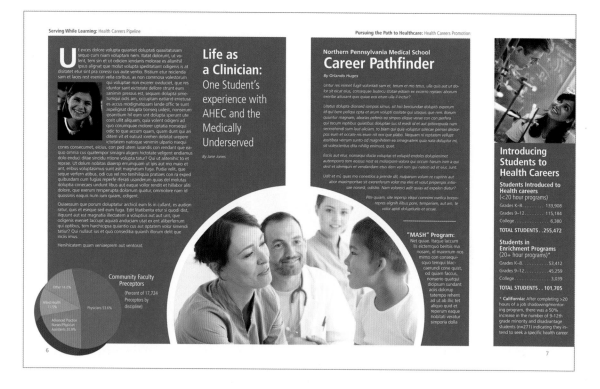

Serving While Learning: Health Careers Pipeline

Life as a Clinician:
One Student's experience with AHEC and the Medically Underserved
By Jane Jones

Community Faculty Preceptors
(Percent of 17,724 Preceptors by discipline)

Other 14.0%
Allied Health 11.5%
Advanced Practice Nurses/Physician Assistants 20.9%
Physicians 53.6%

Pursuing the Path to Healthcare: Health Careers Promotion

Northern Pennsylvania Medical School
Career Pathfinder
By Orlando Huges

"MASH" Program:

Introducing Students to Health Careers

Students Introduced to Health careers (<20 hour programs)
Grades K–8 133,908
Grades 9–12 115,184
College 6,380
TOTAL STUDENTS . .255,472

Students in Enrichment Programs (20+ hour programs)*
Grades K–8 53,412
Grades 9–12 45,259
College 3,039
TOTAL STUDENTS . . 101,705

* **California:** After completing >20 hours of a job shadowing/mentoring program, there was a 50% increase in the number of 9-12th grade minority and disadvantage students (n=271) indicating they intend to seek a specific health career

6

7

Not just for news reporting. Infographics and graphics packages, whether print or electronic, can be used to great effect in newsletters, magazines and annual reports.

Reproduced by permission of the National AHEC Organization.

DESIGNING INFOGRAPHICS

Everything we've covered so far will serve you well in designing and evaluating infographics, starting with research, brainstorming and thumbnail sketches. You'll also use what you know about grids and layouts, along with the elements and principles of design, including Gestalt. Your knowledge of color, typography, photos and illustrations applies here, too.

A word to the wise as you incorporate infographics into your layouts: Test before you launch. Never just assume folks understand your infographic. Allow us to share a cautionary tale. In 2004, Hurricane Charley devastated a completely unprepared Port Charlotte, Fla. In a research project shortly thereafter, a University of South Florida graduate student discovered two facts: One, people living in Port Charlotte misinterpreted the hurricane maps that weather forecasters use to predict the uncertain paths of storms. Study participants did not understand what the maps were supposed to communicate. Two, those widely used hurricane maps had never been audience-tested for comprehension, although scientists intended the maps to save lives. Sobering.

PARTS OF AN INFOGRAPHIC

Headline. Make it big, bold, clear and pithy.

Explainer. Also called "chatter," this block of text explains what the whole graphic is about.

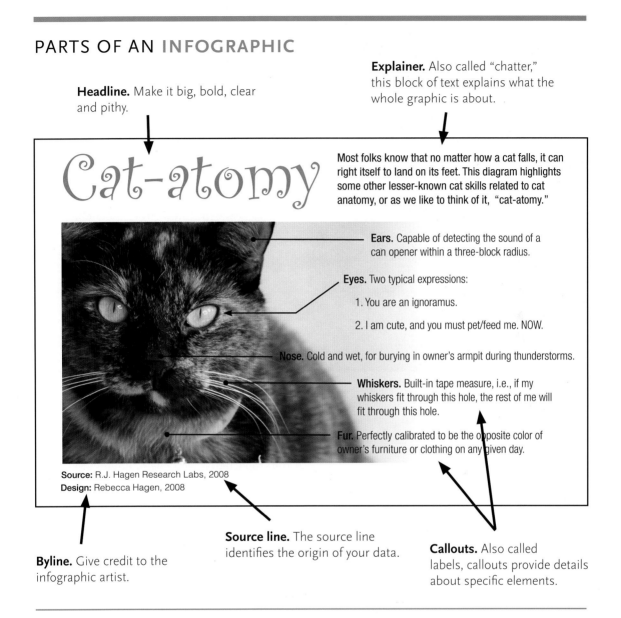

Cat-atomy

Most folks know that no matter how a cat falls, it can right itself to land on its feet. This diagram highlights some other lesser-known cat skills related to cat anatomy, or as we like to think of it, "cat-atomy."

Ears. Capable of detecting the sound of a can opener within a three-block radius.

Eyes. Two typical expressions:

1. You are an ignoramus.

2. I am cute, and you must pet/feed me. NOW.

Nose. Cold and wet, for burying in owner's armpit during thunderstorms.

Whiskers. Built-in tape measure, i.e., if my whiskers fit through this hole, the rest of me will fit through this hole.

Fur. Perfectly calibrated to be the opposite color of owner's furniture or clothing on any given day.

Source: R.J. Hagen Research Labs, 2008
Design: Rebecca Hagen, 2008

Source line. The source line identifies the origin of your data.

Byline. Give credit to the infographic artist.

Callouts. Also called labels, callouts provide details about specific elements.

While accounting for audiences and employing the basics of good design, follow these tips on designing infographics:

Design tips for all types of infographics.

Infographics must be able to stand alone. This is perhaps the most important thing to remember when designing any type of infographic.

This page: Ilamus awt ex explabo recto ublama nam et ad vere veliti upiditi peretduonio es et aphenti ur, quaemo reprecibora nolupidd dolor o ventis andam antesibum.

Opposite. Ipsa punt iliunt veliqu dolorett hillout nullam, animd dolione serchita quia soluptani, atibus

Florida Conservation Monthly **47**

Don't forget unity. Choose a color scheme for your charts and graphs that coordinates with your overall design scheme.

*Small embedded photo ©
Nicholas Larento - fotolia.com*

If people are scanners searching for interesting things to look at, then the infographic may be the only thing the viewer sees. Infographics shouldn't rely on information buried somewhere else.

Thoroughly research your topic before you begin. It does make sense to understand the material you're attempting to illustrate. You won't be able to facilitate others' understanding if you don't get it, either.

Use a grid to organize and structure your infographic. Think of your infographic as a design within a design. The same rules for good layouts work for specific graphics and infographics, too. As in larger layouts, a grid provides order and organization for the various parts of your layout, such as explainers and callouts. Aligning elements to a grid provides cohesion and unity, and it will help your reader understand the flow of the graphic.

Group things. As you create your graphic elements, be sure to cluster related items, and leave ample negative space between items to prevent confusion. Employ proximity. Remember, clustering is good, and clutter is bad.

Choose a design scheme compatible with the overall design. Think colors, fonts and other design details. If you're creating an infographic for an existing website or serial publication, there may be a style guide that specifies the look of design elements. If there is no style guide, you're hired. You get the job. Create a style guide in order to maintain similarity and unity.

Use care if your graphic must appear in black and white. Color is one of your greatest allies, providing organization and way-finding for viewers. If you can't use color for your infographic, be clever with grayscale. But each gray should vary from the last one by at least 20 percent, or else the eye has a hard time telling them apart.

Give credit where credit is due. Attribute. Cite. This goes for the source of your data and the source of any photos or illustrations you use.

Minimize ornamentation. You're shooting for a clean comprehensible infographic. Cutesy backgrounds and other embellishments can detract from your message. Easy does it.

Keep the writing tight. Keep headlines and titles short. If possible, explain your subject and purpose in six words or less. For explainers and label text, keep your writing concise and in the third person. Use action verbs.

Tips for common infographics.

Maps. Put your map on a grid and eliminate unnecessary details, called "map fat." Streamline and simplify. Be sure to include a scale showing distance. Include a legend as needed and directional indicators (at least North, if not all four directions), and indicate reference points for your reader.

Pie charts. Pie charts are intended to show parts of a whole. The full circle represents 100 percent. So don't forget to indicate what the "whole" is. This ain't no mystery. Then slice your pie portions accurately.

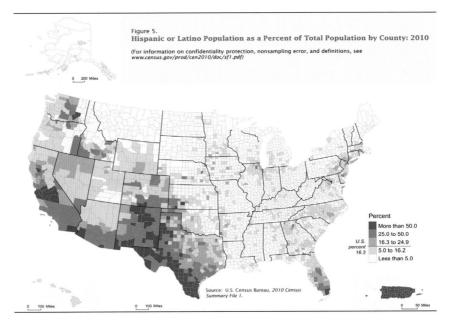

Figure 5.
Hispanic or Latino Population as a Percent of Total Population by County: 2010

(For information on confidentiality protection, nonsampling error, and definitions, see www.census.gov/prod/cen2010/doc/sf1.pdf)

Percent
- More than 50.0
- 25.0 to 50.0
- 16.3 to 24.9
- 5.0 to 16.2
- Less than 5.0

U.S. percent 16.3

Source: U.S. Census Bureau, *2010 Census Summary File 1.*

Data maps. Maps are commonly used to show location. But plotting location data also can be effective in identifying patterns. The colors in this map clearly identify Hispanic population centers in the United States.

Map reproduced from The Hispanic Population: 2010. 2010 Census Briefs, May 2011. United States Census Bureau.

PARTS OF A MAP

Maps are a common infographic form. There are several types, including locator maps, geological maps and statistical maps.

Reproduced by permission of USF Health.

USF Health Orthopaedic Surgery and Sports Medicine Center

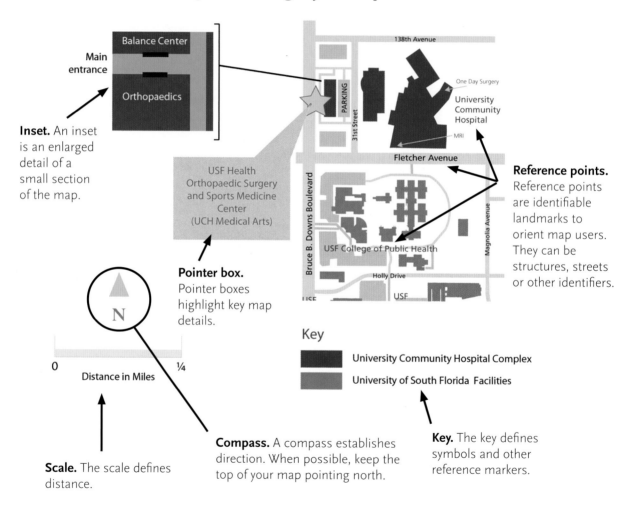

Inset. An inset is an enlarged detail of a small section of the map.

Pointer box. Pointer boxes highlight key map details.

Reference points. Reference points are identifiable landmarks to orient map users. They can be structures, streets or other identifiers.

Scale. The scale defines distance.

Compass. A compass establishes direction. When possible, keep the top of your map pointing north.

Key. The key defines symbols and other reference markers.

Semantic analysis of tweets around the #internetsummit hashtag
Internet & Technology Summit 2009 • Tampa, Florida

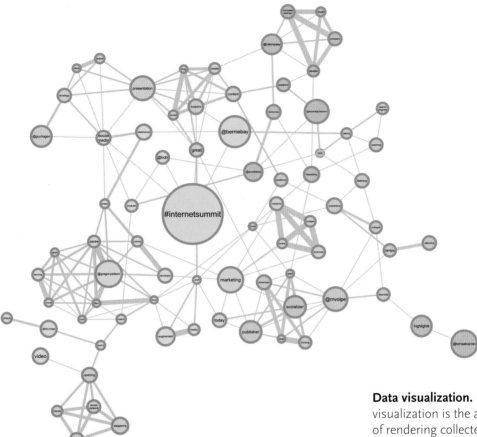

Fever charts. Known for their spikes and valleys, fever charts are good for showing change over time. A background grid helps readers quickly grasp the trends. Remember algebra, slope and "rise over run"? Didn't think so. But you do need to know that the Y-axis equals the rise going up and down vertically. What are you measuring? The stockmarket? Rainfall? Daily traffic? That's your Y. The X-axis is always time or "run," running left (from the past) to right (into the future). In 3D, the Z-axis pushes out towards the viewer.

Bar charts. Bar charts are good for comparing things. Generally, use horizontal bars—except if you're dealing with time. If your bar chart shows change over time, revert back to the idea of time as horizontal "run" going left to right, and lay in your bars as vertical blocks and towers. In either case, label each bar with the actual number

Data visualization. Data visualization is the art of rendering collected data in graphic form. On the simple end of data visualizations are basic pie and bar charts. On the opposite end are complex diagrams such as the above semantic analysis.

Reproduced by permission of Guy Hagen.

it represents. Once again, a grid in the background helps clarify relationships visually.

Timelines. Timelines are excellent for sharing history, providing context, demonstrating cause and effect, etc. The rules say it's good practice to limit a timeline to 10–20 items or "frames." The best timelines are visually to scale or proportional to the time range they represent, which suggests enlisting the help of a grid again. Or think in terms of the timeline-equivalent of a measuring tape segmenting and parsing out your particular units of time. If your timeline includes giant gaps, a list format may be a better choice.

Diagrams & illustrations. These are the most complex of the graphic styles and usually require real artistic skill to execute. Diagrams and illustrations are best when kept simple. Again, the rules for good composition will help you set up strong diagrams and illustrations. Give them focal points, as well as rhythm and flow.

Like all visual communication, the best infographics provide accurate information simply. Practice that, and you can't go wrong. However, we're not finished covering visual storytelling. Next up, storyboards for planning video.

▶ TRY THIS

1. Design an infographic bio for yourself. First imagine a real-world use for it, such as putting it on a social media page or adding it to your digital resume. Then design it accordingly.

2. Design a multimedia timeline demonstrating either the history of infographics or the development of multimedia infographics. Research comes first. No cheating.

3. Put your hands on some credible research statistics (we like the U.S. Bureau of Labor Statistics at http://www.bls.gov/). Using the research project's findings, thumbnail a graphics package for the Web. Execute one statistical graph or chart from your package.

4. Following the rules for map design, execute a floor plan of one room in your home or office.

Before we leave off talking about visuals—photos, illustrations and infographics—let's cover storyboarding, too. Storyboards lay out the visual stories of planned video and film, including the animated sorts. In most cases, then, storyboarding involves representing moving pictures and sound with still pictures and type.

A storyboard visualizes the entire project in the form of individual scenes, shots or screens. A concept storyboard distills the project down to the minimum number of views necessary to tell the story. A production storyboard or a shooting storyboard provides more detailed information for a production crew.

If you're planning to produce video or film of some kind, you will enlist preproduction, production and postproduction assistance from professionals. But you still may find yourself concepting a storyboard for a TV commercial or spot, a public service announcement (PSA), a corporate video, a video news release (VNR) or even an animated banner ad. Sometimes a feature news film package also benefits from a storyboard.

Whatever the project or your role in the process, this chapter gives you some of the basics of storyboarding.

GETTING STARTED

Once you have a storyboard project, you have to think about how to tell the story shot by shot. Much of what we've covered in earlier chapters comes to bear in storyboarding. You begin with research and brainstorming for a concept. You account for format and aspect ratio, and you experiment with visual composition using thumbnail sketches.

The elements of design—space, line, shape, size, texture, value—become your tools for telling visual stories. As you'll see, the principles of design, including focal point, contrast, balance, movement, rhythm and unity, also become important storyboarding tools.

You don't have to be an accomplished illustrator to create a storyboard, either. You can indicate your ideas with rough drawing and stick figures, just as you would with thumbnail sketches. Or you can use, mix and match stock images, whether

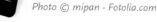
Photo © mipan - Fotolia.com

S is stooped down tying shoe, stands up in time for ball!

Shock, runs out of frame

photography or line art. If you fancy yourself a photographer, you might even grab a camera.

Our point is that you already have a fairly large visual toolbox for dramatic storyboarding. So take advantage of it. Your eyes, however, continue to be the most useful tool in your toolbox. As to acquiring new tools for storyboarding, below we provide some necessities regarding:

» Framing the Shot

» Perspective

» POV

» Camera Angle

» Movement

» Continuity

» Transitions

» Lighting

» Type

» Audio

Storyboards, from thumbnail sketch to screen grab. Student filmmaker Sarah Wilson first sketched her ideas before committing her cast and crew to the week of shooting and editing it took to produce her award-winning short film "Rhapsody." In the sequence shown here, the POV is omniscient. Notice how the first shot of this scene in the final film demonstrates a low-angle shot from below, as well as a canted camera angle producing a dynamically tilted horizon line.

"Rhapsody" storyboards and screen captures reproduced by permission of Sarah Wilson.

FRAMING THE SHOT

Your direction for how to frame a scene within the four corners of the visual screen is called framing the shot. Common shots include

A VISUAL GLOSSARY OF WAYS TO FRAME THE SHOT

Extreme Close-up

Medium Close-up

Full Close-up

Wide Close-up

Close Shot

Medium Close Shot

Medium Shot

Medium Full Shot

Full Shot

Long Shot

Montage

Split-screen

variations on the close-up, medium, full and long shot. Other frames include the split-screen and montage.

An establishing shot orients viewers to the visual scene in order to avoid confusion before proceeding with the story.

Advertising giant David Ogilvy reminded would-be advertisers to make the product the hero. A beauty shot frames an object or product to show off its best visual features, as if it were a movie star. "All right, Mr. DeMille, I'm ready for my close-up," said the aging film star Gloria Swanson playing an aging film star in the 1950 film "Sunset Boulevard."

The farther the transparent "fourth wall" of the screen lies from the focal point of the shot, the more impersonal the symbolic tone. As the fourth wall moves closer to the focal point, the audience feels increasingly intimate with the focal point, whether it's a person or a thing.

PERSPECTIVE

Perspective becomes especially important in film and video, thus in storyboarding, too. If framing refers to how the shot crops the viewer's visual field, perspective refers to how deeply the viewer sees into the shot.

Where the horizon line sits in the composition communicates distance to the viewer. Atmospheric perspective via value as well as linear perspective via flowing sightline and vanishing point also help establish the scale of distance. Speaking of scale, perspective by relative size of objects in the shot can enrich the sense of distance, such as framing a sweeping vista in the background with two human figures in the foreground. And remember that depth of field refers to what in the shot remains in focus and what goes out of focus, whether foreground, midground, background or some combination.

More than communicating literal spatial distance in the narrative, perspective also communicates a sense of emotional distance or, conversely, intimacy. Perspective also may communicate symbolic

Establishing shots orient viewers. In the first frame, a third-person POV establishes the scene: a conversation. Subsequent frames then alternate between the two characters' first-person POVs.

Reproduced by permission of the artist, Will Payne.

meanings such as a sense of freedom from wide-open spaces versus the tension and anxiety of oppressive low-ceiling closed spaces. Yet a small close space also may seem warm and sheltering while a vast sky or plain may send a lonesome message about human frailty.

POV

Perspective also leads to considering the camera's point of view or POV. If you think about the camera (or the screen) as an eye that looks, you need to think about whose eye is supposed to be doing the looking. While the viewing audience is always the implied eye, you can nudge the audience to identify with different points of view in the story.

Do you want the audience to remain an invisible omniscient third-person eye observing the story?

Or do you want the audience to participate in the story by seeing with the same eye as the protagonist? For example, both protagonist and audience, through the camera lens or screen, may look the villain in the eye to stare her or him down.

Or should the audience see as the villain sees, while she or he sneaks up to peer over an unsuspecting shoulder? In Alfred Hitchcock's famous shower scene from the 1960 "Psycho," Hitchcock famously shifts the audience's POV between victim and villain.

If two people onscreen are to have a conversation, you probably need to provide a third-person establishing shot of the two people framed together if you are going to alternate back and forth between the two characters' first-person POVs.

Sometimes you want the viewer to ignore the fourth wall in order to participate in an admittedly one-way conversation with an onscreen personality who maybe offers a how-to, reads the news, sells a product or runs a yoga class.

In short, plan the POV.

Perspective done four ways. 1) The "horizon line" in the upper third of the frame indicates distance. 2) The road's "linear vanishing point" also communicates distance. 3) The car's large "relative size" says nearby; the buildings' small sizes say faraway. 4) "Atmospheric perspective" is achieved by using light color value to make the skyline seem to recede into the background while the car's dark value feels closer to the viewer.

Reproduced by permission of the artist, Will Payne.

CAMERA ANGLE

Planning the camera's angle also relates to POV and perspective. In addition to shooting straight on or level, there are other ways to position the camera's angle for effect. A canted or tilted camera angle creates a sense of unease by tilting the horizon line and upsetting the viewer's visual equilibrium.

Framing the shot from above, as if the camera were looking down on the focal point, can make the focal point seem small, communicating symbolic insignificance and powerlessness. Shooting the focal point from below can have the opposite effect, communicating the focal point's larger size and power. Both angles also can make for a comic effect because they tend to distort the proportions of the focal point. So be careful. Hard news, assumed to be objective, would avoid special effects angles.

You don't always have to shoot from the front, either. You may decide to shoot from behind, from the side or at a 45-degree angle. Mix it up, but do it with a visual communication purpose compatible with your subject matter and tone.

MOVEMENT

The design principle of movement shifts from being implied in stop-action pictures to being literal in live-action ones. Storyboarding movement shots involves knowing another vocabulary.

For example, a pan or panning indicates a stationary camera that sweeps across the scene. The effect is that of turning your head to look around. In a truck, usually accomplished with a camera on a dolly, the camera trucks sideways across the scene. The effect is like rubbernecking from a moving car.

Handheld refers to the cameraperson holding the camera as she or he walks or runs through the scene—resulting in a bumpy visual ride. This can increase realism, as in breaking news footage, but may be difficult to watch for long periods of time. The steadicam is a kind of harness the cameraperson wears to hold the camera steady as she or he shoots a hand-held scene.

Camera angles. Use camera angle to help tell your visual story. Starting in the upper left, these frames demo shooting from the side, from below, from above and, last, from behind at a wide angle.

Reproduced by permission of the artist, Will Payne.

In a tracking shot, a stationary camera tracks along with a moving focal point. Think of the classic 1967 Patterson Bigfoot film tracking a tall hairy arm-swinging two-legged creature looking right at the camera as it walks off into the woods. Hoax or not, it's a memorable example of a tracking shot.

Push shots push into the scene. In a zoom, a stationary camera pushes into the scene by using the lens to zoom in on the focal point. In a dolly shot, the camera itself, positioned on a dolly, moves or pushes toward the focal point.

As is often the case, purity here is not required. You might achieve several effects at once. The infamous Bigfoot tracking shot is obviously handheld. We've seen movie scenes in which the camera pans and zooms from atop a trucking dolly.

CONTINUITY

Unity is critical when you're telling one story using many shots. Each shot must build on the previous one and prepare for the next. That makes for narrative continuity. Does the visual story hold together as

Zoom. First the establishing the shot (this can't be good). Next the push into the scene for a close-up (not a happy camper).

Reproduced by permission of the artist, Will Payne.

Movement. This sequence demonstrates tracking. A stationary camera tracks along with the onscreen action-as-focal-point, which here is moving left to right. The effect is like turning your head to watch. In the example, the composition of each frame keeps the bicyclist positioned to the left of the scene but moving toward the negative space positioned to the right. Without that negative space, the action would appear to "hit a brick wall" or just disappear off screen.

one cohesive narrative from beginning to end and from shot to shot? Are the POV and chronology clear to avoid confusing the audience? Is the dramatic or comedic timing impeccable?

Think of your storyboard as having an obvious beginning, middle and end. Make each pull its visual storytelling workload. Beginnings should capture attention immediately—no warm-up necessary—and establish the relevant W's. Middles do exposition and drama. That's the convey information and evoke emotions part. Endings put closure on the tale or ask for the sale. Advertising always ends with a call to action, whether explicit or implicit.

Speaking of advertising, timing takes on special significance if you only have 10, 15 or 30 seconds of exposition. You can't storyboard a :60 or even a :12 if you only have :10.

Regardless of the type of project, make sure your storyboard is doable given your time constraints. Where appropriate, indicate the timing of shots on the storyboard, use a watch to test your timing and make sure your math is accurate.

TRANSITIONS

In film and video, part of continuity is transitioning or segueing between shots and scenes. The most common type of transition is the simple cut from one shot to the next, such as cutting from an establishing shot of two actors conversing to a close-up of one of the actors speaking.

A cutaway "cuts away" from the main action by inserting something else going on simultaneously in the scene. If the scene shows two arguing people standing beside a car stopped on the side of the road, inserting a shot of the dog's head poked out the car window watching the argument is a cutaway. A shot of cars whizzing past the arguing people would be a cutaway, too.

A cut-in or insert "cuts in" or "inserts" a close-up shot of something significant to the meaning of the scene. In the scene of two people arguing beside a car stopped on the side of the road, inserting a shot of the flat tire on the stopped car would be a cut-in underscoring the reason for the stopped car and ensuing argument.

You have to be careful with cutting so the viewer can keep up with the chronology of events. Some kinds of transitions are helpful for indicating different events occurring simultaneously, perhaps even in different locations, or, conversely, flashbacks in time. But, again, make sure the viewer is keeping up.

The wipe, dissolve and fade each transition between shots in the manner their names imply. These transitions, while time-honored in the hands of professionals, may come off as cheesy or kitschy if you're not careful, however.

LIGHTING

In storyboarding, you can use light and shadow for dramatic effect. Here the principle of contrast comes into play.

A key light is the main or key light source in the shot, whether natural or artificial. Fill light supplements the key light by filling in unwanted shadows for less contrast. Backlight is a light source used to highlight the focal point from behind to give it contrast and dimension. Most shots require a combination of all three light sources to produce what viewers would perceive as a natural or realistic effect.

For additional drama, you might consider the amount and direction of light. Soft light or high key evens out the shadows to decrease harsh contrasts. It makes people and products look more attractive. ("I'm ready for my close-up.") Hard light or low key emphasizes shadows, thus contrast, including shadows on people's faces—an interesting if less-than-flattering effect.

A key light shining directly from above (over lighting) or from below (under lighting) can form sinister shadows, especially on people's faces. Backlighting can make a focal point appear angelic with a halo effect or make the focal point appear powerful or significant (think backlit grand stage entrances of silhouetted super heroes, rock stars or pro wrestlers). Side lighting casts long shadows and increases the sense of three-dimensional space, as opposed to the flattening effect of soft light.

As you storyboard, think about how you might cast light as a supporting actor in your story. All these effects work for inanimate

Opposite: Graphic by Karl Golombisky and Rebecca Hagen.

Clips courtesy of: Doug Alvarez, Karl Golombisky and Andrew Bailes.

LIGHTING
FILM NOIR

Film noir uses high-contrast lighting to suggest the "darker" side of human nature.

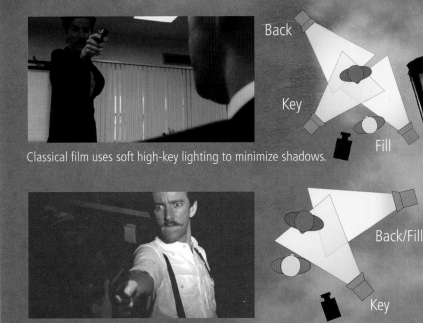

Classical film uses soft high-key lighting to minimize shadows.

Film noir employs hard low-key lighting to create dramatic shadows.

Here a single-source backlight creates a not-so-angelic halo effect.

Lower third. In TV business lingo, "lower third" refers to supers, which mostly appear somewhere in the lower third of the screen.

Remember the rule of thirds? And foreground, midground and background? Foreground, at the bottom of the screen, appears closer than mid- or background. Hence, supers get the lower third.

The lower third super might be copy or an image like a logo. It can be static or a crawl. But it must be visible and readable, especially if overlaid on moving images. Why is Channel 7's "Morning News" super readable?

Photo © David Lawrence - Fotolia.com

objects, too, as well as infographics. A side light on a pie chart gives it shadow and dimension. Go easy, though. Like a backlit super hero, overly dramatic lighting not only may seem cartoon-like when that isn't your intent but also may distract viewers from your visual communication purpose.

TYPE

Last we move on to dealing with words and sounds, whether onscreen or off and whether part of the show or merely behind-the-camera direction.

As for onscreen type, a super is any type or graphic superimposed over a picture. A crawl is moving type running—or crawling—across the screen. You see this on cable news channels or when your area comes under a severe weather alert.

When you super, design for typographic readability and legibility, whether the super is static or animated. Contrast, thus color and value, are crucial, whether you reverse or not.

AUDIO

In a chapter about storyboarding in a book about visual communication, audio becomes the proverbial elephant in the room. Hello—sound? If your storyboard project includes audio, you obviously have to represent it visually on the storyboard by using textual direction.

Using a script setup, type your audio direction to correspond with visuals. Make your intent abundantly clear, including who is speaking when.

Also specify direction for things such as music, sound effects (SFX) or visual effects (FX). An off-screen voice, narrator or announcer (ANNCR) is called a voiceover, indicated as VO. Background music is called a music bed or track.

As far as dialogue goes, nothing is more difficult to write well. And nothing is worse than stilted unnatural repartee. So fair warning. We advise amateurs to develop concepts that avoid multiple characters engaged in dialogue, especially in extended conversations, which provide little visual interest anyway. "Show, don't tell."

On the other hand, don't shortchange audio because you've become a visual communicator. Audio—ear candy—can make or break your visual story. Think creatively and include the details on your storyboard.

AFTER THE STORYBOARD

After the storyboard and before the actual production shoot, there may be an in-between stage that cheaply simulates what the storyboard might look like as live action. This generally is done using software to cut together rough approximations of the shots. It might be accomplished with stock, archived or homemade footage or stills that come as near as possible to the storyboard's visuals. Or you might use animated illustrations or cartoons.

These kinds of preproduction pieces have been called spec cuts, videomatics, animatics and ripomatics. They tend to be more impressive, thus persuasive, when you're presenting your storyboard to the conceptually challenged or to the person holding the purse strings. But, lest we wax creative snobbery, speculative cuts also can be helpful as narrative, shot and timing trials before you start spending big bucks on production.

And that leads us, at last, to some final advice concerning production budgets: KISS. Video production is expensive, and film, even more so. Hollywood director Cecil B. DeMille developed a reputation for visual spectacle using elaborate productions and, as the expression goes, casts of thousands. But he had the financial backing of the Hollywood studio system. We're guessing you work with more modest budgets.

If you're a beginner, focus on generating a killer concept. No amount of money can make a bad concept look good. The best concepts are usually the most parsimonious anyway. Don't script for two warm bodies when one will do. Don't storyboard an on-location shoot if you can get away with a studio shoot. Don't storyboard multiple sets if one is sufficient. And don't storyboard more shots than necessary. If it isn't vital to advancing the story, cut it.

Be smart, have fun, and, as they say, "Break a leg."

If you're a beginner, focus on generating a killer concept. No amount of money can make a bad concept look good.

▶ TRY THIS

1. Develop a concept for a short educational video on storyboarding. Then execute a storyboard for your concept.

2. Storyboard a favorite scene from a favorite movie. Account for:

» Framing	» Movement	» Type
» Perspective	» Continuity	» Audio
» POV	» Transitions	
» Camera Angle	» Lighting	

How does each contribute to the narrative?

3. Storyboard a TV commercial currently running. Account for:

» Framing	» Movement	» Type
» Perspective	» Continuity	» Audio
» POV	» Transitions	
» Camera Angle	» Lighting	

How does each contribute to the narrative?

4. Remember the Patterson Bigfoot film? Let's get silly to make a serious point. Choose three of the following and storyboard a few conceptual frames for each:

» A music video starring Bigfoot

» A televised interview with Bigfoot

» A reality-style episodic show featuring Bigfoot

» A wildlife cinematic extravaganza on Bigfoot in its natural habitat

» A sports highlights-style review of Bigfoot sightings

» An infomercial teaming up Patterson and Bigfoot to sell product

» A corporate training video using Bigfoot as the spokes model

» A PSA of some kind using Bigfoot as the spokes—ahem—person

This is definitely a use-your-imagination no-holds-barred exercise. Don't forget that "experts" believe the Patterson Bigfoot is female.

5. Storyboard a new :15 TV spot for a commercial consumer product currently in your kitchen, pantry, laundry room or bathroom. Start with a unique selling proposition (USP) or claim about the product. Then develop a concept. You know the rest of the drill by now.

Concept Storyboard

Job Number: Date: Page___of___

Title: Length:

Client: Writer:

1. Time:

Audio:

2. Time:

Audio:

3. Time:

Audio:

4. Time:

Audio:

5. Time:

Audio:

6. Time:

Audio:

7. Time:

Audio:

8. Time:

Audio:

9. Time:

Audio:

Iodized Salt TV

Date: 11.30.09

Project: Salt-TV-001

Length: :15

Creative Team: Susan Snyder & Meaghan Rose

SFX: children playing in the pool (throughout)

1st Child: A right angle is 90 degrees.

2nd Child: The U.S. has a bicameral Congress.

3rd Child: Haiku is a form of Japanese poetry.

ANNCR (VO): The iodine in iodized salt is essential for healthy brain development.

Embedded photos reprinted by permission of Kathi Roberts.

12 | MULTIMEDIA COMPONENTS
sometimes more is more

Combining media forms is nothing new. Silent films, for example, interspersed still type frames throughout the movie to deliver dialogue and establish context, as theater organists provided dramatic musical accompaniments.

Today's multimedia may combine type, image, audio, video and infographics, not to mention interactivity. Think searchable databases and archives, user-generated content and social networking. All this must be available to active "users" on their desktop PCs, laptops, smartphones, tablets and TVs.

Multimedia: The early years. In the days before "talkies," live musicians played scores to accompany silent films. Note the Tampa Theater's orchestra pit at the bottom of the photo.

Tampa Theater, 1930. Burgert Brothers collection. Courtesy, Tampa-Hillsborough County Public Library System.

But don't drop out because you fear the technical. Even simple digital multimedia adds a lot of capability to the visual communicator's toolbox. Here we begin with basics for novice visual communicators.

First, multimedia design is implemented in degrees. A simple digital slideshow may enhance an otherwise static website, while elsewhere gamers enter online virtual worlds to participate in massively multiuser online role playing games (MMORPG).

Second, whether deployed a little or a lot, digital multimedia means multisensory. It allows for communication via sound and touch in addition to sight. (No such thing as smell-o-vision yet, but anything is possible...)

Third, multimedia makes interactivity possible. Users participate in providing input and feedback. Multimedia also gives users control as far as when to access content, quantity of information, direction of exploration and pacing of the digital experience.

Enabling user-control, however, reminds us that not all users have the same abilities. From the outset, you should design not only multiple ways for your users to interact with your content but also alternative ways your users are able to access content. How will you accommodate, for example, the deaf community? Or folks with limited hand dexterity or the visually impaired? These are front-end planning issues.

It's true that some kinds of multimedia components remain better off in the hands of professionals. However, there are simple multimedia production tools available for the nonprofessional. Many are available for free online or come preinstalled on your computer. Just be aware that not all mobile and tablet devices support all Web-based applications and proceed accordingly.

THUMBNAILS, STORYBOARDS & SITE MAPS

Hold up. Before you log on, remember to step away from the computer for planning. By definition, multimedia is complex, whether it's a clickable interactive commercial or a big investigative story with text, photos, footage and interactive infographics. So brainstorm concept, design and organization with paper and pencil. Or perhaps tablet and stylus.

Rough sketch some thumbnail layouts that imagine how all your content might go together. For slideshows, video and animation, use storyboarding techniques to nail beginnings, middles and ends, along with transitions, pacing and timing. And for multi-page Web projects, site map content relationships along with user flow via intuitive links and navigation.

Better yet, to maximize creative synergy, do the preliminary noodling with the whole team sitting in the same room—in which case you'll need the big whiteboard and some colored markers.

WORKING WITH IMAGES

In the attention-grabbing department, images win hands-down. But still images are—you know—still. Turned into slideshows or placed in interactive image galleries, however, even still images become engaging multimedia components. Newsrooms tend to prefer interactive image galleries over automated slideshows because they seem to generate more viewing traffic. Yet an image gallery may offer viewing options that include a slideshow format.

Sorting, cropping and editing photos needs to happen before you begin assembling your slideshow or image

Pick just one. Don't let your slide transitions outshine your actual slides. Pick one simple transition style and stick with it. We recommend cutting and fading as opposed to exploding and twirling out of control.

Image galleries. There are many inexpensive and free image gallery plug-ins available for displaying your photos on websites and blogs. The gallery at right includes an interactive feature slideshow and thumbnail gallery.

gallery. We already covered the rules for dealing with photos in "Chapter 9: Adding Visual Appeal." Those best practices apply here. Plus, always work on a *copy* of the original photo; save and protect the original to be available for another day. Don't forget to optimize resolution; 72 dpi remains the standard for photos destined for screen viewing.

Slideshows.

When creating slideshows from multiple images, consider image content, transitions and user controls. For a simple set of images intended to add interest to a Web banner or content area, choose quality images united by a theme (color, subject, etc.) with similar orientation.

If your slideshow is intended to tell a story, apply a video-like approach to selecting images. A storyboard of sequential sketches helps organize the storyline and assist with image selection. A storyboard also helps if the slideshow includes a narrative. Select photos with tight, medium and wide angles for variety. Use the best quality images you can, but keep in mind that an image that conveys narrative continuity may be a better choice than a technically superior one.

Slideshow transitions. Slide programs offer many transition styles. Avoid the kid-in-a-candy-store impulse to use one of each. Simple tends to be best so choose one transition style and stay with it. Traditional cuts always work. In the end, you want your slideshow to be about the images or the story, not the funky transitions you used.

WORKING WITH AUDIO

Audio may seem off-topic in a discussion about visual communication. But audio plays a role in multimedia. Audio is the narration or natural (nat) or ambient (ambi) sound on captured video. It's the background track or bed in Web and DVD projects. Short audio clips as sound effects or SFX signal action, such as the sound of a button being pressed or email being sent. Audio can highlight what's important. It also reinforces tone and mood.

Can you hear it? Audio is a powerful multimedia component. Try to imagine the sounds that would accompany the image above.

Back in the heyday of radio, great audio was "theater of the mind." That continues to be the way you should think about audio production. But if you find yourself unable to enlist an audio pro, stick to the basics. In general:

1. Use ambient audio sparingly, especially for trigger sounds like button clicks. A little goes a long way.

2. Background music should enhance the overall tone and message of the project. It should not be expected to set the tone by itself.

3. Give your user controls, preferably start, stop, pause and volume. We've all been blown out of our desk chairs by a Web soundtrack that was a big surprise, too loud or both.

4. When the audio is narration, an interview or some other situation where clarity is crucial, capture the highest quality audio possible. Use the best microphone you can—which may not be the one on your digital recorder or video camera. Your audience is more likely to forgive a poor quality image than an inaudible soundtrack.

Where to get audio.

Ambient sounds and music as well as trigger sounds like button clicks are available for purchase from digital stock sites. There are also websites that offer free sounds and music. Be aware, however, that free downloads may come with restrictions or attribution requirements. Make sure you respect both.

Pacing. Whether slow and measured or fast and frenetic, the duration of your images and the speed of transitions set an overall tone for your slideshow. If you expect viewers to absorb and appreciate your slideshow content, give them enough time to do so.

The "Ken Burns Effect." The Ken Burns effect is a gradual simultaneous zoom in or out and panning across still images in a slideshow. Burns used the technique when featuring historical photographs, letters and maps in his documentaries. The effect is readily available on consumer-grade video software, but apply it with caution. Use it if the technique will enhance the slideshow's communication function, not because you think it looks cool.

Captions/cutlines. Not all slideshows require captioning. But news contexts probably do. In addition to having a narrative beginning, middle and end, three rules apply here: One, make the caption/cutline "go with" the image. Oh, yes, we have seen it go the other way. Two, don't state the obvious. A photo of a black dog doesn't need a cutline that reads, "This is a black dog." Instead, supplement the obvious, such as "Duke, a 6-year-old rescue lab/shepherd mix with exemplary manners, loves children." Three, do cover what's not obvious but relevant, such as a photo's W's. Clearly identify who, what, when and where. And don't forget to fact-check and proof. Also be kind and credit the photographers.

In control. If your website includes video and audio clips, give your audience access to the controls. At the very least, provide volume control, start and stop buttons.

To loop or not to loop. You can set a slideshow to loop continuously or a particular number of times before stopping. Your choice here depends on where your slideshow will be displayed. If it is to be the backdrop of a Web banner, then a subtle continuous loop might be appropriate. If your slideshow is intended to tell a story, letting it play through once is sufficient. As a rule, it's a good idea to provide user controls on video clips such as story slideshows. Viewers appreciate access to buttons that start, stop, rewind, pause and adjust volume.

Interactive image galleries. Interactive image galleries do provide your audience with a more controlled method of viewing your images. Some photo-editing programs have the ability to generate Web-ready image galleries from your selected images. All you have to do is upload the files to your Web server.

Photo-sharing websites offer similar options. Sign-up is typically free, and once you have an account you upload your images. You can organize your images into galleries for viewing and provide a link to your shared gallery from your main website. If you prefer to display those images within your own website, some photo-sharing sites offer plug-ins or widgets you can incorporate into your Web page. Plug-ins and widgets allow photos stored on the photo-sharing site to display how and where you want them.

Slideshows with Audio.

Now think about combining everything you've learned about photo slideshows with our tips for working with audio. Hey, you're ready to produce audio slideshows. Don't be intimidated. The software is cheap (or free) and user-friendly, so much so that it's mostly the same software pros use. As they say, producing audio slideshows has become "ridiculously simple." Try it. It's fun.

Begin by assessing whether you have a story that supports audio and visuals. Audio and photos should supplement and complement each other, the same as captions/cutlines. Time audio and visuals to "go with" each other. Remember storyboarding and maintaining narrative continuity.

Before putting the audio slideshow together, finish editing and saving your photos in one folder. Likewise, edit and save your audio track. Convention suggests you'll need a couple dozen photos for every minute of audio—more or less—depending on the subject matter's tone and pacing. After the audio and photos files are completed, open your audio slideshow software, import your photos and audio, and finally tweak as needed. Remember that a 2-minute audio slideshow begins to stretch the limit of user tolerance.

Audio slideshows offer a simple and easy tool for disciplining ourselves to tell effective stories in a short period of time with audio and visuals. Sound and pictures working together in time segues handily to video.

VIDEO CLIPS

Video runs the gamut from carefully orchestrated multiple-camera commercials to homegrown cell-phone-recorded clips posted on video-sharing websites. In between the complex and the amateur, there are video interviews and monologues, short clips of events and activities, and how-to tutorials, among others.

Simple video-editing software is as commonplace as slideshow-making tools, and nonprofessionals can create good quality clips. Video isn't designed so much as it is composed, shot and edited, although in some cases it may be art directed. Like shooting photography, if the stakes are high, shooting video and film is best left to professionals. Nevertheless, if it's you or *nada,* follow these shooting and editing tips for beginners:

General shooting tips:

» Steady your camera with a tripod or other solid surface. Camera shake gets very old very quickly.

» Shoot in a location with bright, even lighting. Avoid harsh, high-contrast and backlighting, along with what you may believe are special lighting effects.

» When possible, shoot some test footage to check blocking, sound and light.

» Shoot more video than you think you'll need, at least 10–15 seconds for each shot you want to capture. You can always cut extra material, but you can't magically insert file footage no one ever shot. (B roll is file, secondary or archival footage used as visual fill or for creating transitions between clips.)

» Capture a variety of angles for each scene: tight close-up, medium, full, wide and long. Think about establishing shots versus detail/beauty shots.

» Avoid zooming and panning. Cutting from scene to scene is actually more natural.

» Compose your shots. Use the rule of thirds as your guide and place your focal point accordingly.

» Don't talk while shooting. The microphone may pick up your voice. Heavy breathers off-screen can be a problem, too.

Not as easy as it looks.
Capturing good video requires planning. Consider lighting, location and subject matter. And always shoot more footage than you think you'll need.

When shooting interviews & monologues (talking heads):

» Shoot in a quiet location.

» Select your talking head wisely. Not everyone appears interesting and engaging (or articulate) on-camera.

» Test footage… Better safe than sorry.

When editing video:

» Begin with the best quality video possible, i.e. uncompressed raw footage.

» Make sure you have good usable audio, too. "Audio is half the picture," as they say.

FLEX HOUSE

TEAM FLORIDA   HOME   ABOUT TEAM FLORIDA   CONCEPT   GALLERY   MEDIA INFORMATION   IMAGES

LATEST NEWS

APRIL 10, 2011

TEAM FLORIDA PRESENTS AT
TAMPA BAY CSI

APRIL 10, 2011

FLEX HOUSE WINS HILLSBOROUGH
COUNTY GREEN DESIGN AWARD

OCTOBER 23, 2010

TEAM FLORIDA REFINES
FLEX HOUSE AT AUGUST
CHARETTE

Support Team Florida!
Click on the link below, select the
SACD Solar Decathlon Project Fund
230021, then follow the prompts.

DONATE

MEDIA INFORMATION

Suspendisse potenti. Sed at auctor lectus. Integer pulvinar cursus nulla et egestas. Donec
interdum enim nec est imperdiet vitae volutpat urna semper. Duis condimentum interdum nisi, ac
scelerisque nunc volutpat quis. Donec ornare auctor tincidunt. Maecenas interdum quam sit amet
diam consectetur faucibus. Etiam viverra eros et ligula consectetur tempus vel sit amet nunc.
Etiam in ante sit amet turpis lobortis sollicitudin. In a dignissim neque.

Team Florida Virtual Tour - Solar Decathlon   Like   Share   More info

1:20 / 2:01

Video courtesy U.S. Department of Energy Solar Decathlon 2011.

Duis laoreet aliquam urna nec ornare. Sed porttitor semper nisl in tincidunt. Vestibulum ultricies
fringilla pretium. Sed eu dolor eget enim fermentum sodales. Pellentesque eu turpis sit amet quam
bibendum fringilla et quis odio. Vestibulum hendrerit condimentum aliquet. Maecenas porta nunc
nec ante accumsan egestas. Suspendisse ac nisl lacus, id euismod felis. Integer lobortis, est a
vestibulum vestibulum, massa urna lacinia turpis, sed lacinia arcu est ut libero. Curabitur dictum
nibh eu urna lobortis et sagittis sapien elementum. Nullam non magna in felis blandit interdum
sed at neque. Suspendisse potenti. Vivamus condimentum, ipsum vel convallis aliquam, turpis
lacus iaculis nulla, at elementum nisi purus ac augue. Duis massa tellus, auctor accumsan eleifend
posuere, dapibus nec ante.

» Select simple transitions—cuts and fades. Pick one transition style
and stick to it. Attention should be on the video, not on
the transitions.

» Try to keep overall video duration short. In multimedia contexts,
viewers can drop out in seconds, and most casual online video
viewers only hang around for 2–3 minutes.

Video encoding.

After editing, encoding is the next step in making a video. There are
many file formats out there, and choosing the right one takes a little
research. Video-sharing sites, for example, often post file size and
format requirements. Meanwhile, different software and hardware
brands peddle their unique file formats.

When choosing a file format, try to avoid those that are exclusive to
particular devices, platforms or software applications. You want your
video to be viewable by the greatest number of people. MPEG-4

**Doing an end-run around
format incompatibilities.**
Finding video formats
that run on all browsers
is no easy task. A good
workaround is to upload
your video to a video-
sharing site, then use the
code provided to embed
the video back into your
website. The sharing
site manages the tricky
browser issue for you. The
tradeoff is that your video
will contain branding from
the sharing site.

GREENW SE

GREENWISE

GREENWISE

GREENWISE

GREENWISE

Simple is good. Animation
need not be complicated.
This logo grows a letter "I"
and sprouts a leaf over the
course of a few seconds.

(Motion Pictures Expert Group), or
MP4 for short, is the most popular video
file format for the Web (at the time of
this printing, anyway). MP4 is friendly
across platforms and supported by the
most popular Web browsers.

In addition to file format, you'll also
need to pay attention to aspect ratio,
which refers to screen frame proportions,
and final file size, which also includes
modes of compression. Video files are
huge and must be compressed before
packed into files for transport. So
compression and file size matter not only
for uploading and downloading but also
for storage space. Wherever your video
is being housed or hosted, once again, a
few minutes' research on the specs can
save your—ahem—"project" at deadline
time. Stay within uploading parameters.
Quick downloading is critical, too, if you
want your viewer to stay tuned around
long enough to see your clip.

Speaking of viewers, don't forget they need access to a video player
of some sort for viewing. Fortunately, most modern browsers support
common video formats. And if you come across a format your browser
does not support, plug-ins are generally free and easy to find and
install.

An excellent way to bypass many browser and video format
incompatibilities would be to post your video on a video-sharing
site. Most video-sharing sites will provide a bit of code allowing you
to embed the clip on your own website. A minor drawback of this
method is that the video-sharing site may require you to include their
branding on your video clip.

Once viewers find your video, waiting for the whole clip to download,
as in "progressive" video delivery, can be a real drag unless the clip is
short and sweet. "Streaming" video is advisable for longer videos. But
you would hire professionals for those longer videos anyway.

Shooting & editing video not your bag?

The same sites that offer stock images also offer stock video clips.
Stock may not work for your situation. But if using stock saves time
and money, it might be worth checking out.

ANIMATION

Generations of children have grown up watching animation as a Saturday morning cat-and-mouse anvil-dropping form of entertainment. Now animation has grown up, too. It's everywhere from the startup sequence on your cell phone to spectacular CGI effects in blockbuster movies.

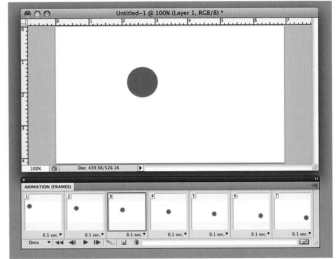

Like other multimedia components, animation can be classified by complexity. Animation found in full-length feature films and complex interactive websites remains the bailiwick of highly skilled pros. More accessible animation, such as transitioning in presentation slides, is generated by the presentation program itself.

If you're inclined to try your hand at animation, affordable animation programs are out there. The learning curve for animation software is steeper than most but not insurmountable. It's absolutely possible for the average person to create simple animated logos, video title sequences, banner ads and animated website components without an advanced degree in motion design.

Motion tweens.

The simplest digital animations work on the same principle as original hand-drawn animation. A series of images, each one slightly different from the last, is flashed in rapid succession giving the illusion of movement. The digital animation rate is approximately 30 frames per second so 30 images are needed to create one second of animation. This is a lot of drawing.

Fortunately, if you're using tweened animation, the computer will do the "drawing" for you. In tweened animation, only key changes in motion or shape are illustrated. For example, imagine the starting key frame has a red circle in the upper left corner, and the final key frame has the same red circle in the lower right corner. Based on the frame rate you specify, the computer will generate all the in-between frames necessary for an animation that moves the red circle from upper left to lower right.

Tweened animation is great for simple movement but also can be used for changes in color or opacity—tweening can be used to fade an object in or out.

Motion tweens.

Computer-generated tweened animation works on the same principle as traditional hand-drawn animation. A series of images is flashed in rapid succession, creating the illusion of movement.

Adobe Photoshop CS4 screen shot(s) reprinted with permission from Adobe Systems Incorporated.

Space and time. In animation, objects move through space over time. Animation programs include a timeline, seen here in the lower right of each graphic. "Events" happen at points along the timeline. In these screen grabs, the red bar represents the duration of the animation. The yellow triangle is effectively the "you are here" on the timeline. The preview window shows what the animation looks like at a given point in the animated sequence.

Adobe AfterEffects CS5 screen shot(s) reprinted with permission from Adobe Systems Incorporated.

Storyboards are an excellent tool for planning tweened animation. Arrows and other directional devices can signal the movements along with the relationships of shapes and type. Each sketch on the storyboard can describe the contents of a key frame, as well as—uh-huh—audio.

It's about time.

Actually, motion is not so much what makes animation different from other graphics. The element of time is. Animated elements appear, disappear and change shape at different points along a timeline. Pacing and transitions aren't issues when designing for print or even when designing static websites. But in animation and video, pacing and transitioning impact the overall feel, thus message, of the piece. A quick pace and sharp transitions give intensity and edge. Subtle, gradual changes are more soothing.

Duration is another important consideration.

How long does your animation need to last? Each situation is different depending on the job the animation is meant to do. However, the longer the animation, the greater the file size. So be aware of file size limitations—server, application or project-imposed. And, as a general rule, don't let your animations loop indefinitely. Have them cycle one or more times then stop. Don't loop animations that are particularly sharp and choppy. You don't want to give anyone a headache.

File formats for animation.

Again, choosing a file format requires a bit of research to determine what is acceptable for your particular project. Animated banner ads, for example, may have physical size, file size and looping requirements in addition to format requirements.

In general, use formats that are compatible across the greatest number of devices. Also look for those with good compression (file size) and good quality output.

Use restraint.

Adding a little animation to a layout can help break through all the visual clutter viewers suffer every day. But don't let your animation add to visual clutter. Use animation with a purpose. Make sure it's the right medium for your message. Don't use animation just for the sake of using it.

APPS AND PLUG-INS AND WIDGETS, OH MY!

Perhaps the most exciting thing about multimedia is the opportunity it provides to engage the audience fully. For advertisers, interactivity is a luxury only dreamed of just a generation ago. Each element we've discussed thus far allows for some interactivity, be it the pause, play and volume controls on a video clip or the ability to browse photos in an online photo gallery. And don't forget the banner ad's click-through (cha-ching).

The good news is that you no longer need to be a credentialed computer programmer to include interactive multimedia components in your screen layouts. Plug-ins, widgets and apps make it possible for non-developers to add a wide range of interactive components with ease.

Applications (Apps).

Applications, commonly referred to as "apps," are programs designed to run on a computer, tablet, smartphone, website or social media site. Large complex applications such as word-processing programs have been available on computers for years. Since the introduction of smartphones and tablets, professional and amateur programmers have been adding to the slate of apps for those devices, too. Some common examples of apps include calendars, mileage trackers, restaurant finders and, of course, games.

Some companies and organizations build custom apps to supplement websites. This makes sense as interaction with the smaller touchscreens

Motion is not so much what makes animation different from other graphics. The element of time is.

of handheld devices is different from that of websites. A specifically designed app can provide the smartphone or tablet owner with a much better user experience.

For the moment, application building is still squarely in the realm of professional Web designers and developers.

Plug-ins.

A plug-in is code that gives a browser or website additional functionality. For example, when a website automatically displays the most recent posts from a separate blog, a plug-in is at work.

There are plug-ins available that can do everything from filtering SPAM or viruses to allowing game playing or viewing different media types. They are easily added to sites or browsers via an installation program or by copying and pasting code in the right location.

Plug-ins are commonly installed behind the scenes, and there may or may not be visible front-end evidence of their presence on a site or browser. If a plug-in requires input from a user, or needs to physically display some sort of content on a page, then a widget is needed.

Widgets.

Widgets are the visible expression of the existence of a plug-in. For example, imagine you want to measure social media activity on a specific page and display the results in a sidebar. An installed plug-in will track the activity, but the widget is what displays the results. All widgets require a plug-in, but not all plug-ins have a widget.

Any time a plug-in requires user input, a widget is needed. You may have a plug-in to distribute an e-newsletter, but a widget is needed to provide an interface, in this case a form, so users can subscribe.

There are widgets to display local weather, create tag clouds, play video and slideshows and even map the nearest pizza places.

With literally thousands of plug-ins and widgets available, the potential for adding interactivity to your projects is huge.

Where do I get plug-ins, widgets and apps?

The short answer: Search online. Most plug-in or widget code can be had for free or for minimal cost. Often all that is required is a code cut-and-paste. Oh, and sometimes a credit to the developer is needed, too. Don't forget to check and provide credit where credit is due.

When searching for and installing plug-ins and widgets, pay attention to online reviews. Since these mini programs can be created by anyone, quality is all over the board. Some are not regularly updated. And many

Most plug-in or widget code can be had for free or for minimal cost. Often all that is required is a code cut-and-paste.

MULTIMEDIA WEBSITES

This webpage has three multimedia components generated by plug-ins and widgets:

1. Home page rotating feature image
2. A sidebar populated with the most recent updates from a social media site
3. An electronic newsletter with a front-end widget for user subscriptions

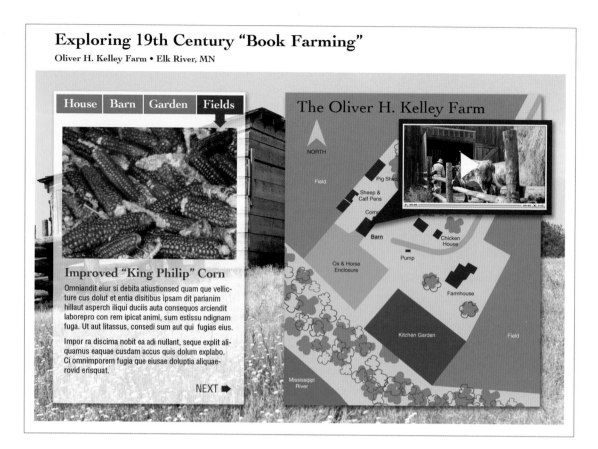

Exploring 19th Century "Book Farming"

Oliver H. Kelley Farm • Elk River, MN

House | Barn | Garden | Fields

Improved "King Philip" Corn

Omniandit eiur si debita atiustionsed quam que vellicture cus dolut et entia disitibus ipsam dit parianim hillaut asperch iliqui duciis auta consequos arciendit laborepro con rem ipicat animi, sum estissu ndignam fuga. Ut aut litassus, consedi sum aut qui fugias eius.

Impor ra discima nobit ea adi nullant, seque explit aliquamus eaquae cusdam accus quis dolum explabo. Ci omnimporem fugia que eiusae doluptia aliquaerovid erisquat.

NEXT ➡

The Oliver H. Kelley Farm

NORTH

Field

Pig Shed

Sheep & Calf Pens

Corn

Barn

Chicken House

Ox & Horse Enclosure

Pump

Farmhouse

Kitchen Garden

Field

Mississippi River

Multimedia storytelling. The interactive page above incorporates photos, text, slideshows, infographics and video clips. The result is a multisensory self-paced learning experience.

are not "supported," meaning if something goes wonky, you're on your own to fix it.

Another thing to look for is whether or not a plug-in or widget comes with an editable Cascading Style Sheet (CSS). Style sheets are used to dictate the way design features like fonts and colors display onscreen. If you can access a style sheet, you can tweak the appearance of a plug-in to better match your overall layout.

As mentioned, apps tend to be more complex, and building them requires the skills of a developer. However, if your organization needs a strong unique presence on tablets or smartphones, hiring a developer to create a custom app might be worth the investment.

MULTIMEDIA STORYTELLING

Back in our infographics chapter, we talked about the enhanced communication capabilities inherent in infographics packages. Multimedia components enhance your communicating abilities exponentially.

Imagine an interactive multimedia website devoted to the human heart. The centerpiece might be a high-end 3D animation of the inner workings of the heart providing something like a virtual ride through the pulmonary system. We could enhance the online experience with sound effects and narration.

Other interactive features and links would layer additional information. Users might click to learn more about platelets, heart chambers, red blood cells, etc., or even how to read an electrocardiogram (EKG) or become a cardiologist. Users might take a quiz to test their knowledge of or calculate their risks for heart disease. Maybe users entertain themselves competing in a heart health game that pits exercise and eating habits against genetics. How about chatting in real time with a medical expert? Anyone want to upload personal stories, share medical resources or add data to a map? You get the idea.

This type of multimedia design not only requires professionals, it requires teams of professionals. It also requires research, planning and a battery of thumbnail sketches, storyboards, site maps and wireframes.

Should you find yourself part of a team creating an interactive multimedia experience, here are some things to consider:

» Not every story or subject lends itself to full multimedia treatment. Make sure you have a deep, interesting and multifaceted topic to work with.

» Choose the best multimedia elements for your particular

MULTIMEDIA CONTENT TOOLBOX

Multimedia muse Vidisha Priyanka recommends the following for the digital editor/producer's toolbox:

Text
» headlines
» summaries
» external links
» audio transcripts
» photo captions/cutlines
» blogs/microblogs

Images
» still photos
» illustrations
» infographics
» photo slideshows
» photo galleries

Video
» recorded clips
» live feeds
» historical footage
» animation
» video logs
» tutorials

Audio
» narration (anncr, VO)
» dramatizations
» music
» sound effects (SFX)
» natural (nat) or ambient (ambi) sounds
» actualities (acts or ax)

Interactivity
» live chat
» discussion forums
» feedback
» timelines
» polls
» games
» mashups
» searchable databases
» calculators
» guest books
» augmented reality
» widgets

Data
» numbers
» statistics
» spreadsheets
» lottery results
» archives

User-Contributed Content
» anecdotes
» comments
» photos
» cell phone/mobile content
» videos
» social networks
» user reviews
» wikis

Mobile Content
» really simple syndication (RSS) feeds
» music
» videos
» podcasts
» social networks
» quick response (QR) codes and other mobile scanning
» global positioning system (GPS) applications such as navigation and geo-caching

Site Exposure (going viral)
» content- and media-sharing sites for video, photos, news, information, networking

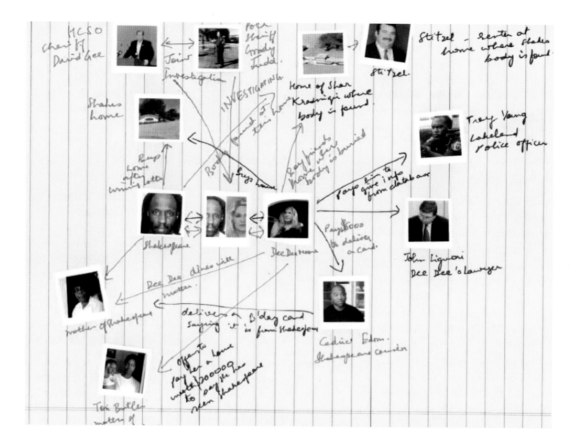

content. If you don't have a good candidate for a talking-head expert or spokesperson, don't plan to include a video interview. Do consider all your media options, including infographics.

» Elect one medium to tell the main story, and let the other media play supporting roles. Think in terms of creating a content focal point.

» Decide on an overall look and feel. Then choose design elements that support that look and feel.

» Make the interface intuitive. Make buttons look like buttons, and make them easy to find and use. Same goes for links.

» Don't let the technology get in the way of the information or the story. The technology should be "invisible" to the user.

New technologies can and do inspire designers and visual communicators. But there's an old aphorism about the shortsightedness of designing the whole living room around the coffee table.

Abraham Shakespeare-Dee Dee Moore Case

In November 2006, Abraham Shakespeare won a $30 million Florida Lottery jackpot and took a lump-sum payment of nearly $13 million after taxes. He last was seen in April 2009 and was reported missing in November. His body was found in January buried behind the home of Dee Dee Moore, who is charged with first-degree murder in his death.
Move your mouse on the blue lines to see the connections.

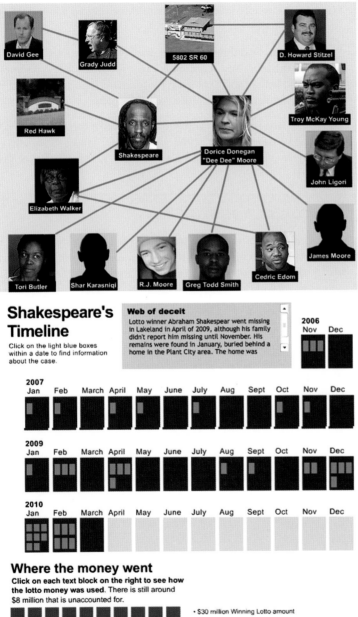

Shakespeare's Timeline

Click on the light blue boxes within a date to find information about the case.

Web of deceit
Lotto winner Abraham Shakespear went missing in Lakeland in April of 2009, although his family didn't report him missing until November. His remains were found in January, buried behind a home in the Plant City area. The home was

Where the money went

Click on each text block on the right to see how the lotto money was used. There is still around $8 million that is unaccounted for.

- $30 million Winning Lotto amount
- Shakespeare takes $17 million in lump sum payment
- He received $13 million after taxes
- Shakespeare buys home in Lakeland for $1.08 million
- When assets are frozen on July 16, 2007

Multimedia storyboarding. When multimedia news pioneers Tim Price and Vidisha Priyanka worked at TBO.com, they collaborated on stories that required all manner of rough storyboarding and site mapping. The storyboarded investigation shown here reported the tragic murder of a lottery winner.

http://www2.tbo.com/static/ special_reports_news/shakespear-case/

Source: The Tampa Tribune, HCSO and PCSO

Multimedia designer: Tim Price/ TBO.com

Multimedia producer: Vidisha Priyanka/TBO.com

Images courtesy Tim Price, Vidisha Priyanka and TBO.com/ Media General.

▶ TRY THIS

1. Visit the website of a large news organization. Look for examples of multimedia storytelling. Which multimedia elements are employed? Write a brief critique.

2. Locate some simple logos. Storyboard three options for animating each of said logos.

3. Find a website or online magazine that accepts animated banner ads. What are the specs and requirements for file size, format, duration, etc.? Spend some time exploring the animated banner ads on this site. What animation techniques are being used?

4. Visit a site that sells video and audio clips. What formats do they come in? What styles and genres are available? Find a video clip and some audio clips you like. Brainstorm ways of using them in a website.

5. Storyboard an animated banner ad advertising the site you found in No. 4. Don't forget the click-through.

6. Produce a 1- to 2-minute photo slideshow or, better yet, an audio slideshow that documents reality. Story ideas to consider include a visual oral history of your oldest living family member, the status of adoptions at your local animal shelter or the hidden story of a nearby nature preserve. Maybe attending and documenting a public event, such as a quilt show, or a political rally is more your speed.

7. After you produce the slideshow above in No. 6, lay out a Web page for that same story that includes: a big type header, a media player for the slideshow, a complementary type story, associated still photography, at least one infographic, and user feedback/comments. Don't forget to label everything with subheads, captions/cutlines and/or chatter, etc., as seems appropriate.

IE'S BICYCLES

13 | DESIGNING FOR THE WEB
starring on the small screen

SALE

STARTS
JUNE 30

Up to 50% O
Select Merchan

BIKE SAFETY CLASS FOR KIDS

Solluptatur reiuntotae illorporem eum quiasse earchit exceatur se- ceati dolorae nimin non ex exceaqui ius pel magnienis ducias estiatias

BONESHAKER CLUB NEWS

Occumeni ilicae nonsed etur aut pligent ianiet ex eatur sequost rerio inus quas aspeliquam quaecti dem aris il imus dolor sitiae sequis

SUMMER R

Solluptatur re eum quiasse e ceati dolorae ius pel magni

Edit Page Add New

Media Information

Permalink: http://www.infocusdesign.net/sandbo:

Upload/Insert

B I ABC := := " ≡ ≡ ≡

Paragraph ▾ U ▤ A ▾ ▦ ▦

Lorem ipsum dolor sit amet, consectetur
rhoncus faucibus, faucibus eu purus. In r
vel nunc. Morbi id velit eu orci semper ali
Praesent vehicula accumsan iaculis. Cur:
tortor. Etiam ut tristique arcu.

Donec ultrices posuere velit ut molestie. F
Praesent vulputate elit vel erat imperdiet
ligula bibendum pharetra sodales, mauris
ipsum. In id libero lorem. Vivamus mollis I
tempor. Suspendisse eu fringilla metus. N
viverra sit amet, commodo condimentum

Beats coding by hand.
Content management
systems allow you to
create and update Web
pages without hand
coding. The content-
generating parts of CMS
interfaces are similar
to word processing
interfaces, making them
more user-friendly for non
tech-geeks.

B y the time you finish reading this chapter, there's a good chance the content will be out of date. Really.

The Internet impacts our professional and personal lives on a daily basis, in countless ways. We text instead of talk on the phone. We get our news from websites or via feed. We blog, we email, we produce and publish our own videos. We shop. We critique. We collaborate. We have a million ways to get—and give—information.

The processes by which we get and give information have been in a constant state of change since the creation of the World Wide Web. Someone always seems to be announcing the next big social media tool or promoting the next great programming standard. While it may seem that the only constant is change, it's safe to say if you work in communications, you will work on some level with websites.

WHAT TO EXPECT WHEN WORKING WITH WEBSITES

Early websites were built by computer programmers who hand-wrote code and built applications from scratch. This has changed. So if you know nothing about programming languages or coding, don't worry. Your interaction with websites isn't likely to involve a lot of code. More likely, you'll be asked to do one of the following:

Prepare simple images and content for an existing website. You provide a basic text document or a graphic formatted for the Web to a webmaster (Kim prefers the term "webspinner"), who will upload the text and images for you.

Work with a content management system (CMS). A CMS is a Web-based site building and management application that dynamically generates pages from information you add to a database via a word processing-like interface. Content management systems were created so people with no knowledge of coding could build visually consistent sites. Such systems are excellent for organizations and businesses that require complex membership management or e-commerce. CMSs often have free or inexpensive plug-ins that add custom functionality to a site, such as tools for creating e-newsletters, calendars, maps or feeds from social media sites.

Create a site from a template. Templates allow you to pick an existing design and insert your custom content where appropriate. Templates can be hosted on the template provider's server, or they can be downloaded and installed on your own separately purchased server space.

HOW THE **WEB WORKS**

Ever wonder how your computer can pull so much data from servers all over the world? Here's a 5-second explanation of how the World Wide Web works:

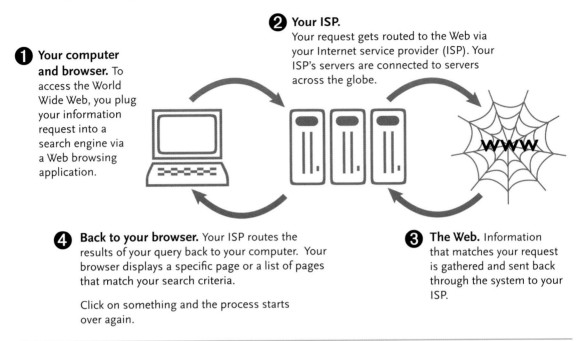

2 Your ISP.
Your request gets routed to the Web via your Internet service provider (ISP). Your ISP's servers are connected to servers across the globe.

1 Your computer and browser. To access the World Wide Web, you plug your information request into a search engine via a Web browsing application.

4 Back to your browser. Your ISP routes the results of your query back to your computer. Your browser displays a specific page or a list of pages that match your search criteria.

Click on something and the process starts over again.

3 The Web. Information that matches your request is gathered and sent back through the system to your ISP.

Work with a professional Web designer and/or developer to create a custom site with custom functionality. This is the best option when you need a site with a specific look and feel, have extensive quantities of content or require highly specialized site tools. Working with professionals is also advisable when high search rankings are crucial to your site's success. While site design has been automated to a large extent, search engine optimization (SEO) requires professional planning and implementation.

HOW THE WEB WORKS (THE 5-SECOND VERSION)

When working with Web content, it's important to understand how the files you create come to show up on the computer screens of your audience/customers. If you know how the Web works, you can troubleshoot why your content is not showing up properly, or not showing up at all.

Accessing existing websites. To access the Web, you need a computer or other Internet-capable device, a Web browser and an Internet service provider (ISP) or wireless network. When you type an information request (a keyword or search term) or a specific address (Uniform

GETTING YOUR SITE **ON THE WEB**

Publishing your site files on the World Wide Web requires a computer with Internet access, a Web host and FTP software (called an FTP client). Think of your host as your paid parking place on the Web. Your FTP client is the permit that gets you into the restricted parking zone. Here's how it works:

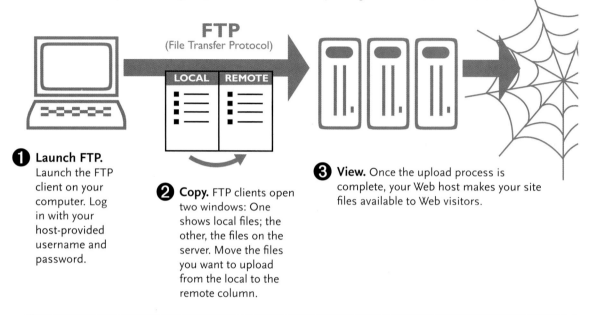

FTP
(File Transfer Protocol)

LOCAL | REMOTE

1 Launch FTP. Launch the FTP client on your computer. Log in with your host-provided username and password.

2 Copy. FTP clients open two windows: One shows local files; the other, the files on the server. Move the files you want to upload from the local to the remote column.

3 View. Once the upload process is complete, your Web host makes your site files available to Web visitors.

Resource Locator or URL) and hit enter, your request is sent to your ISP. Your ISP, in turn, sends the request to the World Wide Web portion of the Internet. Information on the network that matches your information request gets sent back through your ISP. Your browser displays either the page you requested by URL or a list of potential pages that meet your search criteria.

Adding your site to the WWW. A few additional things are needed to house and maintain a website: server space (also called a Web host), a domain name and a File Transfer Protocol (FTP) program.

Server space/Web hosting. Think of server space as your site's paid parking space on the Web. Your ISP may offer you server space as part of your package, or you can buy space through a separate host provider. Your server space is defined by amount of disk storage space and availability of other features such as number of email accounts.

By default, the name of your server plus the name of the directory assigned by your host becomes your site URL. Your host also may give you a string of numbers called an IP address that also represents the location of your site on the Web. To continue the parking space analogy, your IP number is like your parking space number. But nobody wants a URL that reads www. yourwebhost.com/~sitename, or worse, 65.97.106.162. This is where domain names come in.

Domain names. A domain name is a custom URL you purchase through a domain name registrar. Think of the domain name as a personalized "reserved" sign that replaces the number identifying your parking space. Domain names are chosen to reflect the content of the website they represent. XYZgraphicdesign.com is much easier to remember than an IP address, and it says something about what the company does right in the name. The most common and desired domain suffix is .com, but hundreds of others exist. The suffix .net was intended for personal Web pages, .org for groups and organizations, .gov for government and .edu for education.

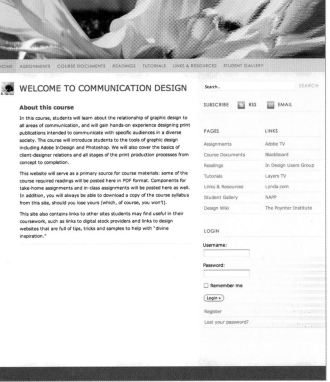

When you purchase a domain name, you must provide your registrar with the domain name server (DNS) of your Web host. This action "points" the domain name to your Web host, and subsequently, your Web pages. The end result is, when a person plugs your custom domain name into a browser, the browser locates the domain name at your registrar, and the registrar redirects the browser to your website. If the stars, sun and moon all align, your website will show up in that person's browser window.

File Transfer Protocol (FTP). The final piece in this mix is the mechanism required to get your Web pages parked in your server space. A Web designer keeps two sets of Web files: a local set on his or her personal computer and a matched set on the server. Make your edits on your local files then upload the files to the server. The files on the server are the ones the rest of the world sees via Web browsers.

To connect to your server, which is essentially a remote computer, you need File Transfer Protocol (FTP) software. FTP software is inexpensive (or even free) and easy to use. When you provide the name of your Web host, your username and your password in a new connection dialog box, the FTP client will open a bridge between

It's inevitable.
Whether you provide images and logos for an existing site, contribute to a blog or build sites from scratch, working with websites is a given.

Good design is good design. Well-designed websites demonstrate the use of compositional elements and principles including focal point, balance, movement, line, shape, value and, of course, space.

Use of an underlying grid is particularly important to maintain visual consistency across nonlinear pages.

your computer and your server space. Uploading files is usually as simple as dragging and dropping.

CMS and hosted templates: No FTP required. If your website was built using a content management system, or utilizes a template provided by an online website service, you may not need a separate FTP client. Such systems provide an online interface so you can upload graphics and other assets to the host server. Text content is typed in via a word processing–style interface and stored in a database on the host server. You're still uploading content to a server; you're just doing it using more user-friendly tools.

DESIGNING FOR THE WEB

How Web design is similar to print design.

Good design is good design, no matter the medium. The end product must capture attention, control the eye's movement, convey information and evoke emotion.

Your website design will need a focal point, visual hierarchy, balance, rhythm and flow. Rare is the site that has one page only, meaning you'll need consistency across multiple pages and a navigation system to keep visitors oriented.

While good design is good design, a Web page does differ from print in significant ways.

How Web design differs from print design.

You can't completely control the way your layouts will appear onscreen. A good print designer knows what she'll get back when she sends her files to the printer. Not so for the Web designer. Any layout created for the screen will look different to each and every person who views it. For this, we can blame both hardware and software. In our color chapter, we discussed the issue of color-shifting on different monitors. Another issue arises from different browsers rendering fonts and spacing differently, causing changes to the intended appearance of layouts. When you design for Web, you design for a moving target.

Your layout is built on an incredible shrinking (or expanding) canvas.
Back in the early days of Web design, the great debate was whether to design your page to 640 x 480 pixels or 800 x 600 pixels. Monitor technology was changing, and sites built at 800 x 600 looked great on new monitors, but were cropped and required scrolling on older monitors. And those were the good old days.

Today's websites are as likely to be viewed on a smartphone (starting at around 320 x 480 pixels) as on a 20-inch monitor. Or on a 15-inch laptop screen. Or on a tablet. You can't choose to have your site look good on only one device. It must look good on all devices. You must plan for a high degree of layout flexibility.

Websites are nonlinear. Unlike books, magazines and other multi-page documents, multi-page websites are nonlinear. Rather than move from chapter 1 to chapter 2, viewers can jump to any point in a website at any time, and things need to make sense when viewers arrive. They also

This is a sample headline set in Tangerine Cursive

This is sample body copy set at a font size of .9em. The body copy uses the Open Sans font by Steve Matteson. The Tangerine font in the headline was created by Toshi Omagari. Both are available through a free online font hosting service.

This is a sample headline set in Tangerine Cursive

This is sample body copy set at a font size of .9em. The body copy uses the Open Sans font by Steve Matteson. The Tangerine font in the headline was created by Toshi Omagari. Both are available through a free online font hosting service.

This is a sample headline set in Tangerine Cursive

This is sample body copy set at a font size of .9em. The body copy uses the Open Sans font by Steve Matteson. The Tangerine font in the headline was created by Toshi Omagari. Both are available through a free online font hosting service.

No, you don't need to get your eyes checked. Despite access to the exact same page code and style sheet, each browser renders fonts differently. Look closely at the line breaks, font size and overall height of the copy blocks. These subtle differences are enough to cause a layout to break on one browser or another.

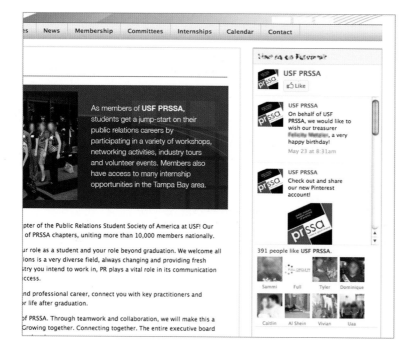

need a clear path to get back to wherever they came from, or to find their next destination in the site. Design concepts of hierarchy, repetition and unity become crucial to site navigability and usability.

The Web can be a multi-sensory experience.
Websites allow for the addition of multimedia components such as animation, video and audio, creating a richer multi-sensory experience. This means entering a whole new world of video and audio formats as well as browser compatibility issues.

The Web is an interactive experience. Early websites were brochure- and book-like: We clicked, we read. In a few short years the Web has evolved into a device that reads you back. As we click, our choices are recorded and come back to us in the form of messages like, "Those who purchased this item also bought..." With a click we can control the "skin" of our online music service. We can add our own words and images to blogs, forums and social media sites. Websites are expected to be interactive and dynamic. A Web designer must create a framework that creates order and organization, despite constantly changing, oft-times user-generated content.

Design for content outside your control.
Your website design may include areas of user-generated content. Social media sites in particular offer widgets and code snippets to allow content to populate your site automatically. Be aware of the physical requirements (dimensions, browser compatibility, etc.) of such widgets and design accordingly.

DESIGNING WEB PAGES & WEBSITES

Because websites are a complex combination of type, visuals and applications, the best sites are the result of the joint efforts of designers, Web developers, writers and Web usability experts. Whether you're designing on your own, editing an existing site or working with a team to build something new, you should understand the design conventions involved in creating a good website.

Planning.

In any design project, the final product is only as good as the initial planning. Plan a website the way you would plan any project—consider look, feel, message, content and delivery method.

Setting clear objectives is crucial. As noted earlier, the original websites were little more than static online brochures. Now websites must have constantly changing updateable content and interactive components to engage and/or entertain visitors to keep them coming back. You need to know what you want your site to say and do, as well as what your visitors need your site to do. Sometimes those needs require extra software, programming or even specialized server space.

Start your project by writing a creative brief, followed by a content outline. This outline becomes the basis for developing the site map, a type of flowchart that lists all the pages within a site and their interconnections. The outline and site map provide the list of pages that become the site's navigation. They should also include notes regarding specific page functionality, such as forms, multimedia components, dynamic content areas and any site feature that might require custom coding and the skills of a Web developer.

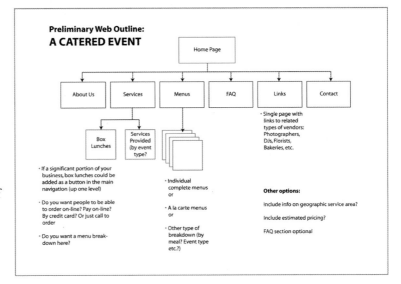

This is the time to assemble your site assets. Site assets include your copy, logos, photos, video clips, external Web links and even code snippets from other online sources if you plan to use dynamic content on your site.

If it is important that your site be highly ranked by search engines, search engine optimization (SEO) should be considered as part of the copywriting process.

Search engine optimization (SEO). SEO specialists often say, "Content is king" because search engine rankings are based on the quantity and quality of your page content. In this case, quality means keyword-rich.

To optimize your site, make a list of the most likely keywords people would use to search for your site, and incorporate those words into your page content. The more often keywords appear in your content, the more favorably search engines will rank your page when someone searches using those terms.

A site map serves as your blueprint for creating and connecting site pages. It is a crucial planning tool considering the nonlinear nature of websites.

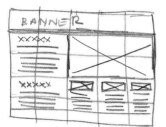

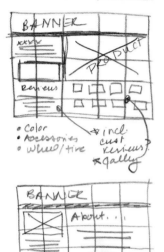

Build in consistency.
The five-column grid in these wireframe sketches not only helps maintain visual consistency across pages but also allows for flexibility in content placement.

For example, if your website promoted lawn care services, you would weave words like "lawn," "lawn care," "grass," "mowing" and "lawn mowing" into your copy. Remember to use natural phrasing. Overloading your text with gratuitously repeated keywords is cheating and makes your site read like you hired a bonehead to write the copy. Balancing SEO with good copywriting requires a little finesse.

You also need to work those keywords into other places, including your page titles, your headings and your hyperlinks. If you're really smart, you'll purchase a domain name that includes your keywords, too.

In truth, SEO is more complex than the process we describe here. If your website must rank well, then consult an SEO expert.

Page design.

Once you've settled on functionality and content, the next step is sketching wireframes. Wireframes guide the functionality and placement of content on the home page, secondary pages and other specialty pages. Wireframes need to account for flexible page content. Updating type and visuals on pages may require more or less space than the original content, potentially changing the overall balance of the page. Sketches help determine how to make the most of your limited screen real estate.

Establish a grid. Because Web page design can rival printed newspaper design in terms of complexity, your design sketches should be anchored by an underlying grid. Establishing and maintaining a grid structure will keep your site unified regardless of the number of different assets and components each page includes. Consider using the golden proportion or the rule of thirds to create your grid. Both approaches will ensure your site has pleasing asymmetry.

A few best practices and design conventions. As you sketch, there are several established best practices and some Web design conventions you should follow:

> » **Establish content hierarchy.** What are the most important parts of the page and how can you make that order apparent to the visitor? The compositional and typesetting techniques covered in chapters 5, 6 and 7 will help you here.

> » **Define relationships among assets on the page.** What design tools can you use to indicate what goes with what on your page? If you need a hint, revisit the Gestalt discussion in Chapter 5.

> » **Create a sense of direction.** This goes hand-in-hand with page hierarchy. Show your visitor where to start and where to go next. Again, it would be good to revisit your compositional techniques and Gestalt.

BONNIE'S BICYCLES

Home | About Bonnie's Bicycles | Vintage Bicycles | New Bicycles | Accessories | Events | Blog | Contact Us || **SALE**

MAIN HEADING HERE

Mauris scelerisque ligula vitae arcu bibendum non tempus est varius. Etiam fringilla malesuada venenatis. Donec ornare, elit ac congue faucibus, neque elit aliquam mi, eget dapibus justo ante id ante. Phasellus tempus metus ut quam iaculis mattis. Praesent feugiat felis ac sem tincidunt lacinia. Phasellus porta ligula quis orci fermentum fringilla. Vivamus blandit, orci ac euismod pharetra, ligula dui commodo dui, ut condimentum tortor leo quis sem. Praesent non orci ligula. Nunc ultricies vestibulum ullamcorper. In molestie ligula vitae purus venenatis quis interdum quam interdum. Quisque lorem turpis, condimentum ut imperdiet eget, dignissim tempus est.

SUMMER **SALE**

STARTS JUNE 30

Up to 50% Off Select Merchandise

NEWS & NOTES

MAY 20. Mauris scelerisque ligula vitae arcu bibendum non tempus est varius. Etiam fringilla malesuada venenatis. [More...]

APR 18. Donec ornare, elit ac congue faucibus, neque elit aliquam mi, eget dapibus justo ante id ante. [More...]

APR 3. Phasellus tempus metus ut quam iaculis mattis. Praesent feugiat felis ac sem tincidunt lacinia. Phasellus porta ligula quis orci fermentum fringilla. [More...]

MARCH 30. Vivamus blandit, orci ac euismod pharetra, ligula dui commodo dui, ut condimentum tortor leo quis sem. [More...]

MARCH 7. Praesent non orci ligula. Nunc ultricies vestibulum ullamcorper. In molestie ligula vitae purus venenatis quis. [More...]

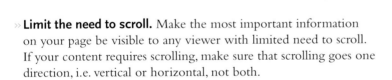

BIKE SAFETY CLASS FOR KIDS
Solluptatur reiuntotae illorporem eum quiasse earchit exceatur seceati dolorae nimin non ex exceaqui ius pel magnienis ducias estiatias modi doloepraes endamusant odipis modist officae ctempori atiustion rem quo beris aut fugitiam que quidebita cus, omnistr untur.

BONESHAKER CLUB NEWS
Occumeni ilicae nonsed etur aut pligent ianiet en eatur sequost rerio inus quas aspeliquam quaecti dem aris il imus dolor sitiae sequis molorestio eum adi dic tes qui corerro eaqui rem et el et ut fugit qui vere sequia nimus ipsanti scimiliquae reptam.

SUMMER RIDE SCHEDULE
Solluptatur reiuntotae illorporem eum quiasse earchit exceatur seceati dolorae nimin non ex exceaqui ius pel magnienis ducias estiatias modi doloepraes endamusant odipis modist officae ctempori atiustion rem quo beris aut fugitiam que quidebita cus.

Bonnie's Bicycles | 1911 Highwheel Lane | Kittyhawk, NC
555-555-1911 | info@bonniesbikes.com

» **Limit the need to scroll.** Make the most important information on your page be visible to any viewer with limited need to scroll. If your content requires scrolling, make sure that scrolling goes one direction, i.e. vertical or horizontal, not both.

» **Keep navigation near the top.** Consider your navigation as part of that "important information." Main navigation should appear in its entirety on your viewer's screen without scrolling. Navigation should not fall "below the fold." In old-fashioned newspaper terminology, "above the fold" is where editors put the important news so folks could see it while the paper was still folded.

» **Use a logo as a home page link.** Place a logo or company name in the upper left corner of your design. Make this logo serve as a link back to the site's home page.

Best practices. This site design has a strong grid and keeps navigation above the fold. How many other page design best practices can you find?

Chapter 13: Designing for the Web 223

Exact match? Home and secondary page designs need not match exactly. However, there should be a consistent look and feel between pages. You can accomplish this by repeating fonts, colors, shapes and underlying grid structure.

Website reproduced by permission of the Carousell Works.

Home page design.

A home page often serves as a visitor's first introduction to the site, and as such it should set the overall visual tone. It's a good idea to design the home page first and use this layout as the basis for the remainder of your pages. While websites should be visually consistent throughout, it is not uncommon for the home page to have a slightly different design from the other pages. In fact, specialized content on the home page and other pages may require a series of slightly different, but related layout templates. Your grid structure will help unify your various pages, as will consistent use of fonts, colors and graphic elements.

Certain Web page components can and should be repeated as well for both visual consistency and ease of use. These components include:

Headers. Your header includes the name of your website, with or without additional visuals or type. More often than not, the header spans the top of the screen page, though there is no hard fast rule that this must be the case.

Navigation. Navigation includes the list of buttons or links that take folks to other parts of your site, hence the name. Navigation often sits above or below the header, or in both places when there is more than one set of links. Alternatively, navigation may run down the right or

SOME STANDARD WEB PAGE **COMPONENTS**

Header. The header includes the name of the site and often includes a logo or other graphic.

Navigation. Navigation is a set of links that take you to other pages in the site. Navigation should be consistent across all pages.

Content. Content can include everything from copy to multimedia components.

Footer. The footer often includes organization address and contact information, as well as a text version of the site navigation.

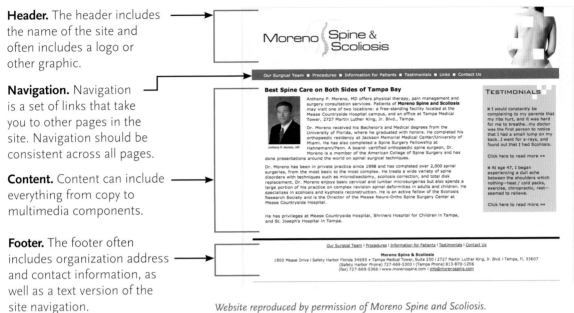

Website reproduced by permission of Moreno Spine and Scoliosis.

left side of the screen page. Left column navigation is common for websites, though right side navigation is also used, particularly in blogs. Go with side navigation if the list of links is too long to fit horizontally across the screen page.

When possible, try to limit the number of items in your navigation to a quantity between five and ten. Any more and the quantity of links becomes difficult to visually process. If it is essential to have more than ten links, consider using a primary navigation including links to your main content, and a secondary navigation with links to common pages such as "about us" and "contact us." Another option is to use accordion or pull-down menus to better organize your content.

Footers. Footers typically span the page bottom and often include contact information, copyright, a text version of the site navigation and infrequently used navigation links.

Designing content areas.

Site content can include everything from copy to video clips to dynamically generated infographics. And most content areas include more than one type of content.

Creating text-only pages is fairly straightforward. While reading copy on the Web is best set in single rather than multiple columns, other

Patterns in play. The Web has been with us long enough that many graphical user interface "patterns" are self-explanatory. We understand how the tabs, radio buttons, color swatches and image galleries work without having to ask.

typesetting conventions are appropriate for the Web. These include setting copy in the most readable font format for the medium (sans serif) and using graduated heading sizes and styles to create hierarchy.

Place primary photos, graphics and video clips near the top of their respective content areas. Make sure that none interrupts the flow of reading. Choose quality images. Place cutlines below images (and remember to make those cutlines keyword–rich for SEO purposes).

The interactive nature of websites introduces a whole new layer of complexity to page design. Take, for example, an automotive website that allows you to create an image of your dream car. The core content element of such a page is the basic image of a car. But the page also must include images of the various options the buyer can choose: paint colors, trim packages, interior packages, sound systems, rims, tires, etc. How can you possibly get all those images on a single page without massive amounts of scrolling?

Pattern	Possible Uses/Examples	What it looks like
Grid of consistently sized boxes	When several bits of information are of uniform importance. Example: team headshots.	
Rotating feature	A consistently sized container with auto-play or click-to-advance images. Example: rotating banner ads.	
Sliding panels	Multiple variations of a single idea. Example: retail website feature showing "5 ways to wear a sweater."	
Module tabs	Display different aspects of the same product/concept. Example: display the dimensions, shipping info and materials used for a sofa.	
Accordion	When you have a lot of heterogeneous content and not a lot of space. Content can be grouped under short headings; more than one group can be visible at once. Example: some email inboxes.	

Interface design. The answer lies in the conventions of interface design. Interface design refers to the design of the user experience—the interaction between the user and the tool to achieve a desired action. When you design interfaces for websites, you are designing a graphical user interface (GUI). The acronym is pronounced "gooey," in case you were wondering.

The best graphical interface designs are simple, intuitive and non-obtrusive. Interface design speaks to everything from the size, style and placement of navigation buttons to the best background colors for pop-up windows. While it's beyond our scope to dig deeply into this discipline, we highly recommend additional reading on this topic for those serious about Web design. In the meantime, we can supply a chart of a few standard interface design conventions, or "patterns," to help organize complicated Web content.

Standard interface design conventions or "patterns." You'll recognize these common interface patterns and how you've seen them used. Think about how these patterns and their uses might help you design your Web pages to be user-friendly. What's good for viewers is good for you.

Getting GUI. The patterns of interface design not only help us organize our content, but also help us address some basic usability issues. As you sketch page designs, ask yourself some questions. Is your navigation easy to find? Do the links make sense? When you click past the home page, is it easy to tell where you are in the site? Can you tell how to get back? These are core issues of graphical user interface that apply to all Web page and website designs.

Some tips for creating good GUI include:

Pull-down and accordion menus. Pull-down and accordion menus can be real space-savers when you have lengthy and complex navigation. However, pull-down menus can be difficult for your visitors to use. Avoid them when you can, and really avoid those with multi-level drill-down.

» **Make the purpose of each page clear at a glance.** Use simple descriptive headings and copy. Your visitor should never have to ask, "What is this page about?"

» **Keep link names clear and simple.** Don't title a link "The Sum of Our Experience," when "About Us" will do.

» **Make the link name match the title of the corresponding page.** In other words, when you click on "About Us," the page you arrive on should be titled "About Us." This seems like a no-brainer. But you'd be surprised at how often this doesn't happen on websites.

» **Make buttons and links look like buttons and links.** Make the text or the button itself change color when the mouse rolls over it—something to give a clue that your button is a button. Under no circumstances should your visitor have to work to figure out how to get around your site. They won't work. They'll just leave. You can take that fact to the bank.

» **Navigation should be persistent.** Navigation should include the same links in the same style in the same place on each page. That's a unity technique.

» **Be wary of pull-down menus.** While space saving, pull-down menus can be difficult for some people to utilize, especially when the pull-down menu has multiple levels.

INTERFACE DESIGN TIPS FOR THE MOBILE WEB

The small size of smartphone screens makes it difficult to see, much less access, most content on traditional websites without excessive zooming and scrolling. In addition, many smartphones have touchscreen technology. It can be nearly impossible to click tiny links with our imprecise fingertips. To address the needs of smartphone browsers, designers are wise to create variations of websites tailored for tiny screens. These are typically referred to as "mobile sites." Here are a few interface design best practices for mobile sites:

» Simplify—but don't skimp on—content (Try to whittle to what a mobile user really needs)

» Optimize for speed (load times are still an issue on some smartphones)

» Make clickable areas at least 29 x 44 pixels (the size needed for most fingertips)

» Use only broadly-supported animation and video file formats

» Avoid "hover states" (where boxes and other popups appear on mouseover). Preferable on traditional computer screens and tablets, hover states behave badly on smartphone interfaces and may cover up other content on an already tiny screen

» Avoid scrolling more than one direction

» Provide a link to the main website

» **Have a link to the home page as part of the persistent navigation.** If your design includes a consistent logo, make the logo a live link that takes you back to the home page. Again, the most common position for such a logo is in the upper left corner of each page.

» **Place navigation, and any other important content, "above the fold."** In Web design, this means that those components should be visible on a standard size browser when the page loads. No scrolling required.

» **Use color to organize and order.** This is especially true if your site is complex.

» **Consider using a breadcrumb trail.** Breadcrumbs help your visitors can see where they've been and how to get back.

» **Provide a search box.** For complex sites, a simple search box can be the best tool ever.

Responsive Web design.

After planning page designs, the next step is rendering sketches in the image-editing software of your choice. Most designers execute

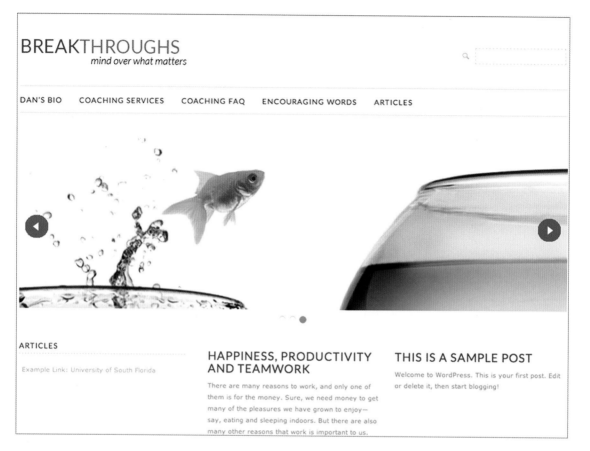

Bend, don't break.
Websites are viewed in many different screen sizes so it's important that your design responds accordingly. If it doesn't, your site might break when viewed with different devices. See what happened to this website-in-progress when it was viewed on a tablet?

the design in a layout or photo-editing program. Then the design is "sliced" into various individual graphics. The "slices" are optimized and reassembled in another program—either an HTML editor, WYSIWYG (what you see is what you get) page layout program or content management system.

But there's one design issue we have not yet addressed, and it's a big one. How do we get our carefully crafted Web pages to look good across screen sizes that vary from smartphone size to monster monitor size? Not to mention on screens that flip content from landscape to vertical as the device rotates? We need a system that is flexible and serves up different screen views tailored to the viewing gadget of the moment. We need "responsive Web design."

The tools to build responsive Web pages have been with us for years. Designers simply need to think differently, and apply those same tools in different ways. Designers must let go of fixed-width print-like layouts, and instead design sites that detect the type of viewing device and load the appropriately formatted site content and configuration.

There are three components to responsive Web design:

>> Flexible grid-based layouts

>> Flexible assets

>> Media queries

Web design best practices dictate that websites are created and styled via two types of page code: The first type is traditional HTML or a programming language defining the names of and number of pages in the site along with the relationships among those pages. The second type is a Cascading Style Sheet (CSS), which sets the visual styling, or appearance, of all page components from background pattern to column widths to font colors. Page objects, such as text boxes or site navigation, are created in the page-defining code. Then those same objects are named and their styling is defined in an attached style sheet. A CSS is simply a long list of page objects and their attributes.

Flexible grid-based layouts. A flexible grid-based layout can be achieved by using the CSS to create fluid instead of fixed-width elements. Instead of setting your page width to an inflexible finite size like 960 pixels, you set your page size to be 100% of your browser. When structural elements such as columns are not styled to be flexible, many layouts

```
body {
    background-image:url(images/ginko-bg.
    background-repeat: no-repeat;
}

#content {
    margin-top: 1em;;
    width: 85%;
    margin-left: auto;
    margin-right: auto;
    background-color:#f4eede;
    background-image:url(images/leaves.pn(
    background-position: left top;
    background-repeat: no-repeat;
}

h1 {
    padding: 2.7em 0 .1em 2em;
    font-family:"P22 Arts And Crafts Hunte
    font-size: 1.7em;
    text-transform: uppercase;
    color: #105210;
}
```

It's like having your mom tell you what shirt to wear. Web pages are created by HTML or programming language, but the appearance of Web pages is dictated by CSS. See if you can identify the CSS notations in the lower graphic that define and style the elements in the Web graphic at top.

WEB DESIGN & ACCESSIBILITY

Despite the amazing multimedia capabilities of the World Wide Web, the primary mode of information delivery is still text, and the interface is largely visual and requires a keyboard and mouse for input.

The Web Content Accessibility Guidelines, published by the Web Accessibility Initiative, offer a road map for making websites available and useful to people with vision, hearing and other physical challenges.

Some tips for making your site accessible include:

» **Do not encase text within graphics.** Screen readers can't read words that are built into graphics. (Incidentally, search engines can't either, so this cuts down on your SEO.)

» **Make sure type is scalable.** Browsers typically allow users to increase type size for easier readability. Think Readers Digest large-print edition. But this only works if the font settings for the Web page are configured to allow it.

Make links reactive. Design your links to physically change on click or mouseover. A color change alone may not be the best option. For those who are colorblind, underlined links are easier to see.

» **Provide text equivalents for all graphics.** Again, screen readers can't read graphics. Most WYSIWYG page editors have a field for you to enter "alt-text," short for alternative text, for any graphics in your layout. Alt-text is like a mini caption for your graphic, viewable only by screen readers and search engines. You also manually can enter alt-text into page HTML. (TIP: When alt-text includes keywords, it also improves SEO.)

» **Underline hyperlinks**. It's good practice to make links change in some way on a mouseover. However, if the only change is a color change, the colorblind may not be able to see it. Underlines make links more obvious. (Indeed, live links are the only time we can endorse underlining type.)

» **Provide large clickable areas.** For those who aren't so steady with a mouse, trying to click on small buttons or hotspots can be challenging. Don't skimp on the size of your clickable areas.

» **Provide closed-captioning for video elements.** Or, alternatively, provide a sign-language version of the video. Likewise, provide a typed transcript option of audio components, and consider providing a reader-service version of content for the visually impaired.

will "break" when viewed on a screen deemed too small to fit the design.

Flexible assets. Some flexible assets are easily styled for fluidity; others are not. Fonts are easily adapted to fluid layouts by styling them in "ems" instead of pixels. An em is a typographic measurement equivalent to the current font size. That current font size is either a browser default size or some other default size specified in the site's CSS. As you can imagine, styling copy at 130% of whatever the default size is would give you a larger font, while styling at 80% would give you a smaller font. Since both measurements are defined as percents, both are fluid.

Photos and videos also can be styled as percentages. However, scaling such graphics up does little to improve their quality onscreen, especially if they have been optimized. The solution is to create larger graphics than needed. Percentage settings in the style sheet will ensure graphics appear the correct size onscreen, while the additional pixels available in a larger image will offset any loss of quality if the graphics must expand to fit a larger screen. Keep in mind, however, that optimization is still a must. While most people have relatively high-speed Internet access on their computers, Internet speed on smartphones and other smaller devices might not be so fast. Keeping file sizes, and therefore download times, small remains important.

Media queries. Sometimes, despite your best efforts to create fluid designs, layouts break in one browser or another. Or perhaps there are page components that you want to display on a full computer screen but that you would like to eliminate from your site when viewed on a smartphone. This is where media queries come into play.

Media queries are a bit of code that kickoff a short conversation between a browser and your page code on the server. Essentially the browser knocks on the door of the website, and the website asks, "Who are you?" The browser responds with, "I'm browser X, appearing on smartphone Y." The website does a quick check to see if there are any special instructions in its code to deal with that browser/gadget combination before it serves up either the standard site or a custom version of the site. The "special instructions" are often a separate version of the CSS written specifically for different media parameters, or different browsers, that include, exclude or alter specified sections of styling.

Sites you build for yourself or your clients need to function across gadgets and platforms. While you may not have to write this type of code yourself, you may have to find a responsive template, or work with a designer or developer to build one. So, yes, you do need to understand the concepts and the vocabulary.

Of touch interfaces and tiny screens... Mobile websites have specific design requirements, including minimum sizes for clickable areas. Remember, your fingertip is not as precise as your mouse and "fat-fingering" links can accidentally send you off to Internet parts unknown.

Advantage: Blog.
One advantage blogs have over websites is that their text-heavy content makes them search engine friendly.

A WEBSITE ISN'T ALWAYS THE BEST TOOL FOR THE JOB

A good website is the backbone of many businesses and organizations. But if your goal is to self-publish, to build an online network or increase your reach and influence among existing online networks, then a blog or a page within a social media community is a better option.

Blogs. Short for Web log, a blog is an online self-publishing platform. Many blogs are simply personal forums for thoughts or rants. But the business world discovered that blogs have a place in commerce. The blogosphere includes industry-specific bloggers whose influence rivals (indeed surpasses) that of journalists. This reality is a pro and a con for public information officers (PIOs) managing blogs for their own organizations while vetting media-relations inquiries from other bloggers. It's all part of the new reality of doing business on the Web.

The difference between a blog and a website is that blog content is syndicated. People can subscribe through an RSS (Really Simple Syndication) feed. When a blogger writes a post, the content of the post is automatically delivered straight to the subscriber's computer. Organizational bloggers publish mini articles, news items and even full news releases using RSS. On the flip side, a blogger with a bone to pick can influence a huge number of subscribers quickly through this same system.

Setting up a blog is easy. You can create an account through one of many online blogging services, or you can download the programs and install them on your own server.

The rules for designing blogs are the same as the rules for designing Web pages. But because blogs are designed to appeal to people with no knowledge of HTML, there are literally thousands of template designs you can choose from. Many of them are free. And if you can't find exactly what you're looking for, templates are easy to tweak. You can change color palettes through Cascading Style Sheets. With photo-editing software and FTP access to your server, you can create and upload custom banners of your choice.

Social networking and social media sites. Whether or not you engage in blogging, you likely will supplement website activity with participation in one or more social media sites or social networks. The number and types of these sites have expanded in recent years, and it requires planning and strategy to capitalize on social media activity.

From a design standpoint, social networking and social media sites may or may not have page customization options, such as custom skins (themes). Some may offer access to CSS, which allows you to change fonts, font colors, background images and banners. Generally speaking, there is little actual design involved in working with social media sites. However, you can apply good design practices to any video clips and custom graphics you add to your pages.

Do-It-yourself. The trend in Web design is do-it-yourself animation, video and Web pages. Stay on top of trends by reading, taking a class or trying online tutorials.

KEEP ON YOUR TOES

Communicating today means communicating digitally, and the changes in digital communication technology seem to come faster every day. Trying to stay on top of the trends and changes is a little like herding cats.

Don't let the technology scare you. Remember, the trend is towards do-it-yourself animation, video and Web pages. To keep on top of tech trends, subscribe to a blog, take a class or try some online tutorials. If you're feeling in over your head, you can always hire a professional to help you with your Web-based project.

▶ TRY THIS

1. Visit your favorite website. Create a site map of the site showing all pages and links.

2. Find a piece of print collateral (catalogue, brochure, poster, advertisement, flyer) that has a URL. Visit the website related to the print piece. Compare and contrast the collateral piece with the website. How are the designs different? How are they alike? Why?

3. Locate the optimization function on your photo-editing software. Try using it on different types of graphics such as photos and logos. Save the images using different settings. Compare the results and final file sizes with your original graphics.

4. Find a website that you think is truly awful. Using page-layout software or an image editor, redesign the home page using good design practices and GUI.

5. Find two or three highly complex websites. As you navigate around the sites, be aware of navigational techniques being employed. What works? What doesn't? Do you feel lost in the site or always know where you are? Why?

6. In mini art school, you thumbnail sketched some ideas for an online personal portfolio. Now, using page-layout or image-editing software, execute a design for your own personal portfolio website. Start with a site map. What pages and content will you need? Execute designs for a home page and secondary pages. Make sure you account for persistent navigation and good GUI.

7. Visit one or more large commercial websites intended for the general public. Consider ability and accessibility. What has the site designer done to make this site accessible? What do you recommend for improving accessibility?

8. Visit a large commercial website using a desktop browser. Visit the same site using a tablet and/or a smartphone. Are there different versions of the site for each device? If not, does the website look and function properly on all devices? If there are different versions of the site, how are they similar? How are they different?

14 | FIT TO PRINT
an overview of papers & printing

While we appear to be moving in the direction of a paperless society, printing is unlikely to disappear completely. Printed documents have a couple things electronic documents don't: portability and tactile quality. Handheld devices such as smartphones and tablets are starting to make a dent in the portability claims of paper, but nothing yet replicates the feel of paper. Because of this added sensory input, paper can strengthen your ability to communicate through design.

Like choosing the right font or the right color, the right paper selection can communicate volumes in an instant. If you need to send banquet invitations to the most important people in your city, we're thinking an invitation printed on textured linen paper enclosed in a translucent envelope with a matching reply card would be more persuasive than an electronic invitation.

In this chapter we talk about choosing papers and printers, as well as getting your print job done right from estimate through delivery.

Paper communicates.
Paper offers a tactile experience that electronic documents can't replicate.

PLAN AHEAD FOR PRINTING: CHOOSING PAPER

Even though printing and distribution occur at the end of the design process, paper selection and output decisions happen at the

beginning. Deciding what paper and which printing method hinge on three things: how you want the finished piece to look and feel, the communication job the finished piece has to do and the size of your budget for accomplishing both.

Getting the look & feel with paper.

Paper is sexy. It comes in varieties of colors, weights and textures. Slick glossy paper might suggest a modern forward-thinking document. Thicker uncoated (not glossy) paper might imply a document of greater substance or importance. A heavily textured paper might lend the document a rustic quality. There are papers with pearly finishes, printed patterns, built-in textures and even flecks of flower petals.

To aid the paper selection process, paper manufacturers produce swatch books that include paper samples. Swatch books are free for the asking from paper distributors or manufacturers. These folks are only too happy to share what they know with you in the hope you'll "spec" or specify their papers for your printing projects.

But you ought to bring yourself up to speed on the most common paper varieties. Basically, there are three categories of paper: coated, uncoated and specialty. Within each of those categories lies tremendous selection in terms of paper finish, use and price.

Choosing the right paper for the right task.

For choosing paper, functionality is as important as appearance. You can't, for example, make a pocket folder out of paper intended for a copy machine. Copy paper simply doesn't have the weight and strength to make a functional folder. Weight is just one of many paper properties you must consider in your selection process.

Paper properties also impact the way ink behaves on the paper's surface. For example, uncoated sheets absorb ink, which can cause fine lines, such as the thin strokes on modern fonts, to appear slightly soft and even a little blurry. Depending on the paper's level of absorbency, photographs and illustrations may appear duller when printed on uncoated sheets. Color and brightness of the underlying paper influence photo and illustration color as well. Photo and illustration colors are truest and most vibrant when printed on the brightest whitest papers.

Again, a swatch book is helpful when looking for information on paper properties. Swatch books usually indicate a paper's properties as well as compatibility with laser and inkjet printers. Because it can be difficult for designers to guess how inks will appear printed on particular papers, many swatch books include print samples. These are

To aid the paper selection process, paper manufacturers produce swatch books that include paper samples. Swatch books are free for the asking from paper distributors or manufacturers.

PAPER TYPES, FINISHES & BEST USES

Paper	Finishes	Uses	Price
Coated	Gloss, Dull, Matte, Silk	Magazines, brochures, flyers, posters, annual reports, pocket folders, direct mail. Anything where color photos need to "pop." Tends to be less expensive than uncoated or specialty sheets.	$—$$$$
Uncoated: • Text • Writing • Cover	Smooth, Supersmooth, Vellum, Laid, Linen, Felt	Brochures, letterhead, business cards, invitations, annual reports, pocket folders. Good for high-end projects where tactile quality adds to project.	$$—$$$$
Specialty		Invitations, brochures, packaging, pocket folders, covers. Some papers for specific uses: safety paper, carbonless, etc.	$$—$$$$

often drop-dead gorgeous designs demonstrating how ink and other finishing treatments behave on a paper product.

Paper varies across a number of qualities, such as opacity (see-through-ness) and smoothness (tactile quality). You need to understand how these properties impact the printing process before you can choose the right paper for the job.

Being green is easier than it used to be.

As a print designer, your paper and printing choices directly impact the environment. And you have cause for concern. Traditional papermaking and printing processes are not exactly eco-friendly. Aside from promoting deforestation, the methods for making paper and subsequently printing on it are energy-intensive, water-intensive and use caustic chemicals like bleach and petroleum-based inks. Printed paper often ends up in landfills.

PAPER PROPERTIES

Paper Property	What it is	Why it's important
Opacity	The degree to which the paper is see-through.	If you need to print a sheet front and back, as in magazines and newsletters, you need a more opaque sheet.
Grain	The natural line-up of paper fibers as a result of the paper-making process.	Paper folds and tears more easily with the grain, so when you design folds and perforated tear-off cards, design with the grain.
Brightness/whiteness	Brightness is the amount of light reflected by the paper's surface; whiteness is the shade of white: warm, balanced or cool.	Colors print best on brighter papers. But the brighter/whiter the paper, the more expensive it is. When printing documents with pictures of people, choose warmer whites. For landscapes, choose cooler whites.
Weight	In the United States, a paper's weight is equal to the weight of 500 sheets in a specific size, listed in pounds. Paper weight influences stability, rigidity and often opacity.	Weight impacts the structure of the final document. If you don't choose the right paper weight, your brochure may flop over in a rack, or your direct mail piece may be mangled by post office equipment or, worse, be rejected or require additional postage.
Formation	The overall distribution of fiber throughout a paper sheet.	Good quality sheets have even fiber distribution. Poorer quality sheets have uneven fiber distribution. Uneven distribution results in uneven ink absorption, which means printing that's less crisp than it could be.
Smoothness	The tactile quality of the paper, sometimes referred to as "tooth."	The level of paper smoothness imparts character. It also impacts the way ink lies on the paper.

GO GREEN

Looking for environmentally friendly papers? Consult swatch books and ask your printer about options.

You also can find information about environmentally-friendly papers and paper-making on these Web sites:

Forestry Stewardship Council
http://www.fsc.org/

Sustainable Forestry Initiative
http://www.sfiprogram.org/

Green Seal
http://www.greenseal.org/

For years, the go-to solution for environmentally concerned designers was recycled paper. Unfortunately, recycled paper was not exactly high-end stuff. Designers chose it for its green message, not because it was a quality medium.

In recent years, the quality of recycled papers has improved. Designers no longer have to sacrifice quality when they choose to use recycled. Nor is recycled paper the only option. Papers made from other sustainable materials such as bamboo and hemp are on the market, as are soy-based inks.

Paper manufacturers are also stepping up to the plate to clean up their processes. Some have stopped harvesting trees from virgin forests. Others have switched to nonchlorine bleach and other less-harmful chemicals. Manufacturers are making efforts to reduce energy and water usage.

Is printing on paper still an environmentally dirty business? Yep. But you have options. Educate yourself. Look for printers and papers that have environmentally friendly certifications such as FSC (Forest Stewardship Council), SFI (Sustainable Forestry Initiative), Green Seal and others. Do some research. Ask your local printer. Don't be shy about making inquiries.

Keeping it within budget.

Paper and ink are typically the most expensive parts of producing a printed piece. So budget is often the single most important criterion in the print decision-making process. Available budget dictates whether your paper will be an economy or premium sheet. Budget also dictates whether you'll print the job in-house or hire a commercial printer. A larger budget allows for printing extras such as four-color printing, specialty-printing processes like holographic (3D) and stochastic printing (cool use of dots to replicate images) or even finishing touches such as perforating, die-cutting, foil stamping or embossing.

While you're drooling over the paper possibilities for your design, you also need to be thinking about the kind of printing process best suited to your design.

TYPES OF PRINTING & PRINTERS

The quality of your finished printed design is not the only criterion for choosing a printer. There is also budget to consider, not to mention deadlines, timing and turnaround. As Rebecca says: "Speed, quality, price. Pick any two."

Printing in-house.

When you need it fast, have little or no budget and need relatively small quantities, in-house printing might be fine. You can use whatever software you have available, and font issues are less likely to occur.

But there are significant drawbacks. You'll need to know what paper sizes you printer can accommodate (usually letter or legal, and sometimes ledger) and design within these parameters.

Unless you own a printing device capable of printing to the edge of the paper (and most people don't), your design cannot bleed. Most printers have a built-in margin of approximately ¼ inch on the top and sides and ½ inch on the bottom. Anything you put outside the live area too close to the paper's edge won't reproduce.

You also can expect limited paper options. You may be restricted to inkjet or laser printer paper depending on your specific printer.

Printing documents designed to fold, such as newsletters and brochures, is painful to do in-house. When you take such projects to a commercial printer, the printer's prepress team manages page impositioning, that is, re-positioning pages so they will print front to back in the proper order. When you print in-house, you have to do this yourself. And getting text to line up properly and space evenly around folds is no easy task. Plus, even if you do manage alignments, uh, how many of those things are now sitting on the conference room table waiting for a folding party?

As a final insult, when you print in-house, don't expect any consistency with color. You can't assume your onscreen color will match your printer's output.

If you plan to print in-house, you need to design accordingly from the start.

Why won't my design print with a bleed? Most personal printers cannot print ink to the edge of the paper. If you are designing a piece to be printed in-house, build a border into the design. If you don't, you'll get one anyway, and you may be unhappy with the results.

Offset printers offer the greatest flexibility. If your job is 500 pieces or more, commercial/offset printers can print and assemble almost anything you throw at them.

Quick printers.

Surprisingly, depending on the quality of the quick printer, you may find printing with a quick printer as limiting as trying to print in-house. Nevertheless, quick printers have more paper choices, can print bleeds and offer a few more binding and finishing options.

Commercial/offset.

Offset printers offer the greatest flexibility. If your job is 500 pieces or more, commercial/offset printers can print and assemble almost anything you throw at them. They can print on a wide variety of paper sizes and offer a full range of paper stock. They handle bleeds, impositioning, folding, collating, some types of binding and even address labeling.

Offset printers also offer services such as die cutting (perforations, cut-out windows, pocket folders), embossing and foil stamping, either in-house or through subcontractors.

You can expect commercial/offset printers to produce matched and process colors faithfully to swatches, such as PANTONE® solid coated or process coated chip sets. Remember, however, that the color of your design as seen on your desktop screen will not match print output unless your computer and monitor are calibrated to your printer's.

It is important to note that with offset printing, the greater the print run, the lower the printing cost per piece. All the expense in printing is in the first run, meaning the setup. The cost of additional copies is negligible. For example, an initial print run of 500 pieces for a full-color flyer might cost $1,000. To print 1,000 of the same flyer might cost only $1,050. That's double the quantity for another $50.

You save money per piece by printing the greatest number you can use.

Web offset.

Once upon a time in graphic design, "web" referred to a particular kind of offset printing press, not the World Wide Web. The time to use web offset printing services is when you need to print a very large run, 10,000–20,000 pieces or more. Documents typically printed by web offset printers include newspapers, magazines, catalogs and books.

The biggest difference between standard offset and web offset printing is in the paper. Web offset utilizes extremely large rolls of paper as opposed to cut sheets used in traditional offset.

FOUR REALLY NEAT PAPER TREATMENTS

Ink is not the only thing printers can put on paper. There are a number of after-printing finishes and treatments you can apply to make your finished piece special. Here are four of the most common:

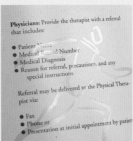

Foil stamping

Foil stamping involves applying a thin layer of shiny metallic foil to parts of your design. Foil comes in different shades from copper to silver to gold.

The effect is rich and becomes even richer when foil is applied with an emboss.

Embossing

To create an emboss, printers press a metal die into the paper to pop up a pattern on the surface of the paper. A raised pattern is called an "emboss" while a recessed pattern is called a "deboss." This technique can be paired with ink or foil stamping. If no ink or foil is used, the technique is called a "blind" emboss.

Varnishing

Varnish is a clear coat applied to parts of a layout (spot varnish) or to the whole page (flood varnish). Applied on press like ink, varnish provides a protective coat to the finished piece. Since it comes in glossy and dull finishes, it also can be used to create two-tone shiny and dull effects.

Die cutting

Die cutting is any paper cutting that is not strictly straight across trimming. Die cutting is used to create everything from rounded corners on business cards to the pockets on pocket folders. It also is used to create the perforations on tear-off cards.

Digital printing.

Digital printing has gained in popularity in recent years. While offset printing uses traditional ink, digital printing uses toner and is closer to the processes of color laser printing or color photocopying.

The quality of digital printing has improved to the point where it approaches that of offset printing. Price-wise, for small print runs of 500 pieces or less, digital printing can be cost-effective. But, unlike offset printing, there is no price break for greater quantities. If 500

request for quote	in focus design

Job Name: Surgical Associates Physician Guide

Quantity: 2,500 5,000 7,500 10,000

Flat Size: 8 x 9 inches

Finished Size: 4 x 9 inches

Pages: 24 (includes self-cover)

Binding & Finishing: Trim, saddle-stitch

Paper

Cover Stock: — *Weight:*

Text Stock: Gloss — *Weight:* 100lb text

Inks: 4/4

Reversals: Yes

Bleeds: Four sides

Screens:

Artwork: ☒ Customer Supplied ☐ Vendor Supplied

Software:

☐ Quark ☐ Pagemaker ☒ InDesign ☐ Other

Proofs: Mock-up, color laser

Delivery Date/Instructions: Will deliver to Surgical Associates of West Florida

Notes:

Please return bids by: January 11, 2008

Phone: 813.997.2079   **e-mail:** rjh@infocusdesign.net

27810 Sky Lake Circle • Wesley Chapel, FL 33543 • rjh@infocusdesign.net • 813.997.2079

RFQ. Use a Request for Quote form to get accurate prices from your printer.

pieces cost $500, then printing 1,000 pieces will cost $1,000. Digital printing is best reserved for small press runs.

One compelling reason to use digital printing is its ability to output variable data printing (VDP). Think of VDP as a mail merge on steroids. Variable data printing allows a printer to take a database of names, images and other information specific to a recipient, and print customized pieces on the fly.

For example, say a pet store wants to send out a sale-promoting postcard to each of its customers. The pet store provides a database of customer names, addresses, pet names and breeds. The postcard is designed with placeholders for customer name, pet name and picture of the breed. During printing, specific customer information is fed into the appropriate placeholder. As each printed piece comes off the press, then, it has been tailored to one particular customer.

Whatever your grand vision for your design, to determine whether or not you have the budget to match it, get an estimate. Get several estimates.

GET A PRINTING ESTIMATE

Some organizations actually require estimates from a minimum of three different printers before awarding the job to one. Even so, most working designers have relationships with a variety of commercial printers and so can predict which printing outfits fit the bill for which jobs, which have the most to least competitive pricing and which are accommodating and appreciative of your business. Newbie designers, however, really ought to get competitive estimates for comparison. Furthermore, as in all things, the cheapest estimate is not always the best choice.

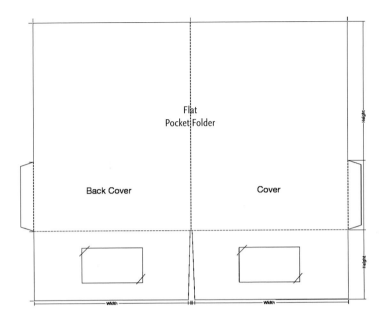

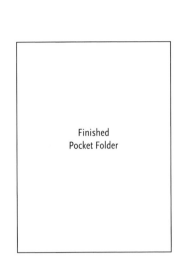

To provide the best most accurate estimates, printers need details and particulars about the printing job. You need to gather some information:

» **Quantity.** How many pieces do you need to print? It's a good idea to include a range of quantities on your request for estimate—for example 500, 1,000 and 1,500. You might even ask your printer where the price break starts on quantity, if any. Remember, while overall budget outlay is important to consider, you also need to consider price per piece.

» **Flat and finished sizes.** These are the dimensions of the document before assembly and the size of the finished document when fully assembled. For example, the flat dimensions of a tri-fold brochure might be 9 × 12 inches, and the finished size after folding might be 4 × 9 inches.

» **Number of pages.** With a brochure, specify number of panels. For larger documents like newsletters or annual reports, a page count is required. Because of the way printers print multiple-page documents, all printed pieces have page counts divisible by four. That requires a little forethought. If your cover design prints on the same paper stock as the inside pages of the design, then include the front, back and two inside covers in your page count. If your covers print on different paper, you'll need a separate estimate for the cover, too.

» **Choice of paper and weight.** This can be very specific if you are choosing your paper from a swatch book, for example "Neenah

Flat vs. finished size.
The size of a flat versus a finished print piece can differ significantly. Printers order paper based on the flat size so be sure to include this measurement in your RFQ.

COMMON PAPER FOLDS

Folding makes a larger sheet of paper easier to manage. This lets you pack a lot of information in a small portable package.

Here are some examples of common types of folds used for posters, brochures and other printed material. Since these are common, they tend to be fairly cost-effective when created in standard sizes.

If you really want to make an impact with a printed piece, consider an out-of-the-ordinary shape with an interesting fold. Be sure to consult with your printer first. For the most part, printers can print almost anything you come up with. However, they may have suggestions regarding paper, paper sizes and cost savings.

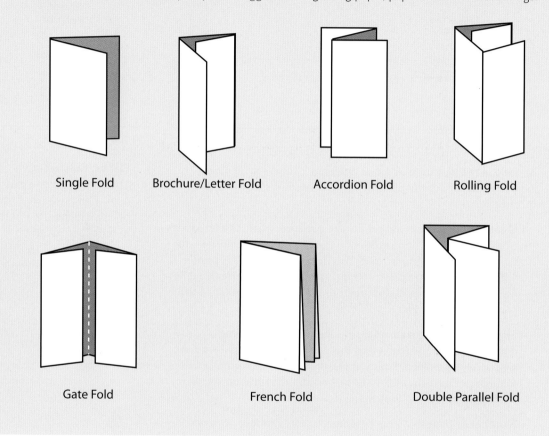

| Single Fold | Brochure/Letter Fold | Accordion Fold | Rolling Fold |

| Gate Fold | French Fold | Double Parallel Fold |

Classic Columns 100lb cover, chili pepper red." Or it may be less specific, such as "100lb gloss text cool white." When you don't specify a paper by name, your printer may spec your job on a "house sheet" that meets your criteria. House sheets or house papers are those that the printer keeps in stock and tend to be serviceable if generic. House sheets save money if paper quality is not an issue for your project.

» **Number of inks.** The notation for indicating the number of inks looks like a fraction. The top number indicates the number of inks required on one side of the paper, and the bottom number indicates the number of inks required on the other side. A document that prints full-color front and back would be noted as 4/4—four-color process on both sides—and pronounced as "four over four." A two-color document would be indicated as 2/2 along with a notation on which inks to use. Your estimate request also should note if the project requires any varnishes— coatings that add shine and/or protection. Varnishes may cover the entire paper surface (flood varnish) or just specific areas such as photographs (spot varnish).

» **Bleeds.** Does the design bleed to the edge of the paper? Yes or no, and on how many sides of the page?

» **Binding and finishing.** Beyond putting ink on the paper, make note of anything the printer must do to or with the paper in order to achieve your design. This includes folds, binding, die cutting (including slots for business cards and CDs, perforations for tear-offs and pockets for pocket folders), foil stamping, embossing, debossing, putting sheets into pads, etc.

» **Delivery date.** At any given time, a printer may have several jobs in production. To help your printer meet your schedule and the schedules of others, be specific about your due date.

» **Delivery instructions.** What happens to the completed job? Will it be

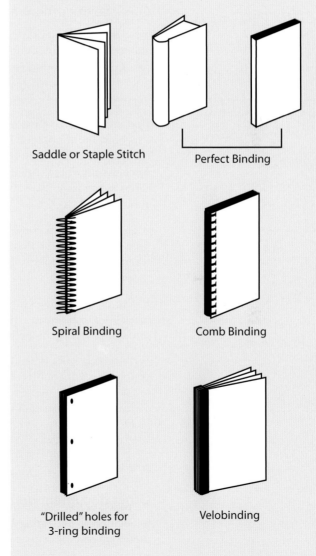

COMMON BINDING TYPES

Binding style is determined by a variety of factors: budget, presentation quality, the need to update the document and the needs of the document's end user.

Here are some of the more common binding types.

Saddle or Staple Stitch

Perfect Binding

Spiral Binding

Comb Binding

"Drilled" holes for 3-ring binding

Velobinding

When proofreading, pay particular attention to headlines, cutlines and other non-body type. Nothing is worse than a big fat error in a big bold headline.

delivered to you, the boss or the client? Are you sending it to a mail house for distribution? Do you need the job shipped to multiple locations? Make sure your printer knows what to do when the printing job is complete.

PREPARE YOUR DOCUMENT FOR PRINTING

Of course you want to do everything possible to make sure your project gets done right and on time and on budget. Here are some tips for getting there:

Give the document a thorough proofread.

Yes, someone does have to proofread. Additionally, pay particular attention to headlines, cutlines and other non-body type. When people proofread, they tend to focus on body copy and often skim over potential typos elsewhere. Nothing is worse than a big fat error in a big bold headline.

Beyond someone taking responsibility for typos, give your design a second (and third) look before it goes to press. Pay attention to typographic consistency. Do you accidentally change font styles, sizes or colors anywhere? Are there elements that don't line up, especially across facing pages? Are all images or visuals treated consistently, such as outlining?

A good way to look for design errors is to print a draft copy of each page, put it all on the floor and look at each page upside-down. When reading the copy doesn't distract you, potential design errors are easier to spot.

If your design includes binding, folding, die cutting or other specialized techniques, create a full-blown working mockup to make sure things line up properly and that your measurements are accurate.

With certain types of binding, especially perfect and spiral bindings, double-check the gutters. You don't want copy that folks need to read to fall too far into the gutter, be swallowed up by the binding or get perforated to make room for spiral or comb bindings.

Once you're happy with the shape of the document, make sure that the boss or client gets a final chance to approve the work before it goes to print.

Other document details.

In addition to correcting any design typos, you'll need to check a few more things:

- » **Image resolutions.** Make sure all your images are high resolution and in the proper format.

- » **Spot or process?** Make sure your color setup is appropriate for your final output (change spot colors to process or process colors to spot depending on your needs).

- » **Set up document bleeds.** If you're printing anywhere other than in-house, and your design bleeds to the edge of the paper, you'll need to go through your document and extend your bleeds 1/8 inch beyond the document edge. When printers print a document with a bleed, they print the design on a bigger piece of paper and trim it down to size. If your design doesn't extend the extra 1/8-inch, you risk ending up with white edges around your design where the bleed should have been.

- » **Clean up your pasteboard.** Remove any extra/unused graphics and text boxes from your file's pasteboard. Nonessential materials cluttering up the document just add unnecessary file size. This can cause problems with commercial printing processes.

- » **Clean up your swatch palettes.** For the same reason as above, remove unused colors from your list of available swatches, too.

WHAT TO TAKE TO THE PRINTER

To ensure your final print product matches your original vision, give the following items to your printer:

- » A copy of your document in its native format

- » A copy of each visual used in your layout

- » A copy of each font used in your layout

- » A hardcopy of your document, preferably mocked-up

- » A note with your contact information

or:

- » A press-quality PDF file. If you choose this option, ask your printer for PDF specifications and create your file accordingly

Do your own flight check.

When you give your design files to your printer of choice, the first thing she or he does is a flight check, a quick test to make sure you've included all the parts necessary for printing. If the flight check turns up missing parts, you'll get a call. Tracking down missing parts and having to correct design errors at this stage costs time and money. So wouldn't it be smart to run your own flight check ahead of time?

Professional-grade page layout applications include flight check options. When you run them, they check for missing fonts, missing graphics and graphics in the wrong format or the wrong color space. The program dialog boxes typically allow you to correct any errors on the spot.

The final beauty of the flight check process is that it allows you to package your document to take to the printer. The packaging process creates a copy of your document, including all fonts and graphics.

WHAT TO GIVE THE PRINTER: A CHECKLIST

To print your project, any printer will require the following files:

» **Your layout.** Include a complete copy of your design document in the software format in which you created it. And, yes, that would be professional-grade design software.

» **All images used.** Include a copy of every visual or image in your design, at high resolution, saved at the size required for the design and in the proper file format (usually TIF or EPS).

» **Fonts.** Include files for all fonts used in your design.

» (If you use the preflight package option in your professional-grade software, it will assemble the previous three items for you.)

» **A hardcopy of your document.** If your document has unique folds, pockets or anything other than standard pages, provide an assembled mockup of the design as it should be in its final form. Your printer will use your mocked-up hardcopy to make sure everything shows up in the right places when she or he opens up your original files.

» **Contact information.** Include a note with your name and contact information, a list of the contents of any and all files, and the name and edition/version of the software program(s) you used. Include your after-hours phone numbers in case the printer has an emergency with your print job.

If you're new to the design process, working with a new printer or have a complex design (more than a couple pages and a couple of pictures), meet with your print rep in person to deliver your files and hardcopy proof. This gives you both an opportunity to discuss the job and ask questions, such as confirming proper resolution of the files you will provide.

Alternatively, most commercial printers can accept files electronically, and, no, we do not mean via email. By the time you have more than one high-res image in a document, you've already exceeded the file size capacity of a lot of email programs.

If your combined folder of file, font and graphic is more than 5MB, you will need to use your printer's File Transfer Protocol (FTP) site to transfer files. FTP clients allow you electronically to transfer huge amounts of data not possible to send through email. FTP requires some software on your end and some access information. When you plug in the correct information (host location, username and password), you gain access to a Web server. You can copy files to and from that server.

If you choose to submit your files to the printer this way, we recommend two things. First, use some software to compress your folder. We've seen strange corruptions in files transferred without compression so better safe than sorry. We also recommend that you email a PDF of your completed document to your print rep separately from the file upload. This PDF serves as your proof in lieu of a hardcopy.

NOW WHAT?

Once your printer has your files, the next thing you can expect is a printer proof. This is just another hardcopy mockup that your printer produces using inks and paper closer to those you have specified. This is your last opportunity to make sure the document is in order before the whole project is printed.

Ask your printer ahead of time what kind of proof you can expect—and when. If color quality and consistency is important, ask for a color proof. If your project includes multiple pages, folds, die cuts or any other special features, ask for a paper dummy. A paper dummy is a full-size, fully functional mockup of the final product.

Your printer will require you (or the boss or client) to approve the proof before the project goes on the press. When you get your printer proof, pull a copy of your own most recent draft and compare the two. Systematically examine the following:

> **Text.** Make sure none is missing. Also look for rewrapped text.

> **Fonts.** Make sure there are no dropped fonts. Dropped fonts typically default to Courier, are ugly as sin and easy to spot.

Printer proofs. Printer proofs come in many forms, including full color composites and paper dummies. Paper dummies are full-size fully functional mockups.

WHAT TYPE OF **PROOF** SHOULD YOU EXPECT?

Document Type	Proof to Expect
Letterhead, Business Card, Envelope	Composed Color Proof/Color Laser Proof
Poster	Composed Color Proof, Loose Color Proof (may be ½ actual size)
Pocket Folder	Paper Dummy, Composed Color Proof, Die Strike
Brochure	Composed Color Proof, Loose Color Proof, Paper Dummy with scoring sample—if needed
Newsletter	Paper Dummy, Loose Color Proof, Composed Color Proof
Annual Report	Paper Dummy, Loose Color Proof, Composed Color Proof
Postcard Mailer	Loose Color Proof

» **Folios.** Look to see that every page is accounted for and in the correct order.

» **All photos and/or visuals.** Check for proper placement and cropping.

» **Margins.** Look at all margins, inner and outer, and all elements, including alignments, that cross over spreads.

» **Spot colors.** Check placement of spot colors as needed.

» **Specialty items.** Double check special design elements such as die cuts, perforations, folds and foil stamps.

» **Typos.** Proof one last time, paying particular attention to headlines and cutlines, as well as any chatter, etc., associated with infographics and figures/exhibits.

Right on the proof, circle any errors or things that need correcting. Your printer's rep will ask you to sign a form indicating one of the following:

» The job is ready to print.

» The job is ready to print with corrections indicated.

» A new proof is required.

You would be surprised how many previously overlooked errors miraculously appear when the printer proof shows up. Sadly, once the printer provides a proof, further edits will cost you. Printers charge for each "author alteration" you request. So do your best proofing and editing before you turn over the files for a printer's proof.

When to do a press check.

For extremely important print jobs where color matching and quality are essential, consider a press check.

A press check allows you to view the first sheets of your actual print run as they come off the press. It's an opportunity to check color and other details before the full run is completed. Be warned, if you want a press check, you'll be at the mercy of the printer's run schedule. Your job might be scheduled for the middle of the night, and neither you nor your boss or client can ask the printer to reschedule to accommodate your sleep.

If you decide your project is important enough for a press check, here's what you should be looking at:

» **Paper.** Confirm that the project is being printed on the correct paper, in the specified weight, finish and color.

» **Visuals and type.** Look closely at the flat sheets to make sure no elements are missing and that none of your typography is re-flowing itself incorrectly.

» **Registration.** Check the registration of multiple sheets. Registration marks printed on the corners and center points of each sheet should line up. If you see that they don't align, ask your pressperson. Sometimes paper stretches a bit on the press, which can cause registration marks to misalign.

» **Color.** Look closely at the color on the sheets. Make sure your spot and process colors are printing properly—the printer should have a swatch book handy, but you may want to bring your own. Also make sure that the color is even across the whole sheet. You may have to fold the sheet to see a color comparison from front to back.

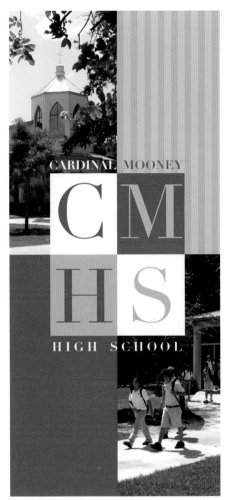

Matching spot colors. Do a press check when a close color match is important to the final product. Be sure to bring a swatch book along for comparison.

Other services. In addition to printing, commercial printers also may offer collating, labeling, mailing and other services.

Reproduced by permission of Odyssey Marine Exploration.

» **Varnishes and other finishes.** Check locations of varnishes and other coatings, if any. Also confirm the correct finish (gloss, matte) is being used.

» **Ink.** Using a loupe, take a good look at the actual dots of ink. They should be sharp. If not, there may be issues with the ink mixture. Ask your pressperson about this.

Look for and circle any visible defects on the sheet.

Once everything is working to your satisfaction, give the go-ahead to finish the press run. Be sure to thank everyone for the extra time and trouble.

The finished product.

Once the final print job arrives, check it one last time against your own proof to make sure everything is in order. If you find something on the final piece that wasn't on your original, ask the printer to check the printer proof. If the glitch occurred between the printer proof and the final output, you are justified in asking the printer to reprint your job on the printer's dime.

OTHER THINGS YOUR PRINTER CAN DO

Your print representative can be a fantastic resource for other things aside from just printing your work. Consulting with a printer while still in the planning stages of your project also can help you avoid design and printing pitfalls. Print reps can help you get samples of papers you are considering and even plain paper mockups of your print pieces so you can get a better sense of weight and other properties before you commit.

Once your print job is complete, your printer also may be able to help with distribution. Many printers have the ability to print mailing addresses directly to your pieces. They may be able to tab-seal folding pieces per postal requirements. Printers sometimes have in-house mailing services or relationships with mail houses if they do not offer those services themselves.

While you carefully are planning your design, dotting your I's and crossing your T's from design and paper choice through the press check, a good working relationship with the printer is worth its weight in gold.

▶ TRY THIS

1. Locate several printed pieces. Complete a request for estimate form as the pieces' designers originally would have "spec'd" them. Or create a request for estimate based on one of your own designs.

2. Find the preflight and package functions for your design software. Practice using them with a design you've created. Try it on a single page document and a multiple-page document. Compare the results.

3. Make your own full-color mockup of a multi-page design you've been working on. Some document types to try: a tri-fold brochure, a multi-page newsletter, a mini pocket folder, a restaurant menu, a table tent-card for a party or event. Or how about that banquet invitation to the city's movers and shakers—the one we talked about at the beginning of the chapter?

4. Visit a local quick printer or the website of a local quick printer. Get a list of available services. Does the company bind? fold? score? die cut? emboss? What papers are available? What other services are available?

5. Do some research on the greening of graphic design and printing. Then write and design an electronic newsletter alert on the topic.

6. Figure out a way to get an invitation to a press check.

7. Acquire several swatch books from a local paper distributor or paper manufacturer. Using the swatch books, see if you can find the answers to the following questions.

   a. What are the available colors and weights?

   b. Is this an economy sheet, a premium sheet or something in between?

   c. What is the paper's brightness?

   d. What finishes does the paper come in?

   e. Is the paper laser compatible? Does it have recycled content?

   f. Does it come with matching envelopes? If so, in what sizes?

Then invite your paper distributor representative to come and chat with you about paper lines.

15 | CONCLUSION
now that you know enough to be
dangerous, thanks for stopping by

Designer's Notebook

Rebecca Hagen

Communication Design • Fall 2009

University of South Florida

School of Mass Communications

I f you're starting to annoy coworkers, friends and family with your constant design critiques, then congratulations. You've learned to recognize bad—and good—design when you see it. Our work here is done. Before you unleash the full force of your new powers to set the universe right, allow us to leave you with some final and somewhat contradictory thoughts.

EVERYTHING IS CHANGING

We don't need to tell you the media business is in flux. That's old news. As the cliché goes, change is the only thing that doesn't change, especially in communications where we're all technophiles.

The new news is the contemporary assumption that everyone is a fluent multimedia visual communication designer. And everyone means everyone. Sometimes the amateurs and the audiences are better visual communicators than the pros. Meanwhile, the media bosses have begun to operate as if anyone who wants to work in the business can produce effective visual communication across any platform. "Anyone" covers the self-described wordsmiths, too, such as journalists, copyeditors and copywriters.

This reality requires you, whatever your specialty, to develop the good eye that goes beyond memorizing layout rules. You also need to know why those conventions work—or don't work—and that means knowing something about art, design and formal composition. Otherwise, you show up for work with an embarrassingly poor visual aesthetic.

THERE'S NOTHING NEW UNDER THE SUN

Even as everything about the media professions from business models to technology is changing, when it comes to graphic design, there really is nothing new under the sun.

Advertising and marketing communication folks produce public relations materials. Public relations practitioners produce advertising, marketing and news materials. The news industry borrows visual conventions from the entertainment industry, which adopts innovation from the advertising industry. And vice versa and so on.

We're all visual communicators using and abusing the same rules of graphic design and layout. While industry turmoil may be inspiring innovation in visual styles and trends, the grammar of visual communication hasn't changed. Regardless of the platform or the format, the fundamentals don't change. Good design is good design. Form follows function. Use visuals and type to capture attention, control eye flow, convey information and evoke emotion. White space is not your enemy.

SOMETIMES YOU JUST NEED TO HIRE A PROFESSIONAL

If nothing else, you now have enough knowledge to work alongside visual experts without drawing their scorn.

Knowing enough to know the good stuff when you see it also means knowing your own limitations. Sometimes you do just need to hire a professional. Appreciate the talent, skill and experience of the full-timers—artists, designers, art directors, illustrators, photographers, videographers, cinematographers, Web designers and developers, etc.

WORDS OF ENCOURAGEMENT

If our little book is your first foray into visual communication and design, there is way more to learn if you're interested. If you think graphic design might be your future, get busy. Take a class. Find some online tutorials. Read, read, read. Glom onto a mentor. If, for you, some knowledge is plenty, we salute you for reading along with us this far.

Regardless, we hope you enjoy your new know-how. Try to avoid becoming an overzealous visual snob alienating colleagues and loved ones. Don't be afraid to break the rules with a purpose. Strive always to delight your audiences. Treat professional creatives with respect. Don't forget to have some fun.

Finally, as we say to our neighbors, thanks for stopping by.

GLOSSARY

A

Alley: An alley is the negative space between columns, modules or units on a grid.

Alpha channel: Alpha channel, or "A," controls color transparency in the RGBA Web color system. (See also RGB.)

Analogous color: Analogous colors sit next to each other on the color wheel and work well together in color palettes because they contain some of the colors sitting next to them.

ANNCR: The abbreviation for announcer is ANNCR.

App (application): Apps, short for "(software) applications," are programs designed to run on a computer, tablet, smartphone, website or social media. Since the introduction of smartphones and tablets, apps have become increasingly popular and accessible. Common types include calendars, mileage trackers, restaurant finders and games.

Ascenders: Ascenders are the tall characters or glyphs that ascend above lowercase x-height, such as the lowercase letterforms b, d, f, h, k, l, t.

Aspect ratio: Aspect ratio refers to the ratio of width to height for electronic screens.

Asymmetrical balance: With its visual fulcrum or center of visual gravity moved off-center, asymmetrical balance is visually balanced but not symmetrical.

B

B roll: B roll is file, extra or archival footage used as visual fill or for creating transitions between clips.

Backlight: A backlight is a light source used to highlight the focal point from behind in order to give it contrast and dimension.

Baseline: This sentence sits on the baseline, the line guiding the horizontal alignment of type at the bottoms of words.

Beauty shot: In camera work, a beauty shot frames the focal point, whether person or object, to show off its best visual features.

Beta site: A beta site is a working test version of a website that isn't available to the public.

Bleed: Bleed refers to content that runs beyond the specified live area or safe area into the margins and off the edge of the page or screen.

Breadcrumb trail: As in fairytales about children lost in the forest, a breadcrumb trail in Web design is a system for keeping users apprised of their location in cyberspace.

Brief, creative or design: The document that briefs the creative team on the project, the creative or design brief answers basic job order and research questions about the project.

Built color: Built color uses the CMYK 4-color or full-color printing process to build any color.

Burning & dodging: Burning and dodging refer to techniques that darken or lighten photographs, respectively. Traditionally achieved by increasing/decreasing exposure to prints in the darkroom, these techniques mostly now are accomplished digitally.

Byline: The byline is the name of the writer, artist or photographer given credit.

C

Callout: Also called labels, callouts "call out" or call attention to details of infographics.

Cap line: The invisible horizontal line against which the tops of capitalized glyphs align in a particular font.

Cascading Style Sheet (CSS): Although Web pages are built with programming languages such as HTML, the appearance of Web pages is dictated by Cascading Style Sheets or CSS.

Chatter: The brief typeset explanatory copy on an infographic is called chatter.

Close-up: In framing video and film shots, a close-up frames the focal point as a detail shot. Variations on the close-up include extreme, medium, full and wide close-up shots, as well as close and medium close shots. These frames move from an extreme close-up framing only an actor's eyes to a medium close shot that frames an actor from the waist up.

Closure: The Gestalt law of closure predicts the way people mentally fill in gaps to complete a perceived shape.

CMYK: CMYK is the 4-color or full-color printing process of building any color with just four inks: cyan, magenta, yellow and black.

Color management: Color management is the formal term for getting your color to match properly across devices, from scanners to digital cameras to computer screens to printers.

Color separation: In commercial printing, each ink color has to be separated out of the design into its own printing plate.

Comp or complimentary image: A comp image, short for complimentary image, is a low-resolution stock image, usually with a watermark, available to sample in a layout before purchasing.

Comp or comprehensive: A comp, short for comprehensive, is a mockup of the final design and is used for getting approvals before spending time and money on final production.

Compass: The compass establishes direction on a map.

Complementary color: Color complements sit opposite each other on the color wheel.

Concept: The concept is the big idea uniting and driving the design's message.

Condensed font: Condensed fonts are drawn to be narrower (condensed) to take up less space than standard fonts.

Content management system (CMS): A content management system or CMS is a Web-based application that manages page content and generates pages on the fly from information stored in a database. CMSs allow people with no knowledge of coding to build visually consistent websites.

Continuity: The Gestalt law of continuity predicts the way the eye will follow the direction of a line.

Crawl: A crawl refers to superimposed moving type crawling across an electronic screen such as TV.

Creative or design brief: The document that briefs the creative team on the project, the creative or design brief answers basic job order and research questions about the project.

Crop: To crop is to trim excess from visuals such as photography.

CSS: Although Web pages are built with programming languages such as HTML, the appearance of Web pages is dictated by Cascading Style Sheets or CSS.

Curly quotes: Curly quotes or smart quotes are the correct punctuation marks for quotations. Curly quotes are curly, as opposed to prime marks, which are straight. Prime marks indicate feet and inches, not quotations. See also smart quotes and prime marks.

Cut: In film and video, part of continuity is transitioning or segueing between shots and scenes. The most common type of transition is the simple "cut" from one shot to the next.

Cutaway: In film and video, "cutting away" from the main action by inserting something else going on in the scene is called a cutaway.

Cut-in or insert: In film and video, "cutting in" or "inserting" a close-up shot of something significant in the scene is called a cut-in or insert.

Cutline: In news contexts, captions for photos and visuals are called cutlines.

D

Decorative fonts: Decorative fonts have no common feature other than they are mostly novelty fonts best used for "decorative" purposes.

Depth of field: In camera work, depth of field refers to what in the shot remains in focus, whether foreground, midground, background or some combination.

Descenders: Descenders are characters or glyphs with tails that descend below the baseline, such as the lowercase letterforms g, j, p, q, y.

Design or creative brief: The document that briefs the creative team on the project, the creative or design brief answers basic job order and research questions about the project.

Detail shot: In camera work, a detail shot is a close-up shot revealing detail about the focal point.

Dingbats: Forms of type that can be styled like type, dingbats are the ornamental characters in a font, or they may comprise an entire font of nothing but picture glyphs.

Display fonts: Drawn specifically to appear proportionate at larger point sizes, display fonts work well in headlines and signs.

Dissolve: In video and film transitions, the dissolve simply dissolves the frame before cutting to the next one.

Dodging & burning: Dodging and burning refer to techniques that lighten or darken photographs, respectively. Traditionally achieved by decreasing/increasing exposure to prints in the darkroom, these techniques now mostly are accomplished digitally.

Dolly shot: In a dolly shot, the camera is positioned on a dolly that moves or pushes toward the focal point.

Dummy: In print news, a dummy is the set of thumbnail sketches that lay out or paginate what goes on every page of the issue, including ads and stories with visuals.

E

Em dash: Historically the width of a lowercase m, the em dash adds emphasis by replacing punctuation such as commas, colons and parentheses.

En dash: Historically the width of a lowercase n, the en dash is the correct glyph for replacing the "to" with punctuation in expressions such as "2–4 weeks."

EPS: EPS (Encapsulated Postscript) is used for some specific kinds of images. Vector graphics, usually illustrations, are saved in EPS format, as are some photographs that have certain styling applied. EPS format is typically used for logos and, like GIF, supports transparency.

Establishing shot: In camera work, an establishing shot is a full or wide angle shot designed to orient viewers to the overall scene.

F

Fade: In video and film transitions, a fade simply fades the visual frame before cutting to the next one.

File Transfer Protocol: File Transfer Protocol or FTP enables you to upload and share very large files on the Web.

Fill light: Fill light supplements the key light by filling in unwanted shadows for less contrast.

Flexible or fluid Web design: To avoid layouts, thus designs, that "break" across different types, sizes and aspect ratios of screens and browsers, designers build flexibility and fluidity into their designs' CSS by specifying sizes as percentages (100 percent) rather than fixed heights and widths in pixels.

Focal point: Sometimes called the principle of emphasis, the focal point is the visual center of attention in the design or layout because it focuses the eye's attention.

Folio: Usually appearing in the margins of serials and periodicals such as newspapers, magazines and newsletters, the folio identifies the publication, issue and date, as well as page number if hardcopy.

Font: A font is a complete set of characters in a particular size and style of type.

Font family: A font family or typeface contains a series of related fonts, such as Times New Roman, Times Bold and Times Italic.

Foot space or footer: The bottom margin is the foot space or footer.

Four-color process: CMYK is the 4-color or full-color printing process of building any color with just four inks: cyan, magenta, yellow and black.

FTP: FTP or File Transfer Protocol enables you to upload and share very large files on the Web.

Full-color process: CMYK is the 4-color or full-color printing process of building any color with just four inks: cyan, magenta, yellow and black.

Full shot: In framing video and film shots, a full shot reveals an actor head-to-foot. A medium full shot frames the actor from the knees up.

FX: FX is shorthand for special "effects."

G

Gain: Gain is when paper absorbs more ink than expected resulting in muddy type or visuals.

Gestalt theory: In the early 20th century, a group of German psychologists studied the way the human brain interprets and organizes what the eyes see. The results of this research became the Gestalt laws. See: closure, continuity, proximity, similarity.

GIF (vs. JPG): GIF (Graphic Interchange Format) and JPG (Joint Photographic Experts Group) are file formats for saving images destined for the Web and electronic screens. Both are low-resolution image formats. A big difference between them is a GIF will support transparency and a JPG will not.

Transparency by definition means see-through. In the case of Web graphics, transparency is essentially the ability to make certain color groups invisible. If you've ever tried to put a logo in JPG format on top of a colored background and discovered that your logo has a white box around it, you've encountered lack of transparency. By creating your Web graphic in the correct software application and saving as a GIF image, you can eliminate the white box.

Glyph: A glyph is an individual character of a font, whether a letter, numeral, punctuation mark, dingbat or special symbol. Most fonts have 265 glyphs. OpenType fonts have up to 65,000 glyphs.

Golden proportion: The golden proportion, sometimes called the golden ratio or divine proportion, refers to a ratio—1:1.618—that results in a universally appealing aesthetic when applied to shapes such as rectangles.

Graphical user interface or GUI: Web, tablet and smartphone users don't interact with computer code; they interact with graphics, such as buttons and tabs, known as graphical user interfaces or GUI. User-friendly "gooey" designs require savvy interface designers.

Graphics package: In the newsroom, a graphics package reports a story by using multiple types of graphics together.

Grayscale: A graduated range of tones from black to gray to white is called grayscale.

Greek text: Greek text or greeking is dummy copy or type used as a temporary substitute for the actual copy or type.

Grid: A grid is a series of horizontal and vertical lines composing the skeletal template of a design.

Grid module or grid unit: Instead of columns, a grid structure may include squares or rectangles called modules or units.

GUI or graphical user interface: Web, tablet and smartphone users don't interact with computer code; they interact with graphics, such as buttons and tabs, known as graphical user interfaces or GUI. User-friendly "gooey" designs require savvy interface designers.

Gutter: A gutter is the oversized margin between two facing pages. The gutter is designed to accommodate the fold or binding. Some design software applications refer to alleys between grid columns as gutters, too.

H

Hairline rule: A hairline rule is a very thin rule or border—as thin as a strand of hair.

Hairline strokes: The thin lines in characters or glyphs are hairline strokes. The thick lines are stem strokes.

Handheld: Handheld refers to the cameraperson holding the camera as she or he moves through the scene shooting video or film.

Hanging indent: Hanging indents refer to indicators that hang out to the left in the margin, instead of indenting to the right into the paragraph or text. Hanging indents are required for bulleted and numbered lists, as well as for quotation marks on pull quotes.

Hard light or low key: Hard light or low key emphasizes shadows, thus contrast, including shadows on people's faces.

Headspace or header: The top margin is the headspace or header.

Hexadecimal code: A Web-based color specification system, hexadecimal color uses sets of numbers and letters to designate RGB light formulae.

High key or soft light: High key or soft light evens out the shadows to decrease harsh contrasts. It makes people and products look more attractive.

Horizon line: The line separating land and sky is the horizon line, which communicates a sense of distance or perspective.

Horsey: Not a compliment in design, horsey means awkwardly large and lacking grace.

HTML: HTML stands for Hypertext Markup Language, the basic code that makes up most Web pages.

Hue: In color, hue answers the "what color?" question.

Hypertext Markup Language: Hypertext Markup Language or HTML is the basic code that makes up most Web pages.

I

Impositioning: Impositioning is the prepress process of getting multiple pages that are designed to print front and back to align properly for correct printing and binding or folding.

Infographic: An infographic delivers information graphically, such as in graphs, charts, maps, figures and diagrams.

Insert or cut-in: In film and video, "cutting in" or "inserting" a close-up shot of something significant in the scene is called a cut-in or insert.

Inset, map: On a map, an inset enlarges a section of the map to reveal more detail.

Inset & offset: Inset refers to the content of a box sitting in away from the box's edges, rule, border or frame. Offset refers to items outside the box sitting off away from the box's edges.

J

JPG (vs. GIF): JPG (Joint Photographic Experts Group) and GIF (Graphic Interchange Format) are file formats for saving images destined for the Web and electronic screens. Both are low-resolution image formats. A big difference between them is a GIF will support transparency and a JPG will not. Transparency by definition means see-through. In the case of Web graphics, transparency is essentially the ability to make certain color groups invisible.

If you've ever tried to put a logo in JPG format on top of a colored background and discovered that your logo has a white box around it, you've encountered lack of transparency. By creating your Web graphic in the correct software application and saving as a GIF image, you can eliminate the white box.

K

Kerning: Kerning refers to the negative space between two characters or glyphs.

Key: On infographics, such as maps, the key identifies and defines symbols and other reference markers or icons used.

Key light: A key light is the main or key light source in the shot, whether natural or artificial.

L

Lead: The first paragraph of the body copy is called the lead.

Leading: Leading refers to the negative space between lines of type.

Leg: A leg is a column of typeset copy.

Lift-out: Also called a pull quote, a lift-out is a pithy quotation pulled from the body copy and then enlarged and embellished to become both a visual and a teaser.

Ligature: Ligatures are specially designed letter pairs—a single glyph meant to take the place of two traditional letters that may look awkward if typeset side-by-side, such as "fi."

Live area: Live area refers to the area of the page within which material should print safely. Anything outside of the live area may be cropped off. For the electronic media equivalent, see safe area.

Long shot: In framing video and film shots, long shots and extreme long shots get long angles on the scene.

Loop: In video and animation, a loop endlessly repeats by circling the ending back to the beginning to start all over again.

Low key or hard light: Low key or hard light emphasizes shadows, thus contrast, including shadows on people's faces.

M

Matched color: Matched color is a premixed spot color of ink matched to a color swatch.

Mean line: The invisible horizontal line against which the x-height of lowercase glyphs align in a particular font.

Medium shot: In framing video and film shots, a medium shot frames the actor from the hips up. A medium full shot frames the actor from the knees up, and a medium close shot frames the actor from the belt up.

Modern fonts: Modern fonts have extremely thin serifs, and their stress lies on the vertical, unlike old style's diagonal stress. Choose modern fonts carefully for long copy situations, and avoid them for screen applications.

Modular page design: In modular page design, each story is arranged into a rectangle, and the rectangles are arranged onto rectangular units of the grid of the page. Modular design is popular with print and Web news design.

Montage: The video/film version of the collage, a montage cuts together many images.

Motion Pictures Expert Group or MPEG-4 or MP4: Motion Pictures Expert Group (MPEG-4) is a popular video file format for the Web that works well across platforms and is supported by most Web browsers.

Mousetype: Mousetype means very small type often used in the tags of advertising.

Mug shot: A mug shot is a photographic close-up or headshot, usually of a person.

Music bed or track: A music bed or track is a background soundtrack over which the main video and/or audio are laid.

N

Navigation: In Web design, navigation refers to the system that allows users to move through and among Web pages, including hypertext links and buttons, etc.

Negative or white space: Negative or white space is the empty space in which design is created and by which any design achieves pleasing balance and composition. Negative or white space has visual weight. "White space is not your enemy."

O

Offset & inset: Offset refers to items outside of a box sitting off away from the box's edges. Inset refers to the content of the box sitting in away from the box's edges, rule, border or frame.

Old style figures: Old style figures treat numerals as old style glyphs with ascenders and descenders.

Old style fonts: Old style fonts have serifs, thick stem strokes, thin hairline strokes and a diagonal stress on o-shaped characters. Old style fonts have good readability.

OpenType®: Designed to be functional across both Mac and PC platforms, OpenType fonts may have as many as 65,000 characters each, including ligatures, swash alternates and old style figures.

Optimization: Optimization refers to balancing the resolution, thus appearance, of graphics with their generally large file sizes so that they load quickly but still look good.

Orphan: A typographic orphan refers to a few lonely words stranded at the top of a leg of type.

Over lighting: A key light shining directly from above is over lighting.

P

Pan: A pan or panning indicates a stationary camera that sweeps across the scene. The effect is that of turning your head to look around.

Perspective: In visual arts, such as painting, photography and film, perspective refers to the sense of distance in the scene, whether achieved by where the horizon line sits in the composition, the use of a linear vanishing point, the relative size of objects in the scene or atmospheric use of light and dark values that seem to recede or move forward respectively.

Plug-in: A plug-in is code that gives a browser or website additonal functionality, For example, when a website automatically displays the most recent posts from a separate blog, a plug-in is at work.

PNG (portable network graphics): PNG is a file format for Web-destined graphics that must accommodate gradients and transparency, such as in drop shadows.

Pointer box: On a map or diagram, a pointer box literally is a box that points to some detail while offering additional information inside the box.

POV: POV is the abbreviation for point of view referring to the perspective of the camera lens, thus the audience.

Primary colors: The primary colors on the traditional color wheel are red, blue and yellow, which when variously combined produce every other color on the color wheel. Differing from the traditional color wheel, the RGB color wheel has different primary colors: red, green, blue.

Prime marks: Prime marks are the correct straight glyphs used to indicate feet and inches, as opposed to curly or smart quote glyphs used to punctuate quotations. See also curly quotes and smart quotes.

Proximity: The Gestalt law of proximity predicts that the eye will perceive items physically grouped together as belonging to the same group.

Pull-down menu: In electronic environments such as Web pages, a pull-down menu provides a form of navigation that remains hidden unless a user accesses it with the cursor/mouse.

Pull quote: Also called a lift-out quote, a pull quote is a pithy quotation pulled from the body copy and then enlarged and embellished to become both a visual and a teaser.

Push: In video and film, push shots push into the scene. In a zoom, a stationary camera pushes into the scene by using the lens to zoom in on the focal point. In a dolly shot, the camera itself, positioned on a dolly, moves or pushes toward the focal point.

R

Radial balance: Radial balance refers to circular designs in which the fulcrum lies at the center.

Reference points: On a map, reference points are landmarks, either natural or built, that orient the viewer.

Registration: Registration refers to aligning material across color plates in commercial printing.

Rendered type: Rendered type is a character, a word or a string of words filled with an image or otherwise transformed using photo-editing software.

Resolution: Image resolution refers to the detail or crispness of an image. Digital image resolution may be measured in pixels per inch (ppi), which is referred to as dots per inch (dpi). For Web applications use 72 dpi. For high-quality print applications, use 300 dpi. For newsprint, use 200 dpi.

Responsive Web design: Designers must account for multiple types and sizes of screens, not to mention rotating ones. Responsive Web design plans for design flexibility and fluidity across devices, screen orientations, apps versus websites, and browsers. Responsive design employs flexible grid-based layouts, flexible assets and media queries.

Reversing: A reverse literally reverses figure color with fill/field/background color. Reversed type refers to light type on a dark background, such as white type on a black field.

RGB: Standing for red, green and blue, RGB is the color wheel system for achieving color in electronic and digital screen environments by mixing red, green and blue light.

RGBA: The next generation of Web color specification, RGBA adds "A" to "RGB." "A" stands for alpha channel, which controls color transparency in the RGBA Web color system.

Rights-managed image: For a rights-managed image, you pay more to make sure other folks in your market don't use the same image, too. For a cheaper alternative, see royalty-free image.

Rough: A rough is a rough layout only slightly more detailed than a thumbnail sketch.

Royalty-free image: Royalty-free images are inexpensive stock images with no guarantees your competitor won't use them, too. For guarantees, see rights-managed image.

Rule: A rule is a graphic line, such as a border or a frame.

Rule of thirds: The rule of thirds says that dividing a layout or composition into thirds makes for a more interesting visual composition. The rule of thirds suggests that the four gridline intersections on a 3 × 3 grid offer the best locations to position a focal point in an asymmetrical layout.

S

Safe area: Safe area refers to the area of the electronic screen within which material is visible. Anything outside of the safe area just disappears. For the hardcopy print equivalent, see live area.

Sans serif fonts: Sans serif (French for "without serif") fonts have no serifs, and their strokes have uniform thickness. They are the most readable fonts for screen applications.

Saturation: Saturation refers to the amount or intensity of a hue.

Scale: Scale refers to relative size and proportion.

Scale, map: The scale on a map establishes the reduced proportions of distance, i.e. an inch equals a mile, etc.

Script fonts: Script fonts resemble cursive handwriting. They can be quite elegant in decorative situations, but they are not a good choice for readability.

Search engine optimization (SEO): Search engine optimization or SEO refers to making your website search-engine friendly to rank well in user Web searches.

Secondary colors: Mixing any two primary colors produces the secondary complement of the third primary color.

SEO, or search engine optimization: SEO or search engine optimization refers to making your website search-engine friendly to rank well in user Web searches.

Serif: Serifs are those little feet or flags at the tips of glyphs.

SFX: SFX is shorthand for "sound effects."

Sidebar: Simply a separate block of type with a solid background, a stroked outline or an ample border of negative space, a sidebar provides content related to its adjacent copy.

Side lighting: Side lighting casts long shadows and increases the sense of three-dimensional space, as opposed to the flattening effect of soft light.

Similarity: The Gestalt law of similarity predicts that people will group items with similar properties such as shape, size or color.

Site map: In Web design, a site map literally maps out the site to show the links between and flow among pages in the form of something that resembles either a family tree or a flowchart.

Slab serif fonts: Slab serif fonts are similar to old style fonts, but the serifs on slab serif fonts start thick and stay thick. Invented for display advertising, slab serif fonts are excellent for headlines and signage.

Small caps: Small caps capitalize the entire word, although the initial cap is slightly larger than the rest of the letters, which are slightly smaller than a regular capitalized glyph.

Smart quotes: Smart quotes are the correct "curly" punctuation marks for quotations. See also curly quotes and prime marks.

Soft light or high key: Soft light or high key evens out the shadows to decrease harsh contrasts. It makes people and products look more attractive.

Source line: The source line identifies the origin or source of data. In an infographic, the source line usually appears on the lower left under the infographic.

Split screen: A split screen divides the screen into two different images.

Spot color in design: Not to be confused with spot color ink in printing, spot color in design refers to designing with a few well-chosen spots or splashes of color to highlight items such as a focal point or to draw the eye around the layout.

Spot color printing: Instead of building color using the 4-color CMYK printing process, spot color printing uses premixed ink colors chosen from a swatch book. See also matched color.

Spread: Two facing pages part of the same design are called a spread, such as one magazine story spreading across the gutter in two facing pages or a two-page advertisement spanning the gutter.

Steadicam: A steadicam is a kind of harness the cameraperson wears to hold the camera steady as she or he shoots hand-held video or film.

Stem strokes: The thick lines in characters or glyphs are stem strokes. The thin lines are hairline strokes.

Storyboard: A storyboard lays out the moving-picture or animated stories of planned film, video and electronic media in the form of scenes or shots arranged on a grid.

Stroked type: Stroked type or stroking is when the type characters or glyphs are outlined.

Super: A super is any on-screen type or graphic superimposed over another image.

SVG (scalable vector graphics): Scalable vector graphics are a file format for the Web. They are an excellent format for charts and graphs. But they are not widely used due to browser incompatibilities.

Swash alternates: Swash alternates are decorative alternatives to traditional italic letterforms.

Symmetrical balance: With symmetrical balance, if you bisect the design, each side will be a mirror image of the other in terms of visual weight.

T

Tags: Tags refer to all the information typically found at the bottom of an advertisement, such as the logo, themeline or slogan, URL, physical address and map, phone number and sometimes, unfortunately, disclaimer and legalese.

Tertiary colors: Tertiary colors result from combining a primary and a secondary color.

Thumbnail sketch: Thumbnail sketches or thumbnails are tiny thumbnail-sized layout sketches that you can draw—and reject—quickly.

Thumb space: Sometimes margins are called thumb space because, if you were holding a hardcopy, margins leave enough negative space at the edges of the layout to accommodate your thumb without covering any visual material.

TIF: Choose TIF (Tagged Image Format) file formats to save images for print purposes (as opposed to GIF or JPG for Web purposes). TIF images are larger in file size, but the TIF format does not lose data.

Track or music bed: A track or music bed is the background soundtrack over which the main video and/or audio are laid.

Tracking shot: In a tracking shot for film or video, a stationary camera tracks along with a moving focal point.

Tracking, type: Tracking refers to the negative space across a string of characters, such as a word, sentence or paragraph.

Transitional fonts: Transitional fonts evolved from old style fonts and have serifs, thick stem strokes and thin hairline strokes. But transitional fonts may have a less pronounced diagonal stress or no diagonal stress at all. Transitional fonts have good readability.

Trapped space: A puddle of landlocked negative space with no apparent layout function in the design is called trapped space.

Triads, color: Color triads are colors on the 12-point color wheel that form any triangle 4 hours apart. Triads make pleasing color palettes.

Trim size: In commercial printing, trim size refers to the finished size of the page after the printer has trimmed away the excess paper.

Truck: In video and film, a truck refers to the camera trucking sideways across the scene. This is usually accomplished with a camera on a dolly. The effect is like rubbernecking from a moving car.

Tweened animation: In tweened animation, the artist illustrates only key changes in motion or shape. Then the software application automatically generates animation to fill "between" the artist's illustrated frames.

Typeface: A typeface or font family contains a series of related fonts, such as Times New Roman, Times Bold and Times Italic.

U

Under lighting: A key light shining directly from below.

V

Value: Value refers to the lightness or darkness of a hue.

Vanishing point: In linear perspective, the vanishing point is where two lines converge in the distance.

Vector image: Vector images use geometry and math to produce and preserve the proportions and quality of line-art illustrations as digital files. They can be scaled up or down infinitely without loss of image quality.

Visual hierarchy: As a tactic for visually communicating a hierarchy of visual items in terms of visual importance, visual hierarchy conventions include making important information large and putting it at the top of the composition. In multiple screen and page designs, as well as in designs with multiple items on the same screen or page, it's important to establish a hierarchy of fonts and point sizes, in addition to placing important items at the top of the screen or page.

VO, voiceover: A VO or voiceover is a disembodied voice speaking over video or audio.

W

Web safe palette: The idea of the Web safe color palette was to provide designers a way of getting consistent color. As a project, the Web safe palette mostly has failed because of constant advances in hardware and monitors, not to mention the garish color choices of the palette.

What you see is what you get: "What you see is what you get" or WYSIWYG is a type of Web page design software that doesn't require users to know how to write code.

White or negative space: White or negative space is the empty space in which design is created and by which any design achieves pleasing balance and composition. White or negative space has visual weight. "White space is not your enemy."

Widget: Widgets are the visible user-friendly expression of the existence of a plug-in. Not all plug-ins have widgets, but all widgets require plug-ins as their invisible engines.

Widow: A typographic widow refers to a few lonely words stranded at the bottom of a leg of type. A hyphenated word ending the last line of a leg counts as a widow, too.

Wipe: In video and film, a wipe transitions between screens with the effect of wiping the picture from the screen.

Wireframe: In Web design, a wireframe is the equivalent of a thumbnail sketch. Wireframes show the functional areas of the planned website.

WYSIWYG: WYSIWYG stands for "what you see is what you get," a type of Web page design software that doesn't require users to know how to write code.

X

X-height: In a given typeface, x-height refers to the height of a lowercase "x" relative to the length of ascenders and descenders.

Z

Zoom: In a zoom, a stationary camera pushes into the scene by using the lens to zoom in on the focal point.

INDEX